The Roman Catholic Church in England
1780–1850
A Study in Internal Politics

The Roman Catholic Church in England
1780–1850
A Study in Internal Politics

Joan Connell

American Philosophical Society
Independence Square•Philadelphia
1984

© American Philosophical Society, 1984 for its *Memoirs* series, Volume 158

Library of Congress Catalog Card No. 83–71299
ISBN: 0–87169–158–2
US ISSN: 0065–9738
Printed in U.S.A. by Braun-Brumfield, Inc., Ann Arbor, Michigan
Composition by Jay's Publishers Services Inc., Rockland, Massachusetts

To the memory
of my parents

Richard C. Connell
who would have been so very proud

and

Marie Monahan Connell
who never doubted that it could be done

CONTENTS

Acknowledgments ix
Introduction 1

PART I. 1553–1780

Chapter
  I. Church without head, 1553–1685 9
  II. Vicars apostolic, 1685–1780 29

PART II. 1780–1850

III. The vicars and the civil government 49
IV. The vicars and John Milner 75
V. The vicars and the Jesuits 122
VI. The Division of the districts 152

Conclusion 189

Appendixes
  A. The vicars apostolic of England and Wales . . . 200
  B. Description of English sources 207

Bibliography 211

Index 214

ACKNOWLEDGMENTS

This essay has been written with the help of a great many people over a number of years. Some of them are no longer active; some of them are no longer living, but their help is warmly remembered.

During the time I worked in England, I was greatly assisted by the archivists of the various diocesan offices. Elizabeth Poyser, archivist at Westminster Cathedral, was particularly helpful in suggesting places to go and people to see. Reverend J. Denis McEvilly of the Diocese of Birmingham made available the letters of John Milner and the records of the Midland District. The Right Reverend Joseph Rudderham, Bishop of Clifton, gave me access to the records of the Western District and permitted me to microfilm extensively from them. In Leeds, Reverend George Bradley gave generously of his time and his historical knowledge about the old Northern District. Reverend Gordon Albion, pastor of St. Edward's in Guildford, the Right Reverend Monsignor Francis Bickford, president of the Old Brotherhood, and the Right Reverend Monsignor Richard J. Foster, rector of Oscott College were all particularly helpful.

In Rome I was most kindly received by His Eminence, Eugene Cardinal Tisserant and Reverend Charles Burns who made available to me the resources of the Vatican Archives. At the Venerable English College, I was received by the Right Reverend Monsignor Joseph Alston who provided me with the excellent assistance of a seminarian, Laurence Hadley.

I wish especially to thank Emmet Larkin, Professor of History at the University of Chicago, without whose encouragement and friendship this essay would never have reached the publication stage. I am also grateful to Thomas Parker, Professor of History at the University of Arizona, who first suggested that history was the proper field of study for me.

Others who provided encouragement along the way were Anne and John Coyne, Mary Rall, and Thomas Munson. Susan Martindale and Joan Buckley gave much assistance in the final stages of proofing and indexing.

INTRODUCTION

Pope Pius IX, on 29 September 1850, in the fifth year of his pontificate, issued a letter apostolic under the Vatican seal restoring the traditional hierarchy of the English Roman Catholic church. In that document, the Papal Secretary of State, Antonio Cardinal Lambruschini, explained that

> considering the whole actual condition of Catholicism in England, reflecting on the considerable number of Catholics, a number every day augmenting, and remarking how from day to day the obstacles become removed which chiefly opposed the propagation of the Catholic religion, We perceived that the time had arrived for restoring in England the ordinary form of ecclesiastical government.[1]

Some years later, Henry Cardinal Manning highlighted the remarkable rejuvenation in the church which the formal restoration had merely proclaimed. "After three hundred years," wrote Manning, "not of suspended animation only, but of organic dissolution, the Church in England was once more knit together in the perfect symmetry of its Divine structure. All at once, as if by a resurrection, all its vital operations resumed their activity."[2] This change was not nearly so perfect as Manning remembered it. Nor were the conditions so favorable as Lambruschini seemed to indicate. Without doubt, however, the events of 1850 did mark an important watershed in the history of the political structure of the English Catholic church.

The Roman Catholic church in England had not had a

---

[1] English translation of Pius IX's *Letters Apostolic* in Gordon Albion, "The Restoration of the Hierarchy, 1850," *The English Catholics: 1850–1950*, ed. George Andrew Beck (London: Burns, Oates, 1950), pp. 107–8.

[2] Bernard Ward, *Sequel to Catholic Emancipation, 1830–1850* (2 vols.; London: Longmans, Green, 1915), II, 288.

regularly constituted national hierarchy since the days of the Elizabethan religious reforms. Instead, the church had been considered a missionary territory unable to direct its own government and was under the protection and guidance, first, of the Holy Office and, after 1622, of the newly organized *Congregatio de propaganda fide*. Under the jurisdiction of first one and then the other of these two curial offices, the English church was governed, for the most part, by a series of vicars apostolic, titular bishops who ruled over districts of England as personal representatives of the pope. Each vicar had sole responsibility for his district and was answerable before 1622 to the Cardinal Secretary of State and later to the Cardinal Prefect of Propaganda. These vicars, although bishops, lacked some of the power and authority normally held by a territorial bishop in a national hierarchy.

Gradually in the course of almost three centuries, the opposition to, the discrimination against, and the fear of the Roman Catholic element in the English population subsided. This lessening of prejudice and persecution was helped greatly by the removal of the threat of a Catholic monarch after the Glorious Revolution, by the concepts of liberty and toleration made popular by the French and American revolutions, and by the continued existence of Protestant nonconformist groups, as well as by the mere passage of time and cooling of tempers. Slowly but steadily Catholics once again began to assume an equal place in society with their Protestant fellow Englishmen. Finally, in 1829, with the passage of the Emancipation Act, Catholics were entitled to most basic rights and privileges.

In the years between 1829 and 1850 the English Catholic church moved steadily toward a more normal and stable form of government. In 1837 the vicars apostolic petitioned Pope Gregory XVI for increased episcopal powers. In 1840 the number of districts was doubled from four to eight—the first change in more than 150 years. That same year Nicholas Wiseman, who was to become the first cardinal archbishop of the restored hierarchy, was consecrated a bishop and appointed as co-adjutor to Bishop Walsh in the new Central District. In 1845 the vicars requested the Holy See to reestablish the national hierarchy in England. In that same year John Henry Newman entered the church, bringing with him much of the spirit and some of the people of the Oxford Movement. In 1847 the vicars sent Bishops Wiseman and James Sharples to Rome to represent there the needs and problems of the English church. In 1848 Bishop William Ullathorne went to Rome to act as agent for the English vicars in matters concerning the hierarchy. Finally in 1850, Wiseman received the cardinal's hat and was appointed archbishop of Westminster, having under him twelve suffragan sees. The national hierarchy was once more functioning in England.

The story of the survival of the English Catholic church is at once inspiring and curiously depressing. Rendered almost totally impotent by persecution, penal restrictions, and a government policy intended to liquidate it, the church should have died. That it did not is a tribute both to the dogged perseverance of the remnants of the Catholic population and to the neglect or refusal of the English civil government to enforce, to their fullest extent, its own laws against Catholics. Furthermore, the Catholic church was systematically debilitated from within by poverty, ignorance, timidity, misunderstanding, lack of leadership, and bitter internecine strife. Much of the internal difficulty was reprehensible. At the very least it was the product of narrow and provincial minds which were unable to control the immediate irritations or keep in view the long-range goals. The main difficulties stemmed from the actions of selfish, ambitious, or stubborn men—both in England and Rome—who would seldom sacrifice their own claims to power and authority.

No one has satisfactorily explained why or how this church survived. Historians have attempted to describe and analyze some of the difficulties it encountered during its struggle for life. Most of their emphasis has fallen on the effects of external persecution and on the role which the Catholic demand for civil and religious liberty played in the larger scene of English politics. Some have dwelt on the internal disagreements—those between laity and the church and those between the secular and regular groups of the clergy. All of these are legitimate areas of study. All are certainly parts of the whole story of the efforts of the English Catholic church to restore its own vitality and to take its proper place in the world.

However, if one were to concentrate on the period after which external forces ceased to be so overwhelmingly important—that is, when persecution began to be eased, roughly in 1780—and before which the national hierarchy was restored—1850—another point of emphasis emerges. In reading through the correspondence of the vicars, it becomes increasingly clear that one of the greatest of the internal problems was the inability of the vicars to work with one another. It was understandable that they would sometimes want to reach the same ends by different means. It was to be expected that they would occasionally clash over policy, that they would now and again disagree over possible alternatives. What is more surprising, however, is that these men were not occasionally but constantly opposed to one another.

This essay will attempt to discuss this neglected aspect of the English Catholic question. It will strive to demonstrate that one of the fundamental problems the vicars had to resolve was their relationship to one another. The first two chapters concern the background and condition of the church between 1553 and 1780. The emphasis then shifts to several illustrations of the problem of episcopal disagreement. In chapter three the vicars are seen taking sides over a problem of lay interference with doctrinal matters in 1791. Chapter four demonstrates how the vicars disagreed over a whole spectrum of jurisdictional problems in the years roughly between 1800 and 1815: the supervision of districts temporarily without a vicar, the methods of nominating new vicars, the manner of dealing with schism and heresy. The problem of the relationship between vicars and the religious orders forms the subject matter for chapter five. Here, in an issue absolutely central to the peace and good government of the church in England, the bishops divided sharply on their attitudes toward the place of the regular clergy, especially during the years immediately following the Jesuit restoration in 1814. Chapter six attempts to detail the manner in which the bishops, even when in agreement over policy, could not refrain from quarreling over means, for while all agreed to the division of the districts in 1840, they argued at length and with much heat over the technical difficulties the division created. The particular themes selected for these chapters were chosen with a two-fold purpose in mind. First, they illustrate the disagreement over a variety of issues and, second, they allow for a chronological development of the narrative.

Possibly a few words of explanation will help to clarify some confusing terms. The church, the English church, the Catholic church, the Roman Catholic church are all used here to refer to the same institution and are never to be confused with the Church of England. Since the latter hardly enters into the story, it seemed unnecessary to make the distinction in the text. Bishop and vicar, also, are used interchangeably. The vicars were, in reality, bishops of titular sees, *in partibus infidelium*, usually Asian sees once held by the primitive church. They were not bishops of any see in England but rather personal representatives of the pope with jurisdiction to govern certain areas in his name and by his authority. However, the vicars themselves used both terms in reference to one another, and it seemed proper to continue their usage.

PART I
1553-1780

CHAPTER I.
CHURCH WITHOUT HEAD, 1553-1685

Standing before Parliament on 30 November 1554, Reginald Cardinal Pole, legate of Pope Julius III, lifted the ban of excommunication and restored the English church to communion with Rome. For the next four years the English hierarchy ruled again as part of the ancient church. Pole later emphasized the significance of that moment in the decree he prepared for the National Council held in 1555-56. "The cause of all the deformation of the church in this kingdom," he wrote then, was "that we, withdrawing from the unity and teaching of the faith of the Catholic Church, deserted the authority and obedience of the Roman Pontiff, the Vicar of Christ."[1] Pole sincerely believed that the failure to recognize the primacy of Rome was the central cause, while the scandals of absentee bishops with all the ecclesiastical abuses resulting from such a system and the lack of properly organized and supported seminaries were among the main subsidiary causes of the sorry plight of the English church. To the restoration of Rome's authority and the reform of these abuses he devoted the remaining few years of his life and episcopate under Queen Mary.

Between 1554 and 1558 Pole consecrated eighteen bishops for English sees. These had fallen vacant when the incumbents had died or when they had been excommunicated for heresy.[2] The new prelates were distinguished chiefly by their youth and inexperience. Some had been exiled under Henry or Edward for adherence to the old faith. Most had suffered

[1] Philip Hughes, *Rome and the Counter-Reformation in England*, 76.
[2] T. E. Bridgett and T. F. Knox, *The True Story of the Catholic Hierarchy Deposed by Queen Elizabeth*; and G. E. Phillips, *The Extinction of the Ancient Hierarchy*. All facts in this and the following paragraph are taken from these two sources.

imprisonment or loss of position for opposing the new religious doctrines. One, Owen Oglethorpe, as president of Magdalen College, had even for a time repudiated Roman beliefs. Yet when Pole died some few hours after his queen had expired on 17 November 1558, six of the twenty-six English sees were again vacant,[3] and before the end of the year, four more dioceses were without bishops.[4] While the surviving sixteen bishops all recognized Elizabeth as queen, fifteen of them refused to participate in her coronation. The bishop of Llandoff was the only one who took the new oath of supremacy and separated himself from Rome.

The existence of the English branch of the Roman Catholic church rested in 1559, then, with these fifteen bishops who remained loyal to the papacy. Five of these, however, were dead within the year,[5] and the remaining ten were either imprisoned or exiled.[6] When Thomas Watson, Bishop of Lincoln, died on 27 September 1584, there was no longer any bishop in England, and when Thomas Goldwell, Bishop of St. Asaph, died in Rome on 3 April 1585, the English hierarchy was no more. That national hierarchy was not to be restored for 265 years.

Virtually without leadership, the Catholic population dwindled and very nearly disappeared in the next two hundred years. It was dependent upon fugitive priests smuggled out of England to the continent for training and back in again for service. Furthermore, that population relied for protection and economic support upon the few gentry families who had remained faithful. When one of these families abandoned the faith or merely died out, the Catholic peasants and servants who were dependent upon them for their religious life were left without church or clergyman and more vulnerable than ever to persecution under a variety of penal laws. By 1604, in Yorkshire, the most Catholic area in England, Catholics numbered only about one percent of the total

[3]Oxford, Salisbury, Bangor, Gloucester, Hereford, Canterbury.
[4]Rochester, Norwich, Chichester, Bristol.
[5]The bishops of Durham, Lichfield and Coventry, St. David, Carlisle, Winchester.
[6]The bishops of Chester, Worcester, Peterborough, London, Bath and Wells, Exeter, Ely, York, Lincoln, St. Asaph.

population.⁷ By 1780, Catholics constituted about .8 of one percent of all Englishmen or about 60,000 souls.⁸ Among the many causes for this decline in the Catholic population was certainly the absence of orderly ecclesiastical government. The violent quarrels which raged within and among the remnants of government which did survive must have greatly contributed to the decline. A people so bereft of clerical leadership and a clergy so absorbed in its own internal struggles for power, position, and prestige could not reasonably be expected to withstand the ravages of persecution.

Although Bishop Goldwell lived until 1585, the hierarchy appointed by Pole during Queen Mary's reign had not had official or effective contact with the laity or the clergy of England since 1559. Pope Pius V did appoint two of the exiled priests, Nicholas Sander and Thomas Harding, as apostolic delegates in 1566 with power to absolve from heresy and schism.⁹ But the first attempt at any kind of official reorganization was made in 1580 when William Allen, founder of the English College at Douay, petitioned Gregory XIII to appoint an English bishop. Allen had become the unofficial head of the English clergy in exile and had been given power to grant faculties to English priests returning to England to work in the "underground" church. A man of tremendous vigor, influence, and personal magnetism, he was able to organize and control the priests whom he sent off to work in his native land. Allen realized, however, that it was his own personality rather than any ecclesiastical authority that was the source of unity, and this knowledge impelled him to petition Gregory for a bishop. The most he could secure was his own appointment in 1581 as "prefect" of the English mission, a title without precedent and with no real canonical power.¹⁰

When Cardinal Allen died in 1594, the office of prefect

⁷A. G. Dickens, *The English Reformation*, 312.
⁸Philip Hughes, "English Catholics in 1850," *The English Catholics, 1850-1950*, 46.
⁹Phillips, *The Extinction of the Ancient Hierarchy*, 274.
¹⁰W. Maziere Brady, *Annals of the Catholic Hierarchy in England and Scotland, A.D. 1585-1876*, 42.

and the influence of this much loved and respected Englishman died with him. Since there was no legal basis for his authority and no fixed chain of command among the clergy, the obvious result was a struggle for power. Four years elapsed before Rome made any further attempt to establish an official government for English Catholics, even though Robert Persons, a prominent English Jesuit then exiled in Spain, made continual recommendations for the establishment of local government under episcopal control.[11]

In spite of all that Allen had done, it was during the period from 1559 to about 1660—a time of "church without head"— that the differences of opinion and the animosities emerged among the English clergy. These arguments set the tone for 250 more years of bickering, scandal, dissension, and disunion. The first sign of trouble was the breakdown of mutual trust and respect between the Jesuits and the secular clergy— an attitude that was soon evident between the seculars and all religious orders and which eventually divided the English church into pro-regular and anti-regular camps. The trouble stemmed mainly from the need to compete for the meager economic support of the laity; from the absence of clear lines of jurisdiction and authority over the clergy; from the belief, fairly widespread and possibly true, that the Jesuits were involved in political intrigue; from the general disrepute into which the Jesuits had fallen on the continent; and from the misunderstandings and mismanagement of the seminarians at the Venerable English College in Rome, then under Jesuit supervision.

A second sign was the problem at Wisbech Castle, where the Marian bishops and clergy had been imprisoned. The dispute there had its roots in the fact that there was no real figure of authority in the group. Moreover, it was perforce a closed community without much hope of survival or outside interest, composed of men who were fiercely independent and strong-willed (they were there, after all, because they would not take the oath of supremacy). Further, they had never intended to live a communal life and were ill prepared

---

[11]Richard Dodd [Hugh Tootell], *Church History of England*, 3:cxvii.

by temperament, training, or circumstances to live peaceably with one another. Disagreement soon arose between those who saw the need for the establishment of some rule of life similar to that of a religious community—and those who felt no need for such an arrangement. The dispute waxed violent with laymen and clergy all choosing sides, and it finally had to be settled in Rome.[12] These "Stirs of Wisbech," of no particular long-range importance in themselves, divided the English secular clergy into opposing factions, so that even when the original dispute was resolved, the spirit of dissension had already hardened into a tradition. It was further nourished by the continued disagreements over the government of the English mission. The suspicion and rivalry between these various groups of secular clergy and the regulars also resulted in a deep-seated mistrust of a Rome which apparently could be influenced by factions of Englishmen with a particular ax to grind. With such a background, none but the strongest and most canonically secure form of church government could hope to maintain order. Such government was, unfortunately, not forthcoming.

As early as 1580 both the Jesuits and Allen had recognized the need for a resident bishop. Even Rome agreed, but apparently lacking any real understanding of the work this bishop would have to perform, proposed to send Goldwell, a man past seventy and broken in health, to govern a church persecuted from without and nearly destroyed by internal strife. Goldwell wisely refused and in refusing made his feelings remarkably clear. "It would be impossible for me alone," he wrote to Gregory XIII on 13 July 1580, "to supply the wants of the Catholics, who are more by many thousands than I thought, and scattered over the whole kingdom."[13] "I cannot but marvel," Goldwell went on to say,

how it is that, after God had given your Holiness grace, as it were, to plant anew and support the Catholic faith in that kingdom, you make so many difficulties about creating three or four titular Bish-

[12] P. Renold, ed., *The Wisbech Stirs, 1595–1598*.
[13] Letter, Thomas Goldwell to Pope Gregory XIII, 13 July 1580, quoted in Hughes, *Rome and the Counter-Reformation in England*, 293.

ops to preserve and propagate it. God inspire your Holiness to do that which shall be most to His honour.

In 1597 Father Persons proposed two bishops for England, one to reside there and one to live abroad.[14] The local bishop, in addition to the normal duties of the episcopacy, would work to unite the clergy and to see to it that the true picture of their situation reached Rome. His counterpart on the continent would screen the applicants for missionary work in England and exercise external jurisdiction. This scheme, which hindsight says might have worked because it was at least a sort of hierarchical episcopal structure, failed to gain the approval of Pope Clement VIII. It is not completely clear just why Clement disapproved of the plan. He possibly feared that there was some danger in appointing a bishop—danger of increased persecution from without and increased scandal from within should the rebellious and independent clergy refuse to accept his authority. Clement finally decided upon sacerdotal rather than episcopal government for England. He determined to appoint a superior for the English secular clergy—not a bishop, but simply one of the clergymen—to be called an archpriest.[15] Many problems were involved in such a proposal. First, there was no precedent for the authority of such an archpriest and both Rome and England had great respect for precedent. Second, he would be superior only of the secular clergy, excluding the regulars from any and all local supervision although they were doing the same kind of pastoral work. This would serve to put them in a separate and possibly privileged category. The archpriest plan, therefore, only served to compound the evils of the developing division between the two groups of clergymen. Moreover, such an archpriest would lack the dignity, the prestige, and the power of a bishop, both in his own mind and in the eyes of his subjects. Nevertheless, Clement's plan prevailed.

The first archpriest, George Blackwell, who governed from

[14] John Hungerford Pollen, *The Institution of the Archpriest Blackwell*, 23.
[15] Ibid., 25.

CHURCH WITHOUT HEAD 15

1598 to 1608, although well received at first, soon met with much opposition.[16] One group of seculars called the "appellants" appealed to Clement VIII disputing Blackwell's authority over them. Clement, by failing to make judgment either for Blackwell or for the appellants, weakened the position of both and strengthened the spirit of disunion. The second problem developed out of the terms of Blackwell's brief of appointment which had ordered him to consult with the superior of the Jesuits on all matters of importance.[17] Later, in response to the appellants' protest, he was forbidden by Rome to seek Jesuit advice.[18] Neither Blackwell nor the clergy could resolve this conflict. Further, the oath of allegiance prescribed by James I for all recusants under pain of loss of property and life imprisonment introduced another complicating factor.[19] Pope Paul V had condemned the oath in 1605 and again in 1607, but many Catholics were taking it anyway.[20] The battle lines were now redrawn with the Jesuits and the appellants uniting against the oath while Blackwell, the pope's representative in England, actually took it. Following this act, Pope Paul V deposed him on 1 February 1608, and named George Birkhead as the second English archpriest.[21]

Birkhead, friendly with the Jesuits, sent his agent, Richard Smith, to Rome to ask whether the former prohibition against consultation with them applied to him also. Paul ruled that it did. At the same time, Paul ignored repeated requests for a bishop in England despite Birkhead's pleading. Describing the dire plight of England to Cardinal Borghese, Birkhead concluded his letter of 26 July 1613, by saying that "ultimately the only and sole remedy is the episcopacy."[22] He made the same point again in October, 1613—that only a bishop could

---

[16] Brady, *Annals*, 55.
[17] Dodd, *Church History of England*, 3: cxix.
[18] Pollen, *Archpriest*, 91.
[19] Dodd, *Church History of England*, 4: cxvii.
[20] Ibid., 4: cxl, cxlvi.
[21] Brady, *Annals*, 64.
[22] Letter, George Birkhead to Cardinal Borghese, 26 July 1613, quoted in Dodd, *Church History of England*, 5:clviii.

save the the faith in England—in a letter to Paul V.[23] Paul, however, would not even give him an assistant archpriest, even though Birkhead had reported that his health and strength had failed.

After Birkhead's death in 1614, the lines of division were even more clearly drawn. The secular clergy, more numerous than the regulars but less united, wanted a resident bishop with full epsicopal powers. They had shown little respect for Birkhead before his death. Their opposition had been strong enough to arouse this usually mild gentleman to write to his agent in Rome, in August, 1613, "I have received more frumps from some four or five of our brethern than ever I have done from the Jesuits."[24] "Their ingratitude forceth me to write to his holiness as you see. I do things with good reason, and sweetly admonish them; and they prevent my meaning with most bitter invective." The regulars, fewer in number, but bound together by both training and community loyalty, were opposed—or so the secular clergy believed—to any episcopal government for such government would impinge upon their freedom. Whether the seculars' beliefs were totally grounded in truth or not mattered little, for the two groups were at bitter odds.

More than a year was to elapse before Rome appointed William Harrison as the third archpriest.[25] Father Antony Champney, one of the appellant group, whose own name had been sent to Rome as a possibility for the position, complained about the delay and expressed the growing dissatisfaction of the English clergy with their treatment at Rome. "I almost forgot to tell you," he wrote on 25 August 1615, to his friend and fellow priest, Thomas More, "what conference we had with the nuncio last week."[26] "Dr. Bishop and

[23]Copy of letter, George Birkhead to Pope Paul V, 20 October 1613. Archives, The Old Brotherhood of the English Secular Clergy, Oscott College, Warwickshire, England.

[24]Letter, George Birkhead to Thomas More, 20 October 1613, quoted in Dodd, *Church History of England*, 5:57.

[25]Brady, *Annals*, 66.

[26]Letter, Antony Champney to Thomas More, 25 August 1615, quoted in Dodd, *Church History of England*, 5:clxxvii–clxxviii.

I," Champney continued, ". . . having told him of the great complaint our brethren in England make, for want of a superior, being now eighteen months since they are without any, whereupon they esteem that his holiness hath either forgot them, or doth wholly neglect them." When the nuncio replied that the divisions in England were the chief cause of the delay, Champney reported to More that he had replied, "So, take away the pope, and will not there be divisions amongst the cardinals?" "If we may speak truly," Champney then added, "we have occasion to think that the pretence of our divisions is used as colourable reason and means to deny us of all things we desire and propose."

When finally appointed in 1615, Harrison devoted much energy to the task of obtaining a bishop for the English church. For some years his work bore no fruit and he did not live to see the results of his labors. After his death and after the accession of Pope Gregory XV, both in 1621, John Bennett, whom Harrison had previously appointed as his personal agent, went to Rome. There he met with much opposition and found the Jesuits formidable opponents. "The Jesuits here are making catalogues of lay people's names, who forsooth would have no bishop," he wrote in December, 1621, to Matthew Kellison, president of Douay College, "and this, as a great weapon, they purpose to use."[27] Rome's great reluctance to decide anything did not pass unremarked, for Bennett wrote again to Kellison on 21 May 1622, saying that the pope's "absence hath put our business to the next week; and I fear Corpus Christi day, which is the day the congregation of the holy office is usually held before his holiness may chance cast it off one week longer."[28] "It is the humour of this place," Bennett wrote two months later, "but the delay is all the harm in this point."[29]

The decree granting England a bishop was finally passed in the summer of 1622, but Rome did not appoint a bishop until March of the following year. Harrison had died in 1621

[27] Ibid., 5:ccxxxi.
[28] Ibid., 5:ccxxvi.
[29] Ibid., 5:ccxlv.

and during the interim, even after Gregory XV had agreed to a bishop, the opposition persisted in its attack. Writing to enlist the aid of his brother Edward in England, Bennett commented, "For our suit of bishops, they leave nothing untried, to hinder it; and, having been foiled here (for we have a decree), they flew to his majesty of England for help. You must help there, that from thence we be not hindered."[30] Bennett then suggested certain features of the new bishopric which could be mentioned to allay fears among the Protestants in England: there was to be only one bishop; he was to be a titular bishop only; his power would be limited and known; he would be able to maintain order among the various Catholic factions. Twenty-one months after Harrison's death, William Bishop was declared bishop-elect of Chalcedon in Asia and, on 23 March 1623, he was appointed to govern the Vicariate of England and Scotland.[31]

Bishop governed for only eight months before he died on 16 April 1624, but in that brief time he attempted the reorganization of church government. He divided the country into seven parts, placing over each one a vicar general, and, most important of all, erected a chapter called the "Chapter of the English Church," later known as the "Old Brotherhood," made up of twenty-four canons. He gave his reasons for this action to his agent in Rome, Thomas Rant, whom he had commissioned to obtain papal approval for the group. "The Dean and Chapter have many privileges by the Canons of the Church," wrote Bishop, "and among the rest, one that we chiefly aim at, which is that Episcopal Jurisdiction doth remain among them until a new Bishop be chosen and consecrated."[32] Recognizing only too well the need to prevent a repetition of the abuses of the past, Bishop went on to say, "We have but one Bishop. If God should call him, then were all Episcopal Jurisdiction lost in our country, unless there be

---

[30] Ibid., 5:ccliii.

[31] Brady, *Annals*, 68. At the request of the Scots, however, jurisdiction over them was almost immediately withdrawn.

[32] Old Brotherhood of the English Secular Clergy, *A List of Members*. Privately published pamphlet (1954), Archives, Old Brotherhood of English Secular Clergy, Oscott College, Warwickshire, England.

Dean and Chapter to conserve it." "Wherefore labour I pray you," he begged of Rant,

> very carefully to obtain of His Holiness that he will be pleased to confirm and establish our Dean and Chapter with power in the Chapter if our Bishop be dead (otherwise to remain in the Bishop), to choose a Dean if he that is now chosen by me should hap to die. For this get the Pope's Breve: holding it to one of the chiefest matters that you have now to do.

Bishop died, however, on 16 April 1624, without obtaining that approval for this Chapter. This failure to have the Chapter canonically confirmed was to play havoc with English church government for years to come.

John Colleton, dean of the Chapter, immediately notified Rome of Bishop's death. To succeed him the Holy Office appointed Richard Smith, who arrived in England in April of 1625 as the second bishop of Chalcedon and Vicar Apostolic of all England.[33] Smith had been educated by the Jesuits and had spent more than ten years at the College d'Arras in Paris. Here, in an institution designed for the scholar-priest, he had devoted himself to study and writing. Here also he had come under the influence of the Benedictines who helped support the college. This close contact with two of the major religious orders working in England, however, failed to make Smith's association with the regulars as their bishop any smoother.

Indeed, Smith's difficulties in ruling the English church centered mainly around the regular-secular controversy. English Catholics were served in 1632 by approximately 400 secular priests and 225 regulars of whom about 165 were Jesuits. These regulars did not live a community life, but worked as missionaries alongside the secular clergy. Although the struggle for the episcopacy had been won by the seculars, many of the regular clergy would not accept the bishop as their lawful superior. They claimed exemption from his decrees and would submit only to the commands of their

---

[33]Brady, *Annals*, 76.

own religious superiors. When Smith promulgated the Roman regulation that no priest could hear confessions of the laity unless he had received the approbation of the bishop, many ignored his ruling. In addition to causing great distress among the laity over the validity of the sacrament they were receiving, the problem raised once again the whole question of the extent of the jurisdiction of a vicar apostolic. Smith attempted to settle the issue by an appeal to Rome and a letter of explanation to the Catholics of England. "As for the authoritie wherewith I demaunded it, that is as great as any ordinarie hath or can have to demaund the same of regulars in his cittie or diocesse," wrote Smith, "for his holiness in expresse termes by his breve giveth me in England all and everie facultie which ordinaries have or can have in theyr citties and diocesses."[34] "He giveth me an authority of mine owne that is peculiar to myself in England," he instructed his flock, "and thereby maketh me as true and absolute an ordinarie in England as other ordinaries are in theyr diocesses. The onlie difference is in the manner of making."

Despite the bishop's efforts, confusion continued. The laity particularly feared he would attempt to exercise the powers which bishops had possessed in former times over wills, trusts, and other legal matters, thus endangering them in the civil courts, although there seems to be no indication that any of the vicars made the slightest effort at all to interfere in these matters. Finally, by the brief *Britannia*, issued by Pope Urban VIII on 9 May 1631, Rome decreed that regulars need not receive approbation before hearing confessions (a victory for them), but that their faculties for administering baptism, matrimony, and extreme unction must be approved by the vicar apostolic (a victory for him).[35] Furthermore, the entire dispute had become public knowledge and was a source of danger as well as scandal, so much so that Rome also reduced Smith's authority in England to that of an archpriest. This act the regulars interpreted as vindication for their arguments and as victory in their struggle against episcopal au-

---

[34]Letter, Richard Smith to the Lay Catholics of England, 16 October 1627. Archives, Old Brotherhood.
[35]Brady, *Annals*, 77–78.

thority, for Smith was the last bishop to govern the English church until 1685. The controversy had raged so openly that the civil authorities became aware of it and orders were issued for the bishop's arrest. Finally Smith declared that under those circumstances, he could no longer be of use to the English church and retired to France. He did not leave, however, without stating his case to Propaganda.[36] In a letter dated 14 June 1631, he wrote,

> It is not indeed that I am longing to keep my position as bishop here, for I live shut up perpetually in one small bedroom, and can never allow myself to breathe fresh air; I am at the mercy of the plots of the heretics and of the harassing Regulars, without any consolation from elsewhere; my life is in danger. It is a state of things that I would gladly exchange for France.[37]

"But I urge these considerations," Smith continued,

> because I am wholly convinced that for me to be deprived of my authority because of the empty and imaginary pretexts of a few laymen, stirred up by the Regulars, could not but entail infamy to the Apostolic See, dishounour to the episcopal dignity, danger and scandal to other bishops, and finally the most serious loss to the whole body of the secular clergy in England and to by far the greater part of the laity.

Until his death in 1655, Bishop Smith lived abroad. His situation with respect to England was most peculiar. Although he had no meaningful authority or jurisdiction over English affairs, he still remained England's only bishop. During this

---

[36] In 1622 Gregory XV organized the *Congregatio de propaganda fide* and transferred to its jurisdiction mission lands such as England which formerly had been governed by the Holy Office. For more than a century thereafter, rivalry existed between the two offices for the "political power" which control over mission lands carried with it. In this power struggle the Holy Office was greatly aided by the regular clergy who had much influence in Rome. Gradually, Propaganda gained more power so that by 1685, when the next bishop was appointed for England, the nomination came from Propaganda and its approval was sought by Pope Innocent XI. Had Propaganda been more powerful earlier in the century, it is conceivable that England might not have been left leaderless for so long.

[37] Letter, Richard Smith to the Cardinals of Propaganda, 14 June 1631. Archives, Congregatio de Propaganda Fide, Rome. Acta, Vol. C.

period, 1631 to 1655, and for the thirty years following Smith's death to 1685, England was again, for all practical purposes, without episcopal leadership.

The major purpose of Urban's brief *Britannia* had not been to make a definitive judgment upon the claims of either Smith or the regulars. Nor had it attempted to define in general the jurisdiction of bishops appointed to the English see. Rather, it was an order to discontinue a feud which was creating scandal within the church and danger of reprisals from without. But without some clarification of the authority of the bishop over the members of religious orders who were working as missionaries, the uncertain state of affairs could only continue and grow worse.

The problems of this period, 1630 to 1685, were only an exaggerated version of the problems of the English church from 1559 to 1850—abuses which resulted from the absence of a canonically established episcopal hierarchy with clearly defined authority. Peter Fitton, agent for Bishop Smith, had reported to Propaganda in 1632 that "the whole fabric of Catholicism in England is threatened with utter ruin for the lack of bishops to restore and repair ecclesiastical discipline."[38] "The clerical body," he explained,

is by no means homogeneous. The vast majority of the priests are seculars. The regulars are taken from no fewer than ten different orders, each one independent of all other authority in England. The lack of some single general directing authority is evident. In this multitude of equally important chiefs, none of whom owes any consideration to the rest, lies the real cause of all the troubles and factions. There is no one responsible for the mission as a whole, and no kind of subordination among these many leaders.

Fitton suggested that Rome appoint bishops with certain clearly defined areas of jurisdiction over all missioners. This would end the practice of the seculars banding together against the regulars, and of the regulars being antagonistic toward the

---

[38]Summary of a report made by Peter Fitton to Propaganda in 1632; translated in Hughes, *Rome and the Counter-Reformation in England*, 409–425.

bishops. As an alternative to this, he proposed that either all secular or all regular clergy be withdrawn, leaving the work of the English mission entirely to one or the other group.

Smith had not abandoned the English mission in a moment of anger. He offered his resignation, which was never formally accepted, in March of 1633, accompanied by recommendations for the correction of the abuses.[39] Through Peter Fitton he also asked Propaganda to appoint a new bishop before his own resignation should take effect so that there would be no lapse of authority. He presented to them the clergy's desire for three or four bishops for England, one to be a regular—although not a Jesuit or Benedictine—and one to be archbishop with jurisdiction over the others. Nor was Smith the only one who appealed to Rome for bishops. One of the Benedictines, David Codner, had asked in February, 1633, for more bishops to help correct abuses even in his own order.[40] In his report of the English correspondence in 1633, Francesco Ingoli, Secretary of Propaganda, clearly stated the issues in the case of the English bishops.[41] According to him, the regulars in England objected to the creation of a bishop because they had enjoyed such great freedom under the archpriest system, a freedom and influence they would lose under a bishop. Moreover, since they could not openly oppose the idea of episcopal authority in general, they tried to weaken the position of a specific bishop so that Rome would restore the former system. Ingoli went on to say that had the first bishop, William Bishop, been given the powers usually granted to bishops-in-ordinary instead of being designated a vicar apostolic, and had he been supported by Rome, the conflict would not have arisen. Now, maintained Ingoli, it was too late for that, but he proposed as a remedy the

---

[39]Copy of letter, Richard Smith to Peter Fitton, 11 March 1633. Archives, Old Brotherhood of the English Secular Clergy.

[40]Letter, David Codner to Propaganda, 3 February 1632. Archives, Congregatio de Propaganda Fide, Rome. Acta, Vol. CL.

[41]Summary of a series of reports made by Francesco Ingoli to Propaganda during 1633; translated in Hughes, *Rome and the Counter-Reformation in England*, 402–407. Ingoli, one of the first and most active secretaries of Propaganda, advocated for all mission lands the use of secular priests and a native clergy.

appointment of three bishops for England, one secular, one Jesuit, and one Benedictine. Each would have jurisdiction over a clearly defined section of the country. This plan, according to Ingoli, would not only have placed the regulars under an authority they could hardly have dared to refuse to respect, but would also have disabused them once and for all of the notion that they could ever be free, in their missionary duties, from episcopal direction.

Why all these almost identical recommendations were not acted on still remains unclear. The various plans for the conversion of Charles I, the Puritan revolution, the efforts to establish diplomatic relations between Rome and England, rivalry in Rome between the Holy Office and Propaganda, Rome's tendency to wait out the problem and her lack of any real understanding of what conditions were like in England—all these contributed to the failure to act. Moreover, there can be no doubt that the stalemate existing between the "Chapter of the English Church"—erected by Bishop in 1623 but never confirmed by Rome—and the Holy See added in great measure to the problem. Joseph Berington, writing in 1793, noted that during the years between 1631 and 1685 when the English church had no leader, "the dean and the chapter also, which the first bishop had erected, and which Dr. Smith had confirmed, and which he afterwards sanctioned by a more express declaration was attacked by the regulars."[42] "They insisted," Berington wrote, "that, as neither of the bishops were ordinaries, the institution of a chapter was an illegal act, and that the authority which it assumed was null."

"It will hardly be asked," Berington observed tartly,

why the court of Rome took sides with the regulars, rather than with its agent whom it had delegated to govern in its name. For it will be recollected, that that agent in his writing . . . had maintained the divine and independent rights of episcopacy; that a hierarchy

---

[42]Joseph Berington, "An Introduction and a Supplement Exhibiting the State of the English Catholic Church," in Gregorio Panzani, *Memoirs* (Birmingham, England: Swinney and Walker, 1793), 274–77.

was necessary to every church; and that the holy see in its late arrangements, had departed from the venerable maxims of antiquity and the common practice of modern times.

"The regulars, on the other hand," he pointed out somewhat bitterly,

had combated these doctrines, which they denominated direful insults to the authority of Rome. Rome, therefore, must patronize their labours, and vindicate their claim to privileges, when it was become manifest how much those privileges had attached them to its nearest interests, the supremacy and universal sovereignty of its bishop.

"The court of Rome," Berington concluded,

though repeatedly addressed by that very chapter, and fully informed through a succession of years, of its existence and many acts, did not suppress it, or treat those acts as invalid and abusive; but as they never, by an decree, confirmed it, it should rather perhaps, be inferred they ridiculed its existence, and despised its weak display of jurisdiction. Or may it not be said that, aware that the nominal dignity amused the clergy, they permitted the enjoyment of it, that so they might be less urgent in their applications for a bishop? The regulars, however, would in no form, acknowledge the jurisdiction of the chapter.

When Bishop Smith died in 1655, the Chapter sent Father Laurence Plantin to Rome to request a successor. Pope Alexander VII promised one within the year and remarked that the Chapter could govern in the meantime.[43] But no bishop arrived and Father Francis Gage journeyed to Rome with the same request in 1659. Unwilling to compromise, the Chapter members expended much of their energy in demands for bishops-in-ordinary in place of vicars apostolic, and in attempts to prove the validity of their own claim to jurisdiction in the absence of a bishop. Gage, while in Rome working for these ends, wrote a series of letters home to his

[43]Old Brotherhood, *List of Members*, 3.

brother George, describing his efforts. "His Holiness gave me an attentive ear," wrote Gage.[44]

He then replied in Latin with a marvelous grace and facility of speech to this purpose. "Amidst the many cares of his pastoral solicitude he had several times thought upon the sad condition of the persecuted Catholics of England, not without a most sensible grief and compassion of their sufferings, and therefore had several times been casting about how to relieve them at least in the way of some spiritual comfort. Wherefore having been an eye-witness of the great good effected both in the upper and lower Germany by means of apostolical vicars, he had designed one likewise for England, when to his great astonishment he was advertised that the priests openly rejected it, in so much that he was forced to leave them alone to themselves".

After this audience with the pope, Gage reported that there was less and less hope for a bishop. He complained that Rome was not interested in English business, that the Chapter's representative was not accepted as the agent of the English clergy, and that the cardinals would not even discuss the issues with him. On 15 November 1660, he wrote to his brother almost in desperation to ask how he could possibly convince Rome to give England an ordinary "which certainly cannot be by sending a titular Bishop as our last two were; which you know, the Regulars denied to be Ordinaries."[45] Finally Gage left Rome unsuccessful but stating that the only way to succeed was to stop begging. "The time may come," he wrote, "when they have more need of us than we of them."[46] Unfortunately, the English church never became that necessary to Rome. Even during the Napoleonic wars, more than a century later, it was the English government, not the English

[44]Letters, Francis Gage to George Gage, March, 1659–May, 1661. Archives, Old Brotherhood of the English Secular Clergy. These archives are preserved on microfilm now. However, they were severely damaged during the second World War. It is impossible to do more than catch lines from here and there. The references to Gage constitute the sense of many letters which I cannot date or identify more completely.
[45]Ibid., 15 November 1660.
[46]Ibid. [date not legible].

Catholic church, which was necessary for the temporal survival of the papacy.

It was not only the conflict with the regulars which caused the Chapter members to reject vicars apostolic. Another reason lay in one of the technical distinctions between vicars and bishops-in-ordinary. The latter had the authority to designate the person who was to assume the government of the diocese when the bishop died. Vicars did not have this right and so could not make provision for an interim government. Being familiar with Rome's tendency to procrastinate, the Chapter members saw great dangers in England's being without episcopal government for long periods of time with nothing to take its place. It was better, they thought, to have no bishop and to continue government by the Chapter, capitular rule, than to have a series of vicars who could not provide continuity of command.

Again in 1670 the Chapter applied for a bishop. They sent Alexander Holt to Rome to congratulate the new pontiff, Clement IX, and to make known to him that Philip Howard, later to become a cardinal, would be an acceptable bishop, but not an acceptable vicar apostolic. Clement would not agree and England received neither bishop nor vicar. That same year, the Internuncio of Flanders, Signor Ayroldi, visited England and presented the Chapter with the terms under which Rome would recognize it; namely, that Rome could appoint some of the Chapter members. This the Chapter refused to consider. As a result, Clement issued the decree *Non confirmatur capitulum Anglicanum*, which was a formal prohibition of the Chapter. Nevertheless, the Chapter continued, in the absence of any other ruling power, to regulate the internal affairs of the English church until 1685. No mention was made of the schismatical character of its existence after the decree was published. In one sense, then, Gage had been right, for Rome had to use the Chapter, even though it nominally condemned it. In commenting on this situation, Berington, who was admittedly Gallican in the extreme, attributed this neglect to Rome's "immutable resolution never to cooperate in the establishment of an authority that, in a single act, would be independent of its own paramount will."[47] "For this," argued Berington, "was the archpriest instituted; for this, was a saving clause, which annihilated the very essence of the supposed grant, inserted in the briefs of the two succeeding bishops; for this, was the present supplication of the clergy resisted, and a superior offered, whose very name of vicar apostolic should define his dependent and delegated powers." The English, unwilling to accept what Rome was willing to offer, were left to their own devices until 1685, when a new era opened, if only momentarily, for the Catholic population.

[47]Berington, "State of the English Catholic Church," 306–308.

CHAPTER II.
VICARS APOSTOLIC, 1685–1780

When England finally did receive a bishop, although he came as vicar apostolic and not bishop-in-ordinary, the Chapter of the Old Brotherhood played no part in his appointment. Rather the bishop came with the succession of a Roman Catholic king, James II, to the throne of England. In 1685 Rome appointed John Leyburne vicar apostolic for all England.[1] With his appointment the long struggle of the Chapter with Rome ended in failure. Before leaving Rome for England, Leyburne, a longtime member of the Chapter and one of its own nominees for the office of bishop, took an oath not to recognize the Old Brotherhood. A prudent man, Leyburne chose to act independently of but not in opposition to the Chapter, and it ceased to claim jurisdiction, even though its heart's desire had been frustrated. The members accepted the vicar, but did not stop agitating for a bishop-in-ordinary, for in 1694 they appealed to the president of Douay for his help in securing a bishop.[2]

Leyburne, under the friendly patronage of James II, moved freely about England. In 1687 he traveled to the northern counties to administer confirmation. This pastoral visit caused him to represent to the Holy See the need for more help. On 30 January 1688, Pope Innocent XI appointed three additional vicars to govern four territorial districts whose boundaries were to be determined by Ferdinand d'Adda, the apostolic nuncio to James II. Their authority as well as Leyburne's was to be exercised "at the pleasure of the Holy See." That is to say, they also were vicars apostolic, not bishops-in-

[1]Brady, *Annals*, 140.
[2]Archives, Old Brotherhood.

ordinary. England now, for the first time in more than one hundred years, had four bishops: John Leyburne of the London District, Bonaventure Giffard in the Midland District, James Smith in the Northern District, and Philip Ellis, a Benedictine, in the Western District.[3]

With a sudden burst of enthusiasm, Rome had, under the protection of James II, reorganized England ecclesiastically under four vicars apostolic, and then settled back expecting, if not the re-establishment of Roman Catholicism, at least its unimpeded growth. The dream faded with the fall of James. The open practice of the Catholic religion ceased once again and the four vicars went into hiding or were imprisoned. A century of persecution and exclusion from all opportunities for economic, educational, social, or political advancement began. The restrictions upon their lives forced Catholics into more and more narrow channels of thought and action. Veneration of the martyrs of the Reformation, love of the English colleges abroad, the loyalty of the people to their missionaries, the ability to exist, unnoticed and unobtrusive, the strict adherence to the customs, practices, and traditions made sacred by their predecessors—these were the "virtues" cultivated by the dwindling Catholic population.

With these "virtues" came the corresponding "vices"—a more and more narrow and provincial outlook, a ghetto mentality, blind devotion to tradition, inability to adapt and adjust to new conditions and ways of thinking, a persecution complex. The need for secrecy in the exercise of religion opened the door to all manner of religious abuses. The poverty of the clergy and their total dependence upon a few wealthy Catholics created endless problems in the assignment of priests and in the administration of missions. The civil restrictions placed upon the property of Catholics and upon their right to inherit resulted in the most complicated and scandalous disputes over the intentions of donors and the support of the church. The prohibition against education produced in large part an ignorant and ill disciplined congregation.

The civil authorities seldom inflicted the death penalty

---

[3]Brady, *Annals*, 145–46.

against Catholics after 1688, but lesser punishments for Catholics apprehended in the practice of their religion continued for another century. In addition to the laws against papists which were already in existence, more were enacted in the eighteenth century. George I appointed commissioners "to inquire of the estates of certain traitors and popish recusants, and of estates given to superstitious uses, in order to raise money out of their security for the use of the public."[4] Catholics could not inherit land,[5] could not practice as doctor, teacher, or barrister.[6] More often than not, it was true, these and other penal laws were not enforced, but the possibility of enforcement was a constant fear with Catholics. Berington, with his characteristic overstatement, described the situation. Despite the evident exaggeration of the psychological effects of the persecution, there is more than a kernel of truth in his words. "Shall I sit down satisfied," he wrote in 1780, "because the good humour of a magistrate chooses to indulge me; whilst there are laws of which any miscreant has daily power to enforce the execution?"[7] "My ease, my property and my life," he lamented,

are at the disposal of every villain, and I am to be pleased because he is not at this time disposed to deprive me of them. To-morrow his humour may vary, and I shall then be obliged to hide my head in some dark corner or to fly from this land of boasted liberty. It is surely better *not to be* than to live in a state of such anxious and dreadful uncertainty.

But dark as the picture was, the English church continued to exist, even if it did not precisely thrive, during the century from 1688 to 1780. With the exception of two brief periods in the Northern and Western Districts, vicars ruled continuously in the four districts. Bonaventure Giffard came from the Midlands to London to succeed Leyburne in 1703, followed by Benjamin Petre in 1734 and Richard Challoner in

[4] I George I, c. 50.
[5] 11 and 12 William III, c. 4
[6] 7 and 8 William and Mary, c. 15.
[7] Joseph Berington, *The State and Behaviour of English Catholics from the Reformation to the Year 1780*, viii.

1758. When Giffard left the Midlands, George Witham replaced him. After Witham came John Stoner in 1715 and John Hornyold in 1756. James Smith of the Northern District died in 1711 and after a lapse of four years, Rome moved Witham from the Midlands to take his place. Thomas Williams, a Dominican, succeeded Witham in 1736, followed by Edward Dicconson in 1740, Francis Petre in 1752, and William Walton in 1775. In the Western District, Ellis, a Benedictine, governed until 1705. The district remained without a vicar then until 1713, when Matthew Prichard, a Franciscan, received the appointment. Laurence York, another Benedictine, succeeded him in 1750, and was succeeded by Charles Walmsley, also a Benedictine, in 1770.[8] The Catholic population over whom this succession of vicars ruled, numbered in 1746 no more than 60,000 served by slightly more than 300 priests.[9]

Almost all the eighteen vicars mentioned above suffered some harassment and danger during their time in office from Leyburne, who went to the Tower when James II was deposed, to Walmsley, whose house in Bath was demolished during the Gordon riots of 1780. Eight of the vicars, Leyburne, Giffard, Smith, both Petres, Walton, and Hornyold, belonged to that select group of the Old Brotherhood before their appointments as vicars apostolic.[10] All, of course, had been trained and ordained abroad and, for the most part, had received the best clerical education available at the time. At least four were converts from Protestantism: Leyburne, Giffard, Benjamin Petre, and Hornyold. Leyburne, Witham, Dicconson, and Walmsley had all lived in Rome and were familiar with customs and practices in the Vatican offices. Two, at least, were authors of some significance. Walmsley was interested in astronomy and physics and his commentaries on Newton's laws appeared in the *Philosophical Transactions* in 1745.[11] In Richard Challoner English Catholics found an author and scholar who produced an impressive collection

---
[8] Brady, *Annals*, 140–301.
[9] Berington, *Behaviour of English Catholics*, 158.
[10] Old Brotherhood, *List of Members*, 19–23.
[11] Brady, *Annals*, 299.

of religious works. His writings, from *Think Well On'T: or Reflections for Every Day of the Month* published in 1728 to his *Abridgment of Christian Doctrine* in 1772, were numerous, varied in subject, and quite popular. *The Garden of the Soul*, Challoner's best known work, remained in widespread use well into the nineteenth century and is still found in reprints today. His translations of the Bible, of St. Augustine's *Confessions*, and of the *Following of Christ* made these spiritual classics available to many Englishmen for the first time. *Memoirs of Missionary Priests . . . that have suffered death in England . . . 1577–1684*, which Challoner wrote in 1741–42, remains one of the best sources of information about the English Catholics of that period.[12]

The single most important internal change in the church during this entire century was the resolution, for a time, of the struggle for power between the regular clergy and the vicars. Chief among the objections to the appointment of vicars apostolic in the first place had been their inability to settle the contradictions created by a regular clergy serving "two masters," the vicars and the religious superiors of their own congregations. The long years of abnormal conditions, including both the desperate need to use the regulars as mission priests and the impossibility of regulars living a conventual life in penal England had aggravated the entire problem. In 1627 and again in 1633, Rome had tried to settle the issue, but both attempts permitted the dual authority to remain. Pope Innocent XII had made a more positive move toward reform when he decreed in 1696 that regulars were subject to the vicars apostolic in all matters concerned with the care of souls and the administration of the sacraments.[13] Although this decree should have settled the issues, enforcement often proved impossible. Confusion and strife were so widespread that one report stated that the arguments "have come to that excess as to make it doubtful whether ye administration of the Sacraments is truly and validly observed."[14]

Finally, in 1745, Pope Benedict XIV confirmed a series of

[12]Edwin H. Burton, *The Life and Times of Bishop Challoner*, 2:323–339.
[13]Decree *Alias a particulari*, 5 October 1696. Archives, Old Brotherhood.
[14]Burton, *Challoner*, 1:251.

directives which the vicars apostolic had presented to him. These rules were a complete vindication of the position of the vicars and a clear statement of their authority over the regulars in what related to their missionary duties.[15] The promulgation of them did not, however, end the argument. Many of the religious orders, but particularly the Franciscans, appealed the case to the Holy See, and while it was pending there, not all abided by the published decrees. Of these appeals, Challoner commented to his agent, Christopher Stonor, "They are all at present resolutely bent to move heaven and earth in order to have the decrees recalled; they are now very busy in concerting their measures and give out that they are sure of success. Some few of the laity side with them."[16] "The articles which they charge with tyranny," Challoner further explained,

particularly relate to the restraining them . . . which they will have to be a taking away the power from the Regular Superiors of removing or calling over their subjects: and a grievance both to them and the laity, by restraining the liberty of the faithful in point of the choice of confessors.

"What they aim at," he concluded, "is to be quite independent and to make the bishops mere ciphers."

Between 1749 and 1751, both the regular clergy and the vicars apostolic presented their cases, with charges and countercharges, to Rome. Benedict appointed a special commission of cardinals to examine the entire matter and to make a final recommendation to him. Two years later, on 30 May 1753,[17] Benedict XIV issued the bull *Apostolicum ministerium* which regulated the internal affairs of the English church until 1850. In twenty-four sections, the pope laid down the rules governing the relations between seculars and regulars and clarified the jurisdiction, and authority, held by the vicars.[18] The latter were both vindicated and victorious, for the

[15]Ibid., 1:256.
[16]Letter, Richard Challoner to Christopher Stonor, 7 March 1749. Archives, Westminster Cathedral, London District.
[17]Burton, *Challoner*, 1:313.
[18]Brady, *Annals*, 496–521.

regular clergy were to be subject to them in all things relating to the missions. The religious orders submitted with varying degrees of graciousness, and although mutual charity and respect were not always present, at least order had been restored. The English Catholic church survived under this uneasy peace, but just barely. Unfortunately its leaders were more concerned with questions of power and authority than they were with the almost total lack of vitality within the church.

For more than two hundred years English Catholics had lived subject to penal restrictions upon their right to practice their religion, to inherit and dispose of property, to hold public office, to select public officials, to be employed, educated, married, and buried. In almost every phase of their lives they had been harried by the actual or potential threat of fine or imprisonment. By 1778 these laws had served their authors' purposes well. In a nation of about seven and a half million people,[19] Catholics numbered less than 60,000 or 0.8 per cent of the total population of England and Wales.[20]

Politically, economically, intellectually, socially, Catholics were of no practical importance and certainly posed no threat to the civil government or to the established church in England. Indeed, most of the fear of Catholics, so widespread before 1745, had become dormant for want of stimulation. The Stuarts, whom the Catholics supposedly supported, no longer endangered the Crown. Among the upper classes, at least, travel and education had dispelled the myth of the pope as an ogre seeking ways to subvert the English people. On the other hand, prejudice was far from dead, as was amply demonstrated by the Gordon riots in 1780, which were the mob's response to the first Catholic Relief Act. But prejudice and persecution from now on were more likely to be spasmodic in nature, a reaction to specific situations, not overtly encouraged by state or church, and not the result of any official policy. A new spirit of toleration coupled with the obvious harmless nature of the insignificant Catholic population of England made possible the gradual relaxation of

[19]Frederick C. Dietz, *An Economic History of England*, 281.
[20]Brady, *Annals*, 169, 212, 263, 301.

the penal code, the eventual absorption of Catholics into the main current of English life, and a revitalization of the Catholic church.

The first such change occurred when Parliament, in 1778, ordered the repeal of some penal restrictions in exchange for Catholic volunteers to fight alongside their Protestant countrymen against the rebellious colonists in America.[21] From that point on therefore, Catholics could begin to see some chance of their religion occupying a legal even if not an equal position in England, and themselves being able to assume the privileges and responsibilities of citizens in good standing. These few Catholics, however, possessed little in the way of strength—whether measured in terms of numbers, property, experience, or leadership—for the task of rebuilding their church. Edmund Burke, not a Catholic himself although always sympathetic to the Catholic cause, described the effects of the penal centuries as "mischievous." "Every person of that communion, lay and ecclesiastic," reported Burke in a speech to a group of Bristolmen, "has been obliged to fly from the face of day. The whole body of the Catholics, condemned to begging, and to ignorance have been taxed to their ruin."[22]

The Catholics were mainly concentrated in London and in Lancashire. Joseph Berington, one of the few contemporary Catholic observers, wrote that "particularly in the West, in South Wales, and in some of the Midland counties, there is scarcely a Catholic to be found."[23] "Some of the manufacturing and trading towns, such as Norwich, Manchester, Liverpool, Wolverhampton, and Newcastle-upon-Tyne," Berington went on to say,

have chapels which are rather crowded. But excepting in the towns, and out of Lancashire, the chief situation of Catholics is in the

---

[21] 18 George III, c. 60. An Act for relieving His Majesty's Subjects professing the Popish Religion from certain Penalties and Disabilities imposed on them by an Act, made in the Eleventh and Twelfth Years of the Reign of King William the Third, intituled, *An Act for the further preventing the Growth of Popery.*

[22] Charles Butler, *Historical Memoirs of the English, Irish, and Scottish Catholics since the Reformation,* 3:280–281.

[23] Berington, *Behaviour of English Catholics,* 141.

neighborhood of the old families of that persuasion. They are the servants, or the children of servants who have married from those families and who choose to remain round the old mansion for the conveniency of prayers, and because they hope to receive favour and assistance from their former masters.

Moreover, the Catholic population was primarily declining in an age when population in general was rapidly expanding. Berington had estimated that there were 60,000 Catholics in England in 1746. When the vicars made their reports to Propaganda in 1773, they reported just over 56,000, or a decrease of 5 percent during a period when the total population of England and Wales increased approximately 15 percent.[24] "The truth is," wrote Berington, "within the present century we have most rapidly decreased."[25] He went on to explain how "in the nature of things it could not possibly be otherwise." Among the principal causes, maintained Berington,

are the loss of families by death, or by conforming to the Established Church; the marrying with Protestants, and that general indifference about religion which gains so perceptibly among all ranks of Christians. When a family of distinction fails, as there seldom continues any conveniency either for prayers or instruction, the neighbouring Catholics soon fall away.

"We have at this day," continued Berington,

but eight Peers, nineteen Baronets, and about a hundred and fifty gentlemen of landed property. Within this year alone, we have lost more by the defection of the Earl of Surrey, only son of the Duke of Norfolk, and the eldest son of Lord Teynham than we have gained by Proselytes since the revolution.

A disproportionately high number of priests ministered to the needs of these few Catholics. The 1773 reports to Propaganda enumerated 393 clergymen: 121 in London, 91 in

---

[24]Dietz, *Economic History*, 281.
[25]Berington, *Behaviour of English Catholics*, 114.

the Midlands, 137 in the Northern District, and 44 in the West. Of these, less than half, 177, were secular clergy and the rest belonged to religious orders.[26] This meant there was an average of one priest for every 143 Catholics, ranging from one for every 202 laymen in London to one for every 97 Catholics in the Western Districts. Neither Berington nor the vicars commented on this ratio. The vicars, moreover, throughout the period 1780 to 1850, were to lament the shortage of priests, although they sometimes refused a priest because they had no work for him. Although no contemporary explanation for this paradox appears to exist, it seems probable that the shortage can be explained by describing the circumstances under which the Catholic population existed. Their numbers were few, it was true, but they lived in scattered pockets of Catholicism or occasionally in complete isolation from any community of Catholics. Their chapels or meeting rooms were invariably small. Travel conditions in the late eighteenth and early nineteenth centuries as well as the poverty of the priest and people and the general unpopularity of Catholics made it impractical for larger groups to assemble at a central place. "The Catholic population," reported Berington, "was very scattered. In the majority of instances the priest had to keep a horse so as to be able to visit the outlying country. Not infrequently he would serve two or more Mass-centres many miles apart, necessitating a long ride, fasting, every Sunday."[27] Even with such doubling up, the number of people a given priest could serve would be extremely limited.

Refusal to employ a priest usually stemmed from one of three reasons. Frequently the vicars could not find the financial support for the man, even though the need for his service was great. Sometimes the priest seeking employment was a "problem" whom the vicars would attempt to foist off on one another. In the case of the regular clergy, the vicars would strive to avoid as much as was possible the use of a group of men whom they had long held in suspicion.

[26]Brady, *Annals*, 169, 212, 263, 301.
[27]Berington, *Behaviour of English Catholics*, 162.

In the absence of any explanation, we can only speculate about the reasons for such a large number of men entering the priesthood. First, it was almost the only career open to the educated Catholic young man. Moreover, he had received his higher education in one of the English Catholic schools on the Continent. These schools, whatever else they might have been, were primarily seminaries for the training of priests for the English mission. It was not surprising that many of their students entered the priesthood. Second, more than half the active priests were members of religious orders, who in other times or in other places, would have performed other services than parish work. Third, in the face of so many years of persecution, those Catholics who had remained in the faith would conceivably have strong feelings about its preservation and would encourage candidates for the priesthood. At the same time, and this would help to explain the small number of lay Catholics, the penal laws made it difficult, if not impossible, for the clergy, no matter how numerous, to proselytize or make any overt effort to spread the faith.

It was not surprising that the priests failed to win new converts, even in the limited circles in which they could work. First, the idea of conversion did not appear to be popular or widespread. Clergy and laity alike saw themselves as a persecuted minority whose goal was to hold fast to the pure and only true faith despite the hardships that task might entail. But to spread it was to endanger that minority and possibly even weaken its hold on the truth by bringing in new members who had not been tempered by trial. The Catholic population, in its conception of itself, was an elite group. But more than that, the priests were often an unattractive and ineffectual group. They lived in poverty, dependent upon some gentleman for their livelihood, and this after spending years abroad and out of contact with their countrymen. "Our priests, in their general character are upright and sincere," wrote Berington,

> but narrowed by a bad education, they contract early prejudices which they very seldom afterwards deposit. Moderately skilled in the Latin and Greek languages, they know nothing of their own,

nor do they become sensible of their manifold deficiencies till it be too late to attempt improvement.[28]

What was even worse, he added, "they are bred up in the persuasion that on coming to England they are to meet with racks and persecution; they land therefore as in an enemy's country, cautious, diffident, and respectful." Finally, Berington concluded, the English priest "contracted in his circumstances," without "the means of drawing information from books; and unfashioned in the forms of elegant life, his company is not asked for. Thus denied all occasion of improvement, at sixty he will be found the same man he was at twenty-five."

Five vicars apostolic governed this poorly trained and narrow-minded group of clergymen in 1778. Richard Challoner of the London District has already been introduced. A learned and wise man, he died in 1781 and already by 1778 had relinquished most of his authority to his co-adjutor, James Talbot, who had been appointed in 1759 and who governed until 1790. Challoner had requested Talbot, brother of the 14th Earl of Shrewsbury, apparently as much because of his family connections and income as for any noticeable ability to lead or administer. Challoner's agent in Rome, Christopher Stonor, sought the help of "James III," the Stuart Pretender, with Pope Clement XIII for Talbot's nomination. "Challoner seems to give the preference to Mr. James Talbot," wrote Stonor to James in 1759,

who, besides enjoying the protection of that noble and widespread family, is provided with a large patrimony—a matter of no small importance in that country, where the Vicars Apostolic have no fixed stipend, and have not been accustomed, so far, to harass the people by the burden of maintaining them.[29]

Talbot objected to his appointment from the beginning and periodically tried to resign his office. He was no leader

[28]Berington, *Behaviour of English Catholics*, 162.
[29]Copy of letter, Christopher Stonor to "James III," 1759. Archives, Old Brotherhood.

and thought that government restrictions upon Catholics were preferable to the persecution from private citizens which resulted when such restrictions were officially removed. He vacillated over the activities of the Catholic laymen who were working for greater civil liberties in the 1780s. This inability to take a firm stand one way or the other with regard to possible accommodations to the civil authority earned him the disapprobation of his fellow vicars as well as the mistrust of the lay gentlemen. His goodness could not be denied, but his suitability for his post could be most severely questioned. He was damned with faint praise by John Milner, who said in his funeral eulogy of Talbot that "he fell a victim to his anxiety and solicitude for the welfare of the Church at a time and in circumstances that seem to require a more than human portion of zeal and abilities to manage the helm of ecclesiastical affairs aright."[30]

Thomas Talbot, younger brother of James, had been coadjutor in the Midlands under John Hornyold since 1766. When the latter died in 1778, Talbot governed the district until his own death in 1795. He apparently had no greater qualifications for leadership or administration than his brother had possessed. He was only really important in two situations. He identified closely with the Catholic Committee, a group of laymen who were agitating for additional reforms in the penal laws after 1778. Although his brother had also signed the Committee's protest in February of 1789, an act which brought the wrath of the other vicars upon them both, Thomas withdrew his cooperation with the laymen more reluctantly than did James when the other vicars pressed them. Thomas also led a movement in London and Rome in 1790 for the appointment of Charles Berington to fill his brother's post in the London District when the latter died. The other vicars interpreted this as a failure on his part to cooperate in unified episcopal action since they wanted Douglass.

The personality of Charles Walmsley, vicar apostolic of the Western District from 1758 to 1797 was in some ways a sharp

---

[30]John Milner, Sermon preached at Winchester on the occasion of the death of Bishop James Talbot, January, 1790. Archives, Westminster Cathedral.

contrast to that of the other vicars. As a biographical figure he is a delight to study. By far the most systematic and efficient of the English bishops of the period, he wrote short, pointed letters in a meticulous hand. Unlike the rest, he had a strongly developed sense of order. He marked each letter with the date received and attached to it a copy of his answer, a technique not followed, unfortunately, by any of his colleagues. He seemed also to have a true understanding of his function as shepherd and pastor. In that respect, his letters demonstrated concern for the spiritual side of his office as well as for the administrative.

In his view of the social and political world in which he operated, Walmsley stood clearly to the right of his brother vicars. He expressed, more than any of them, the prevailing mentality of humble submission in his reaction to the first lightening of the burden of the penal restrictions. "The great humanity of Government toward us," he wrote in a pastoral to the Catholics of the West in 1778, "suggests a propriety of behaviour on our part in using the present indulgence with caution, prudence, and moderation. We therefore strongly recommend to you to be careful in avoiding what may tend to raise disputes or give offense."[31] Some years later in 1789 when agitation for further relief was growing, Walmsley addressed the lay leaders of the movement, warning them that their last state might well be worse than their first. "If Parliament be petitioned to repeal the Old Penal Laws enacted against the Catholics, probably such Petition will be granted," he wrote to the Catholic Committee in 1789, "but I fear not without substituting some Laws or Restriction which may be very grievous."[32] Walmsley sought the advice of priest friends and, no doubt, their comments helped to form his mind in this conservative mold. In 1783 he had asked Rev. Charles Forrester about some of the ideas of the Catholic Committee.

---

[31]Charles Walmsley, Pastoral Address to the Catholics of the Western District, 3 July 1778. Archives, Pro-Cathedral Church of the Apostles, Western District, Clifton, England. [It is essential to avoid the temptation to believe that statements like this one were made with tongue in cheek. They were not!]

[32]Copy of letter, Charles Walmsley to the Catholic Committee, 2 May 1789. Archives, Clifton.

The reply must have struck a note of sympathy in Walmsley's heart. "Upon the whole," wrote Forrester,

> if leaving things as they are is deemed an obstacle to any further relief, is the harm so great, but we may patiently bear it, for fear of a greater? The Burden is certainly much diminished since the act of Parliament in our favor. We are quiet now, let us remain so.[33]

Matthew Gibson ruled the Northern District from 1780 to 1790. The only relevant statement of his which has survived indicates that he may have been more flexible than his colleagues. In 1783 the Catholic Committee asked him as well as the other vicars if they would favor a restored hierarchy as one means of winning civil approval for the Catholic church. Gibson, unlike the other bishops, reacted favorably. Although he agreed with them that in reality it would make little difference in church government, he maintained that if such a move would please the government, it was all to the good. "If any measure," he wrote to Walmsley on 12 October 1783, "consistent with our religious tenets can be devised or suggested condusive towards procuring relief for the Catholics in their still calamitous circumstances, it will certainly meet my approbation."[34] Thomas Talbot's letter to Walmsley on the same subject reflects the marked difference in their attitudes. "We should be content," he wrote on 9 October 1783, "to go on in the old tack which has succeeded well for the last hundred years."[35]

These five vicars and the twenty-five or so who succeeded them until the hierarchy was finally restored in 1850 faced a formidable task. They had to revive a sinking church in the face of external prejudice and opposition. They also needed to reanimate a reluctant and cautious laity who, for the greater part, saw more wisdom and virtue in silence than in agitation. At the same time, the vicars had to learn to deal with an articulate and highly motivated lay minority (characterized

---

[33]Letter, Charles Forrester to Charles Walmsley, 27 September 1783. Archives, Clifton.
[34]Letter, Matthew Gibson to Charles Walmsley, 16 October 1783. Archives, Clifton.
[35]Letter, Thomas Talbot to Charles Walmsley, 9 October 1783. Archives, Clifton.

by the Catholic Committee), who were more than willing to seize the initiative from the vicars in church-state relations. In this task, the vicars did not always receive much help from the clergy, who in most cases lacked training and motivation for leadership, or the skills needed for cooperative efforts, or any real sense of vision. This larger group of the clergy mirrored the timidity and narrowness of the greater part of the laity. A few among them, however, were more than willing to make themselves heard. They disagreed with the conservative policies of their vicars, agitated for reforms, conducted endless doctrinal battles, and by their speaking and writing kept alive a spirit of opposition to vicarial authority. The vicars even met with trouble in Rome, for they were convinced (not without some reason) that the Holy See had no interest in or understanding of their difficulties and circumstances and that innumerable plots were being laid there against them.

Most of all, the vicars were a problem to themselves. They were largely a conservative group, equally convinced with most of the clergy and laity that the best policy lay in retirement and unobtrusiveness. Suspicious of change or innovation, they looked back to the age of the English "martyrs" rather than forward to a more aggressive and growing church. By no means the least among their troubles was their inability to get along with one another, so that important and necessary cooperative efforts were neglected because personalities clashed, bitter arguments delayed communal action, and public displays of pique and disunion weakened the respect of the clergy, the faithful, and the general community.

It was this respect and reverence for their office which the vicars desired from the faithful above all other things. Respect, so they believed, fostered obedience to authority, and in this obedience lay the salvation of the English Catholics. It was not really surprising that they should feel so strongly about the importance of their own authority. After all, the Reformation had begun, as far as they were concerned, when a king refused to accept the authority of the Holy See. It had been confirmed when a queen had demanded allegiance to her authority over that of the Roman pontiff. The evils of the past two centuries had resulted when authority was ignored and respect for it neglected. Obviously, then, the key to a renewed church was the restoration of respect for the authority of the pope and the pope's vicars.

The bishops therefore directed their energies and their talents for the next sixty years or so to this task of redeveloping respect for that authority and re-establishing a viable church with a strong sense of loyalty to Rome.

PART II
1780–1850

CHAPTER III.
THE VICARS AND THE CIVIL GOVERNMENT

The story of Catholic emancipation has been told and retold from a variety of viewpoints and with several objectives in mind. Among the Catholic writers on the subject, the first one to treat it with any degree of consistency and accuracy was William Amherst in 1886. In his work, *The History of Catholic Emancipation*, he made the basic point that all acts of repeal and emancipation were granted out of expediency and necessity on the part of the British government.[1] "In the history of the Act," Amherst wrote of the Act of 1774, "we distinctly see the spirit which animated the lawgivers, and which can be traced down to our own days, in every Act of Relief, and in all the dealings of our Protestant fellow-countrymen with us as Catholics." "The real reason," continued Amherst, "which prompted the introduction of the Act at that time was, that the Government were anxious that Catholics should profess their loyalty at that particular juncture of affairs." This first of the relief acts and every other one since then, Amherst described as "false insinuations, patronizing insolence, hypocritical assertion of benevolent motives, are not these the very pest which is too often so revolting to Catholics even to this day...."

Writing almost twenty-five years later, Bernard Ward did not contradict Amherst, but treated the whole problem of reform from its internal aspects. He concerned himself with the issues and controversies within the Catholic groups as they worked to gain greater freedom. Always a staunch sup-

---

[1] William Joseph Amherst, *The History of Catholic Emancipation*, 1:65–66.

porter of the "establishment," Ward studied repeal efforts from the standpoint of lay-clerical divisions. Indeed, Ward interpreted most of early reform as the unwarranted interference of the laity into those church affairs which traditionally and properly belonged to the hierarchy. The fact that the vicars were for the most part disinclined to work vigorously for greater freedoms for the Catholic population did not, in Ward's opinion, change the basic fact that the laity, from a spirit of anticlericalism, took liberties which even their desperate need for civil rights did not justify. "It is difficult to define the causes of the rising at this time of an anti-clerical spirit in the Catholic body," wrote Ward, "or to analyze the feelings which in their ultimate issue resulted in actions which seem now almost incredible. We cannot believe that such good and devout members of the Catholic laity could have been at heart disloyal."[2] "Yet it cannot be denied," he concluded, "that there had grown up amongst them an undefined sense of distrust of their spiritual rulers, and a suspicion that the bishops were taking too strict a view of the position of Catholics." Whether Ward was correct in his assessment of lay "disloyalty" and "anti-clericalism" is a highly debatable question, but for the present, it is sufficient to note that he studied the story of Catholic emancipation with this attitude as his guide.

Philip Hughes, writing in 1929 on the whole topic of emancipation in England and Ireland, rounded out the story by presenting a third view. In *The Catholic Question*[3] he made the point that repeal of penal laws and the extension of civil liberties occurred in England only because of the threat to the English from Ireland. English Catholics, Hughes pointed out, were a ragtag and sorry group by 1770. Their power or lack of it was unimportant and insignificant because they were unimportant and insignificant. Ireland, however, was a different matter. Referring to the statement made by Pitt's foreign secretary, Grenville, in 1794, that "Ireland must be governed in the English interest," Hughes made a further

---

[2]Bernard Ward, *The Dawn of the Catholic Revival in England, 1781–1803*, 1:87
[3]Philip Hughes, *The Catholic Question, 1688–18͡*

THE VICARS AND THE CIVIL GOVERNMENT 51

point about Irish-English relations. "More important than any theory of religious freedom in its influence on the genesis of the Catholic Question in the British Isles," said Hughes, "was the practical problem of the Government of Ireland . . . as it presented itself to the English aristocracy in the closing years of the eighteenth century."[4] The problems of the Catholics when they finally forced the English politicians to take notice of them, existed as part of the larger problem of controlling the Irish. "The question in its first beginnings—then the question of relieving Catholic social life from the vexations of the Penal Code," maintained Hughes, "was in fact to the English Aristocracy, simply one element more in its old problem of controlling the colony in Ireland."[5]

None of these views contradicts any other. Nor is it necessary to oppose any or all of them in order to present a fourth facet of the problem. Without disturbing the belief that penal reform was a matter of English expediency in the larger task of controlling the Irish problem, and without disproving the opinion that the specific efforts of the English Catholic laity to win reforms were accompanied by some opposition if not actual disaffection from the English vicars apostolic, it is still valid to maintain that there was an internal problem in the dispute not emphasized, indeed, hardly noted by the three authors here mentioned. It is, perhaps, not surprising that they circumvented it. All three were clergymen writing in periods of hierarchical ascendancy. They might be excused for failing to see in the entire issue of repeal and emancipation from the outside and reform and development from within, the matter of discord among the vicars apostolic themselves. It was precisely this aspect of the problem that appeared to affect adversely the efforts of the English Catholics to re-establish themselves as a respectable group both in the eyes of the English government and the Protestant ascendancy as well as in the minds of the Catholic leadership at home and in Rome.

The facts, personalities, and results of attempts at securing

[4]Ibid., 95.
[5]Ibid., 142.

Catholic relief prior to 1791 are well known and relatively undisputed. In 1771 the "Act for reclaiming of unprofitable bogs,"[6] passed by the Parliament for the benefit of Irish Catholics, marked the first relaxation of government oppression of members of the Roman church. This was followed in 1774, again in the Irish Parliament, by "An Act to enable his Majesty's subjects, of whatever persuasion, to testify their allegiance to him."[7] It was not until 1778 that a similar act passed through Parliament for the benefit of English Catholics entitled, "An Act for relieving his Majesty's subjects professing the Popish religion from certain penalties and disabilities, imposed on them by an Act made in the eleventh and twelfth years of the Reign of King William III, 'An Act for the further preventing the growth of Popery.' "[8] This act marked the first legislative relaxation in the execution of such laws as that giving a bounty to anyone reporting a priest for saying Mass or the one preventing Catholic parents from leaving their property to their Catholic children.

The infamous Gordon Riots of June of 1780 followed the passage of this act and demonstrated that the deeply rooted prejudice against and the fear of Roman Catholics were, indeed, not dead, whatever might be the official government position. These riots took their name from Lord George Gordon who was largely responsible for their instigation. When the Relief Act was passed on 3 June 1778, the first reception of it appeared to be peaceful. Charles Butler, writing of the occasion in his *Memoirs*, recalled that "no Catholic who recollects the passing of the Bill will ever forget the general anxiety of the body, while it was in its progress through Parliament; or the smile and friendly greeting with which his Protestant neighbour met him the day after it had passed into Law."[9] But when it was suggested that a similar bill for relief of Catholics in Scotland be introduced into the next parliamentary session, there was great unrest and violence there, culminating in the burning of the bishop's house in

[6] 11 and 12 George III.
[7] 13 and 14 George III, c. 35.
[8] 18 George III, c. 60.
[9] Butler, *Memoirs*, 3:294.

THE VICARS AND THE CIVIL GOVERNMENT 53

Edinburgh and near grave personal danger to the life of Bishop Hays himself. This disorder soon spread to London and other parts of England, encouraged in great part by Lord George Gordon who in November of 1779 assumed the presidency of the Protestant Association, founded to further the "No-Popery" movement and to obtain the repeal of the relief acts of 1778. Much parliamentary and extra-parliamentary agitation ensued, climaxed by a meeting of the Association on 29 May 1780. During this meeting Lord George moved

That the whole body of the Protestant Association do attend in St. George's Fields on Friday next to accompany his Lordship to the House of Commons on the delivery of the Protestant Petition [for the repeal of the Act of 1778]. His Lordship then informed them that if less than 20,000 of his fellow citizens attended him on that day, he would not present their Petition: and for the better observance of order he moved: (a) that they should arrange themselves in four divisions; (b) to know their friends from their enemies every real Protestant and friend of the Petition should come with a blue cockade in his hat.[10]

A clearer call to riot can hardly be imagined, and riot was precisely what took place. For nearly two weeks, until 13 June, street fighting continued, mostly in London, but spreading to other parts of the kingdom as well. It was during these riots that the house of the vicar apostolic for the Western District, Charles Walmsley, was burned down, destroying all records of the district prior to that time. The riots, eventually quelled by the regular militia, resulted in the death of hundreds and the wounding of many more, not to mention property damage from arson and pillage. Parliament took great pains to investigate the causes of the riots. Many of the leaders were convicted and some executed, although Gordon himself was acquitted on the grounds that he had not intended to instigate a disturbance. Efforts were made to grant restitution to those whose property was destroyed and the government, on the whole, seemed to demonstrate a sympathetic attitude towards the stricken Roman Catholic body. Nonetheless, the

[10] J. Paul de Castro, *The Gordon Riots*, 25.

Gordon Riots confirmed in the minds of many Catholics, particularly some of the vicars apostolic, the opinion that to be forward in seeking rights and liberties was to endanger the very existence of the church and her members, and that silence was the better part of discretion. It is essential to an understanding, if not an appreciation, of the later actions of the vicars to recognize their dismay at the violence unleased by this almost insignificant relaxation of penal restriction. One might wish they had been made of sterner stuff in the pattern of their sixteenth-century predecessors, but it is still easy to see why they were reluctant to force the issue. By forbearance and restraint they could practice the faith in practical if not legal safety; by demanding the latter and more, they could be endangering the whole.

But despite such setbacks as the Gordon Riots, the agitation for more and more liberties for Roman Catholics continued. The moves were slow, however, and it was not until 1791 that another relief bill passed Parliament. This slowness cannot be blamed altogether or even largely upon the government, for once the bill was introduced in Parliament on 1 March, the members acted quickly and expeditiously to pass it on 7 June 1791. This act[11] provided, among other things, that all papists who had taken the oath of 1774 could not be prosecuted for attending Roman Church services or becoming members of Roman Catholic religious orders, being ordained priests or becoming schoolmasters. The crucial clause of the act was the one calling for the taking of an oath of loyalty to the reigning government. It was the argument over the wording of this oath which caused the long delay—from 1780 to 1791—and which set laymen against vicars and the vicars against one another.

To understand why this oath was of such concern to the Catholics, it is necessary to examine the Oath of 1606 enacted by James I, the Irish oath of 1774, the English oath of 1778, and at the work of the Catholic Committee in formulating the oaths proposed for the Reform Bill of 1791. The first oath which Catholics could take—and it did nothing to im-

---

[11] 31 George III, c. 32.

THE VICARS AND THE CIVIL GOVERNMENT 55

prove their status—was the one enacted under James I in 1606. Its important provisions relevant to the later oaths were (1) the recognition of the reigning monarch as the legitimate sovereign, (2) the admission that neither the pope nor any authority of the Roman church had any power to depose the king or to release the king's subjects from allegiance and obedience to him, and (3) that it was not part of Roman Catholic doctrine that princes excommunicated by the pope may be deposed or murdered by their subjects.[12] The oath of allegiance in the Irish act of 1774 made the same three points and added a fourth, that it was "unchristian and impious to believe that it is lawful to murder or destroy any person or persons whatsoever for or under pretense of their being heretics [or] that no faith is to be kept with heretics."[13] The oath in the English act of 1778 was practically a repetition of the Irish oath of 1774. There was nothing in any of these oaths that was particulary offensive to Catholics, and there was little objection to the taking of them. What reluctance did exist came from the necessity of making special and extraordinary efforts to prove patriotism and loyalty to the king. Thus, the oaths did not offer much in the way of relief, but it was believed that they would clear the way and the air for more progressive measures. Mostly what they did was attest to the fact that the sworn word of a Catholic Englishman was as trustworthy as the sworn word of a Protestant; in other words, that Catholics could be loyal citizens in spite of their religious beliefs. But the content of the oath intended for use in the next repeal act, that which finally passed in 1791, caused considerable conflict, partly because of the wording of the oath itself, and partly because of the circumstances under which it was composed and approved. In the efforts to obtain the passage of the Relief Act of 1791 and in the formulation of the oath to be contained in that act, the Catholic Committee played an important and major role.

Lay agitation for church reform, with the idea that certain reforms or changes in government and custom would make

[12]Dodd, *Church History*, 4:cxvii.
[13]Ward, *Dawn*, 2:274.

the Roman Catholic body more palatable to their Protestant berthren, began in a systematic fashion with the founding of the first English Catholic Committee in 1782. At a general meeting of English Catholics, five laymen, Lord Stourton, Lord Petre, John Throckmorton, Thomas Stapleton, and Thomas Hornyold, were chosen to be a "committee of five" to work for five years to "promote and attend to the affairs of the Roman-Catholic body in England."[14] Charles Butler, a prominent Catholic lawyer, was selected to act as their secretary. The first committee had but one real goal—the restoration of a national hierarchy with bishops-in-ordinary instead of vicars apostolic. In addition to the argument that such a governmental form was the one intended by Christ at the institution of the church, the committee believed that national bishops would diminish what they felt was the undue influence of and dependence upon the Holy See by the English vicars and thus make their position relative to the English government more favorable.[15] Consequently, the committee contacted the four vicars apostolic to learn their thoughts and opinions on the matter. Thus far the laity conducted themselves with the utmost propriety. Their letter of 14 May 1783, addressed to each of the vicars, began by observing that the Catholics of England "in their application for a further repeal of some of the penal laws against them [found that] the absolute and unlimited dependence of their Superior Clergy upon the Court of Rome, under the denomination of Apostolical Vicars," was one of the major complaints of Protestants.[16] "The Committee are therefore of the opinion," continued the letter, "that the most effectual method to remove the apprehensions that might otherwise impede the obtaining such further relief from those laws would be to constitute the present Apostolic Vicars with the full powers

[14]Butler, *Memoirs*, 4:2.

[15]It is interesting to note here that whereas pressure for this change existed among the clergy throughout the seventeenth and early eighteenth centuries until 1753, at least, the desire for such a change now rested almost exclusively with the lay group.

[16]Letter, Catholic Committee to the Vicars Apostolic, 24 May 1783. Archives, Clifton.

THE VICARS AND THE CIVIL GOVERNMENT 57

of Ordinaries." The Committee then protected itself, it thought, from being accused of interfering, by adding that they "did not pretend to point out the many advantages of an Ecclesiastical nature which might result from such a change. They willingly submit this consideration to the decision of those whose profession it is to judge in these matters."

The vicars from London, the North, and the Midlands all sent their opinions in October 1783 to Bishop Walmsley of the Western District. Thomas Talbot, writing from the Midlands on 13 October, thought the proposal useless and that the members of the Committee "have an unaccountable itching to meddle with affairs out of their sphere," but he added that "I can see no reasonable objection to it."[17] Matthew Gibson, replying from the North a few days later, added that he saw little value in the plan but that "if any measure consistent with our religious tenets can be devised or suggested condusive towards procuring relief for the Catholics in their still calamitous circumstances, it will certainly meet my approbation."[18] James Talbot responded from London that the proposal seemed to him "superfluous."[19] Walmsley himself expressed his opinion early in November in a letter to his co-adjutor, William Sharrock. "I dislike the proposal," he wrote in his most decided and positive way, "and intend at a proper time to answer in the negative; as such a change would be useless and even detrimental, because we enjoy at present the power of Ordinaries and a good deal more."[20] While he did not expand on what he meant by "a good deal more," to give Walmsley his due, he apparently also consulted with others about the wisdom of the move before replying to the Committee. In a letter to Walmsley, the Rev. Charles Forrester, a clergyman of the Western District, wrote on 27 September 1783, clearly in reply to questions addressed to him, that "no encouragement is to be given to the proposal

[17]Letter, Thomas Talbot to Charles Walmsley, 13 October 1783. Archives, Clifton.
[18]Letter, Matthew Gibson to Charles Walmsley, 16 October 1783. Archives, Clifton.
[19]Letter, James Talbot to Charles Walmsley, October, 1783. Archives, Clifton.
[20]Copy of letter, Charles Walmsley to William Sharrock, 10 November 1783. Archives, Clifton.

of the Committee."[21] He offered as his reasons:

(1) accusations of undue dependence on Rome are false, (2) as long as we remain Roman Catholic we will be objects of suspicion and surely the Committee would not advocate renouncing all Catholic practices, (3) the problems are inherent with being Catholic and restoration of the hierarchy will not solve them.

Consequently, Walmsley replied to the Committee that to their proposal his answer "is in the negative."[22]

Since it was clear that there was no great enthusiasm among the vicars for the restoration, according to Butler, "the Committee, upon this account, dropped the measure."[23] From this effort, however, emerged three issues that were of continuing importance. First, the vicars and the laity had held opposing points of view on the direction in which the English Catholic church should go. Second, the feeling was expressed that the laity were meddling in matters outside their rightful sphere. Third, the vicars were not totally in agreement among themselves over the merits of the proposal.

For a variety of reasons the Catholic Committee made few efforts to force the issue of the hierarchy or to enact any other changes. But they were able to form a new Committee in 1787 when the powers of the first had expired. This committee expanded to ten, consisting of Lord Petre, Lord Stourton, Mr. Throckmorton, Sir Henry Englefield, Mr. William Fermor, Lord Clifford, Sir John Lawson, Sir William Jerningham, Thomas Hornyold, and John Townley, with Charles Butler again acting as secretary, was significantly commissioned on 3 May 1787, "to watch over and promote the public interest of the English Roman-Catholics."[24] A year later three clergymen were added to the Committee: Bishop James Talbot of London, Charles Berington, who was Thomas Talbot's co-adjutor in the Midlands, and Joseph Wilkes, a Benedictine

---

[21]Letter, Charles Forrester to Charles Walmsley, 27 September 1783. Archives, Clifton.
[22]Undated document in Walmsley's hand addressed to the Catholic Committee and located in bound volume of letters for the year 1783. Archives, Clifton.
[23]Butler, *Memoirs*, 4:4.
[24]Ibid.

THE VICARS AND THE CIVIL GOVERNMENT 59

monk. Although no one seemed to discuss the reasons for the inclusion of clergy in the Committee, it seems fairly safe to assume that the committeemen thought it would enhance and regularize their position in the eyes of the whole body of the clergy and of the lay Catholics in general by whom the second Committee had been criticized. Ward, in typical fashion, commented that the election of these three, by secret ballot, "contributed to compromise Bishop Talbot's position; for to accept an appointment in this manner was a tacit acknowledgment that the laymen were able by their vote to give some fresh authority to their bishop."[25] His position, maintained Ward, became more difficult. The inclusion of his name could not but give additional weight to the doings of the Committee, while he had not the strength of character required to influence their action. Both Berington and Wilkes, moreover, have been victims of a bad press in the historical literature. Both became deeply embroiled in lay-vicar arguments during this period and have been blamed much more than Talbot, for cooperating with the Committee and joining the lay opposition. As a result of their activities, both were also suspended for various lengths of time from their priestly faculties.

The chief efforts of this second committee were directed toward obtaining further repeal of the penal laws, and it was on this issue that the great split occurred in the ranks of the vicars. A memorial, prepared by the Committee, was presented to William Pitt, then prime minister on 9 May 1788.[26] It listed the still existing prohibitions against the Catholics, described the oath taken by Catholics since 1778, re-affirmed the loyalty of the Catholics to the government and to the nation, noted the universal growth of a spirit of toleration, and finally asked for Pitt's support of the Committee's planned request for further relief. Pitt in reply stated that he had no objection to further relief, but that it would be better to defer the request until the next session of Parliament. He also asked that the Committee furnish him with the opinions of the

[25]Ward, *Dawn*, 1:122.
[26]Butler, *Memoirs*, 4:6.

leading Catholic universities on the extent of the pope's dispensing power.[27]

The Committee proceeded to provide Pitt with the information he wanted. They sent the following questions to the universities of the Sorbonne, Louvaine, Douay, Alcala, and Salamanca.[28] (1) "Has the pope or cardinals, or any body of men, or any individual of the church of Rome, any civil authority, power, jurisdiction, or pre-eminence whatsoever, within the Realm of England?" to which the universities replied unanimously that the pope and others have "not any civil authority, power, jurisdiction . . . within the realm of England." (2) "Can the pope . . . absolve or dispense with his Majesty's subjects from their oath of allegiance, upon any pretext whatever?" to which all the universities replied "no." (3) "Is there any principle, in the tenets of the Catholic faith, by which Catholics are justified in not keeping faith with heretics, or other persons differing from them in religious opinion, in any transaction either of a public or a private nature?" To this last question the universities also answered unanimously "that there was no such principle." The Committee sent these opinions to Pitt as soon as it received them from the universities.

On 20 May 1788, the Committee met in London and directed Butler to draft a bill to

> obtain the repeal of all the statutes of recusancy, of all the statutes which disable them from serving in the Navy and Army, or from practising the Law or Physic; and of all the statutes which prevent their enjoying their property with all its rights and privileges, equally and in the same manner as Protestant Dissenters from the Established Church.[29]

Before this bill could be submitted to Parliament, however, a new element was introduced into the Catholic attempts at repeal. Other dissenting groups were also attempting to acquire equal rights with members of the established church,

[27] Ibid., 4:12.
[28] Ibid., 4:13–14.
[29] Minutes of a meeting of the Catholic Committee, 20 May 1788. Archives, Clifton.

THE VICARS AND THE CIVIL GOVERNMENT 61

and the suggestion was made that toleration should be granted to all. Such a blanket repeal of restrictions would, in a sense, have favored Catholics more than other dissenters, since the laws against Catholics were more stringent to begin with, and because there was considerably more prejudice against Catholics than against other religious groups. Therefore, Lord Stanhope, a member of the Anglican church, recommended that the Roman Catholics should make a special effort to gain public approval and to disassociate themselves from certain widespread opinions held about them, by making a public protestation denying tenets falsely imputed to them. This suggestion, made in good faith, nevertheless resulted in a furious reaction among Catholics, especially among some members of the hierarchy, and initiated a war of semantics which continued for some time.

Lord Stanhope framed the statement by which the Catholics could attest their loyalty to the throne. Butler, acting for the Catholic Committee, had copies of the document, known as the "protestation," sent to each of the four vicars apostolic in December of 1788. There was some dickering back and forth, some alterations in the wording, but by April of 1789 James Talbot, Thomas Talbot, Charles Walmsley, and Matthew Gibson had all signed it.[30] This protest read in part:

... it is a duty that we, the English Catholics, owe to our Country as well as to ourselves to protest in a formal and solemn manner against doctrines that we condemn, and that constitute no part whatever of our principles, Religion or Belief....

I. We do solemnly declare that neither the Pope ... nor any Ecclesiastical power whatever can absolve the subjects of this Realm ... from their allegiance to his Majesty, King George the Third....

II. We positively deny that we owe any such obedience to the Pope ... and we believe that no act that is in itself immoral or dishonest can ever be justified by or under colour that it is done for the good of the Church.... We acknowledge no infallibility in the Pope ... and we hold and insist that the Catholic Church has

[30] Butler, *Memoirs*, 4:19.

no power that can directly or indirectly prejudice the rights of Protestants. . . .

III. We do solemnly declare that neither the Pope nor any prelate . . . can absolve us or any of us from or dispense with the obligation of any compact or oath whatsoever. . . .

IV. We believe that no sin whatever can be forgiven at the will of any Pope or of any Priest or of any person whomsoever; but that a sincere sorrow for past sin, a firm resolution to avoid future guilt, and every possible atonement to God and the injured neighbour are the previous and indispensable requisites to forgiveness.

V. The doctrine that "faith is not to be kept with heretics" we reject, reprobate and abhor, as being contrary to religion, morality and common honesty; and we do hold and solemnly declare that no breach of faith with any person whosoever can ever be justified by reason of, or under pretence that such person is an heretic, or an infidel.[31]

The approval of this oath by the vicars was not gained without considerable hesitation and resentment. Both of the Talbots and Bishop Berington gave their consent with little delay or trouble, but Bishops Walmsley and Gibson had serious reservations. The former wrote to Gibson implying that he felt he had been hurried into signing. "I was surprised," he wrote in a complaining tone to Gibson on 29 March 1787,

with the sudden appearance of Mr. Henry Clifford on the 18th inst. presenting to me the new Declaration to be signed, bringing me a letter from Bishop James Talbot, acquainting me that at a meeting of the clergy in London, he and they had all unanimously signed it, and hoped I should make no difficulty to do the same.[32]

"I objected first that I had not totally made up my mind," he continued in an effort to explain his actions, "that I had by letter consulted the other Vicars Apostolic upon it; but had not yet received your answer. Bishop Thomas Talbot's answer to me was [that] he thought he should make no difficulty to sign it." "At last," Walmsley went on to say, "after a good deal of discussion, I thought I might reconcile myself to it; upon which I signed it, and also Mr. Sharrock, my Co-

[31] Ibid., 4:19–24.
[32] Letter, Charles Walmsley to Matthew Gibson, 29 March 1789. Archives, Clifton.

THE VICARS AND THE CIVIL GOVERNMENT   63

adjutor, at the end of sixty-three previous signatures of clergymen." Bishop Gibson, himself, at first refused outright to sign the Protestation, writing to the Committee on 20 March 1789, "You may rest assured I never shall sign it in its present form."[33] A few weeks later, however, he grudgingly agreed to having his signature added. "If the Declaration and Protestation of English Catholics be generally and impartially understood to refer only to temporals, as you assured me in a former letter," he wrote to James Talbot in April of 1789, "and to mean no more than what is expressed in the printed copy signed by me and delivered to Mr. Clifford, you may, if judged absolutely necessary for the common cause, and to avoid confusion, not otherwise, add my name to the list of signatures."[34]

Although the vicars and the committeemen felt strongly about the Protestation, the document itself was practically of little real influence. It said little or nothing new about Catholics or what they believed in, promised nothing new from them, and its signers were promised, in turn, nothing new from the government. The chief opposition to it concerned itself with the way in which they claimed the lay Catholic Committee had "forced" it through, its creation by a Protestant, its vaguely anti-papal or cisalpine attitudes, and the very natural resentment of the vicars and others against making further protests and declarations proclaiming what evil beliefs Catholics did *not* hold. Its avowed purpose was to encourage the passage of additional relief bills. As events proved, it actually served more to expose the divisions within the Church to the unsympathetic view of the Protestant world and to accentuate the disagreement in policy among the vicars apostolic.

During the spring and early summer of 1789, the Protestation was presented to Pitt with slight changes in the form in which the vicars had finally signed it. "English Catholics" was changed to read "Catholic Dissenters of England," and

[33]Letter, Matthew Gibson to the Catholic Committee, 20 March 1789. Archives, Westminster Cathedral.
[34]Letter, Matthew Gibson to James Talbot, 12 April 1789. Archives, Westminster Cathedral.

the protest was now cast in the form of a petition, "praying to be relieved from certain penalties, to which they lay daily exposed, on the pretence of doctrines which they had solemnly protested against."[35] The Committee's advisers on Parliamentary activity suggested that the bill should be accompanied not only by the Protestation and Petition but also by a new oath because "new benefits called for new assurances of fidelity; a more ample extension of privileges demanded from them a more ample declaration of their principles."[36] According to Butler, another oath, at first merely the Protestation repeated, was drawn up and presented to the ministry who made some alterations in it and returned it to the Committee. Thus far, the oaths and protestations had been, with the exception of the change from "English Catholics" to "Dissenting Catholics of England," copies of the Protestation to which the vicars had given their consent in the spring. The alterations now made, however, were approved of only by the members of the Catholic Committee, including Bishops James Talbot and Charles Berington and Joseph Wilkes. Bishop Talbot declared that "he saw nothing in it contrary to faith or good morals."[37] The revised protestation, now in the form of an oath, appeared in *Woodfall's Register* for 26 June 1789.[38] The major change was in the clause which had read

that no church, nor any prelate, nor any assembly of prelates or priests, nor any ecclesiastical power whatsoever, within this realm, can directly or indirectly affect or interfere with the independence, sovereignty, laws, constitution, or government thereof; or the rights, liberties, persons, or properties of the people of the said realm, or any of them.

In the altered text, this section read,

that no foreign prince, person, prelate, state, or potentate, hath, or ought to have, any civil jurisdiction or authority whatsoever

---
[35] Butler, *Memoirs*, 4:25.
[36] Ibid.
[37] Ibid., 4:26.
[38] Ibid., 4:27.

THE VICARS AND THE CIVIL GOVERNMENT 65

within this realm;—or any *spiritual authority, power, or jurisdiction whatsoever* that can directly or indirectly affect or interefere with the independence, sovereignty, laws, or constitution of this kingdom, or with the civil or ecclesiastical government thereof as by law established....[39]

This oath immediately aroused the objections of the vicars. Walmsley wrote on 18 June, a week before it was made public, that the word "spiritual" had not been in the document he had signed. If civil power by spiritual leaders was all they meant, he explained, then that was what they must say, but if they were implying more than that, then the oath must be rejected.[40] In the same letter Walmsley also took exception to the denial of papal infallibility. He admitted that it was not an article of faith, but thought that an outright denial of the accepted tradition was too harsh. Butler attempted to placate Walmsley with two lengthy letters explaining the nature of the changes made and the reasons for making them without the specific approbation of the vicars apostolic. The second of the letters clearly stated the Committee's side of the case. "I am very confident," wrote Butler on 9 July, in a most correct and mollifying manner,

that if the committee had entertained the least doubt that the Oath materially differed from the Protestation, they would not have signified their approbation of it without consulting the Vicars Apostolic upon it. I can assure your Lordship that on many occasions they have shown the greatest attention not to interfere in anything Spiritual.[41]

"I have explained the circumstances which give rise to the alteration," he continued.

The exigencies of the business made it necessary to adopt it immediately. Mr. Charles Berington was consulted upon it, and both at that time and since has declared himself to be clearly of the

---

[39]Italics mine.
[40]Copy of letter, Charles Walmsley to Charles Butler, 18 June 1789. Archives, Clifton.
[41]Letter, Charles Butler to Charles Walmsley, 9 July 1789. Archives, Clifton.

opinion, that it contains nothing contrary to Faith or good Morals, and that, the variation from the Protestation is unimportant.

"I beg to observe to your Lordship," he went on to explain,

> that in the Protestation it is said, that no Church hath, or ought to have, *any* jurisdiction or authority *whatsoever* within this Realm, that can either directly or indirectly, affect, or interfere with, the independence, etc. of the Realm or the right of the People. The words *any* and *whatsoever* are surely tantamount to the words, any jurisdiction either Spiritual or Temporal. When, therefore, the Oath says that no Church etc. hath *any* Spiritual jurisdiction, it cannot by any [different] meaning affixed to those words be considered as implying anything which is not included in the words of the Protestation.

The furor continued among the vicars all through the summer months. In July Walmsley directed his co-adjutor, William Sharrock, who was in London, to learn all he could about Catholic affairs, who approved of the Oath, and what was being said about it, particularly in the North.[42] In August a clergyman named Pilling wrote to Bishop Sharrock making his observations on the state of affairs.[43] He thought there was real danger of a division in the Catholic ranks over the Oath. Berington, with many of the clergy and gentry, expected no problems, Pilling reported, nor any danger of further accommodation to Protestant opinions. But the North, wrote Pilling, was the stronghold of orthodoxy. There the Oath was vigorously opposed and denounced and strong support offered to the vicars apostolic. Pilling went on to reject the Oath on the grounds that those who took it would then be bound to oppose the conversion of any Protestant. In September Walmsley wrote to Butler objecting strenuously to the latter's statement that "unless your Lordships will undertake to pronounce the Oath heretical or contrary to the word of God, it should not be altered in one syllable."[44] What

---

[42]Letter, Charles Walmsley to William Sharrock, 10 July 1789. Archives, Clifton.
[43]Letter, Pilling to William Sharrock, 14 August 1789. Archives, Clifton.
[44]Letter, Charles Walmsley to Charles Butler, 28 September 1789. Archives, Clifton. This statement of Butler's was quoted in the letter, a copy of which is in the Clifton Archives.

Walmsley seemed to be objecting to more than anything else was not the possible heretical nature of the Oath, but the impropriety, in his mind, of Butler's dictating to him, a bishop, what to do. "Thus to dictate to us in Ecclesiastical matters," chided Walmsley,

is it not assuming an authority which you have not? Must the Vicars Apostolic learn their Duty from You? Are they obliged to adopt your Verdict or have you a right to give here any Verdict at all? Whom did the Founder of his Church speak to, when he said, "Go and teach all nations, he that hears you, hears me."

"I am inclined," concluded the bishop,

to think that our flocks will rather hear us than you. I think you would do well to abstain from interfering so much, and supporting so warmly the new Oath. You should be sensible, that deciding on the propriety of a religious Oath does not belong to your department.

After much delay, the vicars apostolic met to decide what was to be done about the new oath. Several resolutions were passed concerning the content of the proposed bill but the episcopal letter which they issued on 21 October 1789 referred only to the oath.[45] It stated that the vicars "unanimously condemned the new form of an Oath, intended for the Catholics, published in Woodfall's Register, 26 June 1789, and declared it unlawful to be taken." "We also declared," continued the vicars, "that none of the Faithful, Clergy or Laity, under our care, ought to take any new Oath, or sign any new Declaration, in Doctrinal matters, or subscribe any new Instrument wherein the Interests of Religion are concerned, without the previous Approbation of their respective Bishop." Bishops Walmsley, James Talbot, Thomas Talbot, and Matthew Gibson signed the letter. Two days later Walmsley informed the members of the Catholic Committee of the

[45]Letter, Vicars Apostolic to the Catholics of England, 21 October 1789. Archives, Clifton.

specific objections which the vicars had to the Oath.[46] That the bishops' chief complaint was with the manner of the handling of the affair becomes evident from a fragment of an answer from Walmsley to a letter written to him by a Committee member, Sir Henry Englefield. In it Walmsley pointed out the Committee's errors. "Let me remind you," he wrote to Englefield in November,

of the old proverb, "Set the saddle on the right horse." The affair of the bill with its Oath was not carried on in right order. The agents should have from the beginning consulted the Vicars Apostolic concerning the Oath, which was not done; even not one of them was consulted at all. Our knowledge of it and that very late, was merely accidental.[47]

"Such a clandestine proceeding," concluded Walmsley, "is certainly blameable." This statement Walmsley made in spite of the fact that Talbot was on the Committee and must have known about the Oath.

Lord Petre had made this very point when he wrote to the vicars apostolic on 25 November 1789 in reply to the episcopal letter and to Bishop Walmsley's letter of explanation to the Committee.[48] Petre expressed his regret that none of those who were being blamed for the oath had been called by the vicars to make any explanation of it to them. He then went on to say,

Your Lordships have unanimously condemned the form of an Oath, intended for the Catholics;—yet we beg leave to represent that this very form was not many months since, sanctioned with the approbation of one of the four Apostolical Vicars, who as a member of the Committee has all along been consulted, and without whose concurrence, not one step has ever been taken.

---

[46]Copy of letter, Charles Walmsley to the Catholic Committee, 23 October 1789. Archives, Clifton.

[47]Letter, Henry Englefield to Charles Walmsley, 3 November 1789. Archives, Clifton. A copy of Walmsley's answer appears on the letter he received from Englefield.

[48]Letter, Lord Petre for the Catholic Committee to the Vicars Apostolic, 25 November 1789. Archives, Clifton.

Petre concluded his long letter of defense and explanation with the telling criticism that the Catholics of England "have sometimes also suffered from an imprudent interference of Ecclesiastical authority in civil concerns."

Since all the vicars signed the letter condemning the oath, this would seem to indicate their unanimous approval or at least their agreement that the oath could not be taken. Indeed, Ward said of the meeting, "Perfect unanimity prevailed, and the following resolutions were passed by the bishops without a dissentient voice."[49] Ward, however, offered no evidence other than the vote and his own belief that bishops always agree for the existence of such perfect accord. Later events indicated that it was, perhaps, not so perfect an agreement as Ward had thought.

Walmsley immediately promulgated the episcopal letter in his own district on 2 November 1789, and also requested that the Committee remove his name from the Protestation.[50] When the news of the vicars' condemnation reached them, the Committee attempted to persuade them to delay its announcement to the faithful. Their success, of course, was only partial, for Walmsley had already published the letter in the West, and Gibson, after a short delay, proceeded to make it known in the North. In the Midlands, however, where Committee member Charles Berington was co-adjutor, and in London where Committee member James Talbot was vicar, the faithful were never forbidden to take the Oath. Thomas Talbot explained his behavior in a letter written on 14 November 1789. "As a suspension of the publication was strongly urged," he wrote to Walmsley, "it did not appear to my brother and me that this could well be refused; and if matters can be so managed that difficulties may be removed, all will be well, and I shall be glad if what has been done may be attended with such an Issue."[51] Talbot apparently was sensitive to the problems which might arise from the public prohibition of an Oath which, in the form of the Protestation, the vicars

---

[49]Ward, *Dawn*, 1:175.

[50]Letter, Charles Walmsley to the Catholics of the Western District, 2 November 1789. Archives, Clifton.

[51]Thomas Talbot to Charles Walmsley, 14 November 1789. Archives, Clifton.

had all signed. He felt that the dangers in the changed wording of the oath were not so great as the danger of the division in the Catholic body and of the confusion and scandal given to the general public of England by such an apparent reversal of opinion among the vicars. "Whilst we ought not most certainly," Talbot wrote to Walmsley a month later, "to give up any Title of our Faith, or for human considerations make a sacrifice of our religion, we ought not to put any unreasonable obstacles to a measure that is deemed greatly to conduce to the public good."[52] "The desire of suspending for a time," he reaffirmed, "the publication of our Resolutions seemed to my Brother and me so reasonable a request that we thought it ought not to be refused." Later Talbot again attempted to explain his actions to Walmsley. "I before acquainted you with the reasons why my brother and myself never published our condemnation of the Oath," he wrote in 1790.[53] "They appeared to me then satisfactory, and as the Committee Gentlemen then declared, and have since frequently declared, that they are willing to use their endeavors to procure an alteration of any exceptionable clauses, I could see no sufficient reason for any future publication."

Controversy over the oath continued with the clergy taking sides with one or the other of the parties. In the Midland District a group of priests who became known as the Staffordshire Clergy banded together to send a memorial letter of support to their vicar, Thomas Talbot, and to his co-adjutor, Charles Berington. This letter demonstrated the thinking of many about the quarrels over fine points of semantic distinction in the oath and highlighted the very real conflict which existed in the minds of the clergy over the disagreements among their superiors. "Deliberately we compared them together," wrote the Staffordshire Clergy to Talbot early in 1790, "and the result was a conviction in our minds that we who could take the Oath of 1778 and sign the Protestation,

[52]Letter, Thomas Talbot to Charles Walmsley, 14 December 1789. Archives, Clifton.

[53]Letter, Thomas Talbot to Charles Walmsley [no date]. Archives, Clifton. This letter appears in the bound volume for 1790.

might admit the few explanatory words introduced into the new Oath; for the principal and obvious tendency of the three instruments, in our judgments, were the same."[54] "The names of Gentlemen were signed to this Address," the Memorial continued, "whose views to promote our good we know had been most upright." "But among them, my Lord, were the names of two Gentlemen," the memorialists added, referring respectively to Berington and Wilkes,

whose opinions to us must ever carry great weight. One for his moderate and manly character, your Lordship has chosen to be our future Superior; and the other by his manifold endowments, commanded universal respect. Could we now for a moment suspect that anything adverse to the real interests of religion was designed by such men?

Matters were at something of a standstill because the condemnation of the Oath had been published in two districts but not promulgated in the other two. Moreover, James Talbot, vicar in the London District, the seat and headquarters of all the negotiation, died on 26 January 1790, leaving his district vacant for he had no co-adjutor. Finally on 3 February 1790, the Committee arranged to meet with the vicars in an attempt to settle the differences. Both Thomas Talbot and Charles Berington attended this meeting, the latter as a member of the Committee as well as in his capacity as co-adjutor. The West was represented by Walmsley and his co-adjutor William Sharrock. There was no vicar in London. Gibson did not come from the North because he was ill and he failed even to send a deputy. The combined Committee and vicarial group passed a resolution to ask the legislature "to alter the oath to the words of the Protestation; and that, so altered, the oath will be unobjectionable."[55] The vote, however, was not unanimous, for Walmsley voted in the negative and Sharrock abstained.

[54]Letter, Clergy of Staffordshire to Thomas Talbot, 25 January 1790. Archives, St. Chad Cathedral, Midland District, Birmingham, England.
[55]Butler, *Memoirs*, 4:30.

Despite this apparent approval of revising the wording of the Protestation, the matter did not end with this meeting of vicars and the Committee. The revised oath, even though approved by one set of vicars apostolic on 3 February 1790, was once again condemned by another set a year later. Bishop John Douglass, the new vicar of London, Bishop William Gibson who had succeeded his brother Matthew in the North, and Bishop Walmsley issued a joint letter on 19 January 1791, declaring that "the altered oath remained liable to the censure fixed on the former."[56] In addition, they reiterated "their total disapprobation of the appellation of protesting Catholic dissenters given to the Roman Catholics in the bill." Once again Thomas Talbot as well as Charles Berington were at odds with the other vicars apostolic. The Committee made a special point of investigating the position of Talbot and sent a delegation of five priests to interview him for this purpose. "Mr. Thomas Talbot," they wrote in their report to the Committee, "repeatedly, and in the most unequivocal manner, declared, that he approved of the oath in its present form, which form, agreeably to his own requisition, had been accepted in a public meeting, on the 3d of February, 1790;— that from that approbation he should not recede."[57] Talbot himself explained his refusal to join in the pastoral condemnation in a letter to the new Bishop Gibson. "The steps you seem disposed to take," Talbot wrote in January of 1791, "do not appear to me to be conciliatory ones, either likely to assuage contentions and animosities, or to stop the progress of the Bill. . . . Propose a conciliatory scheme, and your Lordship will find a joint concurrent in, Your obedient humble servant."[58]

There appeared to be little hope of compromise or agreement between the Committee and the vicars, or between Walmsley, Gibson, and Douglass in opposition to Talbot and

---

[56] Ibid.
[57] Ibid., 4:33.
[58] Letter, Thomas Talbot to William Gibson, 7 January 1791. Archives, St. Anne Cathedral, Northern District, Leeds, England.

THE VICARS AND THE CIVIL GOVERNMENT 73

Berington. Thus matters stood when the bill reached Parliament in the spring of 1791. It was ironic, perhaps, that the eventual solution and compromise came through the efforts of an Anglican, Dr. Samuel Horsley, bishop of St. David's. Horsley was clearly in sympathy with the desire for relief from penal restrictions, but he recognized the impossible dilemma which the dispute among the bishops and the Committee had created. "My Lords," said the bishop in the House of Lords, "this bill is to relieve the Roman Catholics from the Penal Laws, under the condition that they take an Oath of Allegiance, Abjuration, and Declaration, the terms of which Oath the bill prescribes. The bill will therefore relieve such Roman Catholics as take this Oath, and none else."[59] The bishop went on to explain that the problem was one of language rather than of doctrine and that both factions within the Roman Catholic body were loyal to their church and to the civil government, however obstinate they might be towards one another. Finally he wisely proposed that the whole matter of the much revised, amended, and fought about Oath and Protestation be scrapped in favor of the wording of the Irish Oath of 1774. Parliament quickly adopted this solution and the Relief Bill of 1791 was passed on 7 June 1791.[60]

The most necessary change relating to Catholics in England in the late eighteenth century was the repeal of penal laws, for without some guarantees of basic rights, the Catholic church was not likely to survive, much less prosper, in a rapidly changing world. To obtain these guarantees, it was essential that the Catholic leadership, both lay and clerical, initiate programs and policies designed to reassure a highly suspicious Protestant majority. Not an easy task under any circumstances, the leaders of the English Catholic church complicated and enlarged the problem by their inability to work with the laity. This division between laity and clergy was further exaggerated and increased by the inability of the vicars to maintain an open, working, cooperating attitude with one another. Unfortunately, this lack of unity continued to characterize the efforts of the vicars apostolic as they labored to improve the position of Catholics in England and to develop the spirit of religion among the Catholic faithful.

with one another. Unfortunately, this lack of unity continued to characterize the efforts of the vicars apostolic as they labored to improve the position of Catholics in England and to develop the spirit of religion among the Catholic faithful.

CHAPTER IV.
THE VICARS AND JOHN MILNER

The years between 1791 and 1850 were not without serious problems for the Catholic church in England. Agitation for more freedom and greater equality increased. Once the Act of Union was a reality, the issue of freedom and equality was compounded by the need to treat the Catholic question in England and Ireland as one situation calling for a single solution in both countries. This, in turn, was complicated by the vast differences in the positions of Catholics in the two kingdoms. If these difficulties were not enough, the Napoleonic settlement of the Catholic question in France raised innumerable questions about the status of *emigre* priests and bishops in England vis-a-vis their relations with Rome and their claim to faculties in England. The growing influence of the soon-to-be restored Jesuits further served to stir up old secular-regular controversies among the English clergy. Even the recently improved relations between Rome and England brought new opportunities for misunderstanding. The French wars had brought the pope to a much closer association with the English government which had served him well in time of distress. Such closeness was often viewed with deep suspicion by the traditional "old" Catholic of England who could only see danger and who could never bring himself to trust completely any attempts at friendliness or cooperation between the two governments. In Rome, too, where the ecclesiastical politicians of the curia had their own rivalries and ambitions, the affairs of England were poorly served, caught as they were all too often in the cross-fire of curial rivalry.

The inability of the vicars to cooperate with one another, and their failure to coalesce in the face of opposition compounded all these external problems. It was the same issue which had marred the history of the church in England since the Reformation. Sometimes the difficulty lay in the timidity of the bishops when faced with new ideas. On other occasions the clash of strong personalities created rivalries and contentions, which destroyed peace and union. Indeed, the vicars in the early years of the nineteenth century were stubborn, jealous of their authority, anxious about the prerogatives of their office, determined to let nothing interfere with their episcopal jurisdiction. Trouble often arose because these men had, for the most part, quite different ideas about how all these things could best be accomplished. Most determined among them, least able to adapt or adjust, never willing to compromise, always ready to attribute the worst possible motives to other men's ideas and actions was John Milner, bishop of Castabala in Mesopotamia and vicar apostolic of the Midland District from 1803 to 1826.

Born in London in 1752,[1] Milner received his priestly training at the English college at Douay. After his ordination for the London District in 1777, he spent his early years on the mission in Winchester. His interest in this part of England led him to write a history of Winchester and the surrounding areas. This work in turn admitted him as a fellow into the Society of Antiquaries. Milner first came to public notice during the struggle between the vicars apostolic and the Catholic Committee preceding the passage of the Relief Act of 1791 discussed in the last chapter. He was present with Bishops Walmsley, James and Thomas Talbot, and Matthew Gibson, and the co-adjutors, Berington and Sharrock, when the vicars assembled in October 1789 to condemn the Oath. When the Catholic Committee persisted in its opposition to the vicars and had its own version of the relief bill carried to the floor of Parliament, Milner later acted as the agent for Walmsley, William Gibson, and John Douglass in their efforts to persuade members of Parliament to reject the proposed oath. In all the controversy preceding and following the even-

---

[1] F. C. Husenbeth, *The Life of the Right Rev. John Milner*. All the biographical details of Milner's life mentioned in this paragraph are taken from pages 1–65.

tual passing of a satisfactory bill, Milner took an active, highly orthodox, and heated part. He and Charles Butler, Secretary of the Catholic Committee, exchanged innumerable public recriminations, and remained bitter enemies for the rest of their lives. Milner's comments in the Catholic monthly, *The Orthodox Journal*, a magazine devoted almost exclusively to his own tirades, sometimes signed, but more often presented under a pseudonym, give some idea of the bitterness with which Milner could regard an enemy. A good illustration of Milner's particular style of invective was his review of Butler's *Historical Memoirs* in October 1819. "If a man has distorted eyes," began Milner with a reference to the fact that Butler was both blind in one eye and had a deformed muscle in the lid of the other, "or any other defect in his countenance, he generally conceals it with a patch or a plaster and is by no means forward in exhibiting his portrait to the public."[2] "In like manner," continued Milner, drawing a cruel analogy,

should a man be known to have been guilty of many blunders for a signal misconduct in any agency which he had undertaken, prudence teaches him to descant on any other subject rather than on this. But an excess of vanity will make some persons set these rules of common decency at defiance, so far as to appear vain of their deformity.

"After all, Mr. Editor," Milner then added maliciously,

be sure that I bear no ill will to this meddling man; I can forgive him all the mischief he has done or attempted to do me and the Catholic religions . . . but when I find him misrepresenting the whole history of English Catholics, and see him in particular glossing over his own treacherous conduct in their regard as he certainly does in his late faithless Memoirs . . . I feel it my duty to guard my Catholic brethren against his former intrigues by directing their attention to those which he has already practiced against them.

After attributing not the least bit of good will to any of Butler's action, Milner concluded the review with a suggested

[2]John Milner, *The Orthodox Journal*, 131.

epitaph for Butler. "Here lies the body of _____, having failed in his studies for the priesthood in the pope's Seminary Douay, became the constant opponent of priests, bishops, and popes." He was, so Milner would have it recorded,

> the founder of the sect of Protestant-Catholic Dissenters; the publisher of the three quarto Blue Books in its defence and in opposition to bishops and popes. He was the prime supporter of the Cisalpine anti-papal Club, and the Uncatholic Bible Society. He was the distorter of Catholic history, the joint fabricator of the Fifth Resolution for *concurring* in the support of the Protestant Charter schools and other similar establishments, and the chief framer of the bill for subjecting the jurisdiction, discipline and doctrine of his Church to the control of a lay tribunal under the paramount authority of a state minister . . . and thereby occasioned the schism, the tumults and the misery which have since afflicted one part of the United Kingdom. . . .

In a series of private letters to Bishop Douglass written much earlier, Milner was even more explicit, if possible, about his dislike of Butler and demonstrated even better his own unique ability at character assassination. "For my part," wrote Milner to Douglass about Butler in 1800, "I think he is so habituated to the practice of falsehood that I never believe him except where it is evidently his interest to tell the truth."[3] Milner had no appreciation of mitigating circumstances or that there might be another side when it came to those who opposed him. "Whenever any mischief to religion happens or things are in an unfavorable situation,"[4] he commented in another letter to Douglass, "I cannot help thinking that Charles Butler has a principal share in the business. It is because I have so long known that man's restless dark intriguing character, particularly in every matter in which religion is concerned, that I entertain such suspicions. . . ." By contrast, the worst Butler appeared to have said about Milner was the comment he made to Milner himself in 1791 when

---

[3]Letter, John Milner to John Douglass, 1800, quoted in Ward, *Dawn*, 2:207.
[4]Ibid.

the fight over the Oath was at its height. Concluding an interview with him, Butler said, "I wish you well but I desire never more to see your face."[5]

So much for the style and character of the man who ruled the Midland District for twenty years. Involved as he became in every aspect of church life from the most spiritual to the most political, intimately associated with the Irish bishops whose agent he was for some time, intensely concerned with the kind of settlement reached between the Catholic church and the government, jealously guarding the church from the smallest error or least sign of unorthodoxy, suspiciously scrutinizing every attempt to modify or change church law or custom, Milner placed himself in opposition to almost every issue which was raised by English Catholics during his episcopate. His central position in the internal affairs of the English church and their relation to Rome and Westminster would easily provide enough material for a full length biography— and, indeed, there is need for such a study. Since the purpose here, however, is to demonstrate how successive and continued disagreements among the vicars rendered them almost totally incapable of taking action, only those incidents in which Milner played a key role need be discussed. Milner's part in a series of internal jurisdictional disputes should make clear the divisive nature of his contribution to English Catholic life and the way in which such behavior immobilized the vicars apostolic.

The idea of raising John Milner to the episcopate seems to have first occurred as a possible solution to the awkward problem of bishop Berington's status in the Midland District. As a result of his activities in the Catholic Committee when he was co-adjutor to Thomas Talbot, Berington had been denied the faculties of vicar apostolic when he succeeded to that position after the death of Talbot in 1795. Cardinal Giacinto Gerdil, prefect of Propaganda, insisted that he renounce his signature to the Protestation and Oath before receiving his complete faculties, and this Berington refused

[5] Ibid., 1:279.

to do. Until he and Cardinal Gerdil could come to some compromise, Berington was vicar without powers and the Midland District suffered from lack of leadership and great confusion over who actually had the authority to govern it. The suggestion that perhaps Milner might be the answer to the problem seemed to have come from Gerdil himself. In a letter of 11 September 1797, to Bishop Gibson from Bishop Douglass in London, the latter reported a communication he had received from Rome. "Again the Cardinal asks me if it may not be the best plan to prevail upon Bishop Berington to sign,"[6] explained Douglass, "and then to give him a co-adjutor under pretence of his bad state of health, and if Mr. Milner may not be a proper person for that charge, and that Mr. Milner has many qualifications; in short, of his zeal and virtue and learning we are agreed." Clearly Gerdil placed little confidence in Berington's orthodoxy even if he would admit his errors. The combination of Berington and Milner was almost preposterous, however, for the two had disagreed violently over the matter of lay participation in church affairs. Berington had strong support from the Staffordshire clergy whom Milner considered on the verge of schism. They had taken opposite sides during the entire affair with the Protestation and Oath. Plainly, even Douglass thought the Cardinal's suggestion lacked practicality. In the letter already mentioned, he remarked to Gibson, "Now I beg leave to ask: (1) Do you think Mr. Milner the man fitted to be co-adjutor to Bishop Berington? (2) Do you think him proper to be appointed to govern that District?" "My opinion," Douglass continued

is doubtful for (1). Bishop Berington considers Mr. Milner as an *Enemy*, and one who has *traduced him in print*. Last February he lodged with me a formal complaint against Mr. Milner for having *traduced his character before the public*. (2) Mr. Milner's zeal for the cause of Orthodoxy and the Church is of so inflexible a temper that he may not bear and forbear, he may not conciliate the good will of the Clergy and People of that District.

[6]Letter, John Douglass to William Gibson, 11 September 1797. Archives, Leeds.

"I may say with certainty," he added, "that hitherto he is not acceptable to those of Staffordshire." "But on the contrary," Douglass concluded, judiciously posing the other side of the case, "the state of the Clergy and People there may be in want of an inflexible guide."

There appeared, then, to be no doubt that Douglass was fully aware of the difficulties that might arise should Berington and Milner be forced to work together. More important, it seemed clear that Douglass was equally aware of the character and personality of Milner and of the difficulty such an individual would have working in the Midlands—already the scene of much disorder. The bishop, in fact, seemed to recognize from the beginning that Milner was no unmixed blessing.

Gerdil's suggestion did not become a reality for Bishop Berington and he reached an agreement in the spring of 1798 and Berington's faculties as vicar apostolic were sent to him. His untimely death, however, on 8 June 1798, before the documents from Rome had even reached him, reopened the whole matter of the succession to the Midland District. Once more Milner's name appeared as a possible choice. The entire canonical situation, moreover, was one of incredible confusion. John Bew, whom Berington had appointed as vicar general of the Midlands, claimed jurisdiction over the district after Berington's death. This was the customary procedure when a bishop died without a co-adjutor. Since Berington, however, at the time of his death and certainly at the time of his appointment of Bew, had not been in possession of his full faculties as vicar apostolic, a question arose about the validity of Bew's appointment. Furthermore, Bew was determined to sound his clergy on their opinions for their new bishop, a policy somewhat unusual but not forbidden. He proceeded to poll the clergy with the following result: Bew, 2 votes; Richard Southworth, 25 votes; John Kirk, 1 vote. One of the Midland priests, John Appleton, who was not in sympathy with the entire affair, reported the voting to Bishop Gibson. "Your Lordship," he further complained to Gibson on 2 July 1798, "I entreat you to use your utmost endeavors to extricate our unhappy district from the confusion we have so long been in."[7] Appleton then went on to explain that Bew, Kirk, and Joseph Berington, the late bishop's brother, had met after the funeral and concocted the plan of having the succession decided by the votes of the clergy." These three then proceeded to notify the clergy of their plan, complained Appleton, and even claimed that they knew the late Dr. Berington had marked out Bew for his coadjutor. Appleton, who obviously had little regard for Berington, had even less for Bew. He went on to comment to Gibson, "If true, I pity his taste by the by. What a bare-faced impudence. Heaven preserve us from a self-called Prelate." It was significant that Milner's name did not even appear among those suggested by the clergy of the district.

Meanwhile, Bishop Gibson claimed that since Berington had not had the faculties of the vicar apostolic, his appointment of Bew had not been valid. Hence, the government of the district, in the absence of either vicar or vicar general, reverted to the senior vicar apostolic of England, Gibson himself. Two conflicting authorities now proceeded to make rules for the district, compounding confusion. Ignoring for the most part the choices made by the Midland clergy, the vicars apostolic proceeded to cast about for a proper person to be appointed vicar there. They clearly recognized the possibilities of opposition from within the district, the confusion which had existed there for too long, and the need for a return to strong episcopal control. In a letter written on 16 June 1798, just days after Berington's death, Douglass commented to Sharrock,

If at any time we ought to proceed with secrecy, it is at the present, when we are fixing upon a proper person to succeed the deceased, and to govern the Midland District. I wish and pray that our choice may not be known to the public till the appointment by the Supreme Pastor has actually taken place, for then opposition and malignancy will be devoid of power to obstruct or defeat us.[8]

[7]Letter, James Appleton to William Gibson, 2 July 1798. Archives, Leeds.
[8]Letter, John Douglass to William Sharrock, 16 June 1798. Archives, Clifton.

Significantly, Milner's name appeared high on the list of approved people. In the same letter, Douglass continued, "I have fixed on Mr. Milner for successor, to whose name I shall add the names of Thomas Eyre, president of Crook Hall College, and Thomas Smith, priest in Durham." "As Bishop Gibson is the Senior Vicar Apostolic," concluded Douglass, "he will write the letter to his Holiness." Douglass then added that he was sure Gibson "will concur" and that "you will not disagree with us."

Milner fully realized that he was the bishops' choice, and that he was not the choice of the Midland clergy. In July he wrote to Gibson thanking him for the high opinion the latter apparently had of him, but disclaiming his own abilities for the task of ruling the district. He took pains, however, to indicate clearly what he thought of the "goings on" in the Midlands. "Alas, my Lord," he wrote,

we have a fresh proof of the bad spirit that prevails in a certain quarter in the attempt that has been made to change the established ruler of the mission by invading the just and necessary authority of the Bishops and establishing a species of popular elections in that most sacred and essential business.[9]

"In a word," he explained to Gibson, "I do most devoutly wish to see the Bishops of this country once more happily united on the basis of orthodoxy, and a superior established in a certain part of it, who can neither be overawed or imposed upon by the faction that prevail in it." "But, my Lord," he concluded, "both from conscience and inclination, I wish not for the situation myself, knowing that I am essentially disqualified for it."

Bishop Berington had died in June of 1798. Despite the efforts of the clergy from the Midlands to have their choice appointed vicar, and even though the vicars apostolic themselves suggested names to Rome, no successor was named until George Stapleton was appointed on 7 November 1800. The reasons for this delay of almost two and a half years

---

[9] Letter, John Milner to John Douglass, 24 July 1798. Archives, Leeds.

were complex. Rome never had moved quickly and when there were clear signs of differences of opinion as there were in this case, the whole tendency of Propaganda was to let things drift until the situation had either been settled at the local level or else had disappeared. Furthermore, Rome itself was in grave difficulties. French troops had occupied Rome and Pope Pius VI with most of his curia had been taken from the city by Napoleon's army. Mail service was practically at a standstill and travel was so restricted that there was very little communication of any kind between Vatican offices and local church governments. Before either Rome's or England's problems could be solved, Pius died in captivity on 27 August 1799. Under conditions such as these, the appointment of a vicar for the Midlands was hardly crucial, no matter how important it might seem to the English clergy.

Other problems also existed. A struggle for power developed between the officials of the curia, to whom the business of episcopal appointments would normally belong, and those English in Rome who realized the value or usefulness of a more direct method of communicating with and influencing the pope. One of these latter was Monsignor Erskine. Charles Erskine, resident in Rome in the 1780s, had studied for the priesthood but had left the Scot's college in Rome to practice law. In 1782, Pius VI had offered him the position of "Promoter Fidei" in the curia, and Erskine began a new career in ecclesiastical administration. In 1793 the Holy Office considered sending an envoy to the English court, the circumstances of the French revolution having considerably improved the relationship between Rome and England. Erskine, a British subject, at home both in England and in the intricate power structure of the curia, was a reasonable candidate. The story of his arrival in England, unannounced to the vicars apostolic, and of the ultimate failure of his attempt to establish diplomatic relations with the English government is another tale. Erskine, however, remained for a time in England and then returned to Rome where he became an unofficial but highly vocal source of information on the needs, desires, and weaknesses of the English church and an ever ready authority on solutions to the vicars' problems. Like it or not, the vicars had to consider Erskine when they dealt with Rome.

In the more than two years between Berington's death and Stapleton's appointment, the bishops were clearly aware of Erskine's power in Rome. In January of 1799, Milner wrote to Douglass lamenting the continuing conflict in the Midlands and the great need there was for some new method of making the needs of the English church better understood in Rome. At the same time, Milner acknowledged that, as far as rumor was concerned, he was a possible choice. "I have learnt from a different quarter," he commented to Douglass, "that the story of my promotion is very public in London, though a great many persons with whom I am not apt to concur in opinion upon other subjects agree with me in this that little credit is to be paid to it."[10] In the same letter, Milner offered some very specific recommendations about the best method of dealing with the problem of Erskine's influence in Rome. "The present state of this whole business," he confided to Douglass, "confirms the conjecture which I formed in my own mind from the time it was taken up, viz., that the means used to accelerate it by keeping Monsignor out of the secret, would be the certain means to retard and probably defeat it." "In the present weak (because divided) state of episcopal influence at Florence," he further explained,

it appears necessary to submit, in a certain degree, to the circumstances of the times: to speak plain, I would either establish a direct correspondence with Cardinal Gerdil or other persons who have immediate access to his Holiness . . . or I would condescend to solicit the cooperation of Monsignor.

"As matters are at present," Milner shrewdly observed, "the Bishops stand a very unequal contest in any dispute they may change to have with him." Finally, in still another passage of the same letter, Milner kept open the door to his own eventual

---

[10]Letter, John Milner to John Douglass, 23 January 1799. Archives, Westminster Cathedral.

appointment. "I have often declared to your Lordship," he reminded Douglass,

that in the sincerity of my heart, I would wish to decline the situation in question, which certainly in a worldly point of view is greatly inferior to my own; but that on the other hand, I am infinitely solicitous, as is the great body of Catholics throughout the kingdom, that a person of strict orthodoxy and piety, as also of sufficient sagacity and learning, who may cordially unite with the other Bishops in those measures of general good which are so much wanted, may be nominated.

It is not unreasonable to believe that Milner thought himself such a suitable person.

The failure of Rome to act weighed heavily upon the minds of the English vicars who rightly understood that the problems of the Midland District as well as those of the whole English church would not be settled until some decision was reached. Every day of delay seemed to be further proof, if more were needed, of the low regard with which Rome treated the recommendations of the vicars apostolic. In a strongly worded letter, Bishop Sharrock put the case to Douglass. "I think," he complained on 18 March 1799, "we have been too inactive in what concerns a Vicar Apostolic for the Midland District."[11] "The peace of the Catholic body," he declared, "depends upon the appointment of a proper Person, and if the Agents of his Holiness repose no confidence in the joint recommendation of the three surviving bishops, to what do they not expose the interests of religion and the authority even of the Pope." Turning to the practicalities of the situation, Sharrock proposed that the vicars send a firm remonstrance to Cardinal Borgia. "He was long Secretary of the Propaganda," Sharrock added, "and probably understands the affairs of the Mission better than most of his Colleagues. This business appears to me of so much weight that I would meet your Lordship and Bishop Gibson upon it at any place to consider of it jointly." "London would have many

---

[11]Letter, William Sharrock to John Douglass, 18 March 1799. Archives, Westminster Cathedral.

advantages," he suggested, but then added the reminder, "tho' we should be under the eyes of Monsignor Erskine."

Erskine apparently made it clear that the bishops had little recourse except through him. "He ridiculed the idea of sending up a list of names through a different channel from his own," wrote Milner of Erskine, to Gibson, on 25 April 1799, "saying that he assured Bishop Douglass at the time that any such list would be transmitted back to him for his opinion and concurrence."[12] Milner then proceeded to outline a letter he had prepared for the bishops to send to the pope in which they would affirm their loyalty and the general good order of the church in England. The letter, Milner suggested, would lament the hardships and scandals created by the absence of a bishop in the Midlands and state that since there was so much opposition to the appointment of John Milner, some other person from the bishop's list of suggested names be immediately appointed. Nonetheless, the vicars remained firm in their choice of Milner as the one to govern the Midlands. "If your Lordship or Bishop Gibson agree to place Mr. Milner in the first rank," wrote Sharrock to Douglass on 26 October 1799, "it may be of service to mention that Cardinal Gerdil was the first who proposed him."[13] "However," Sharrock added, "the opposition Mr. Milner is likely to meet with should not be overlooked." The very next day Bishop Gibson wrote to Douglass in the same vein, lamenting the fact that Rome paid no attention to the suggestions of the English bishops. He agreed that Milner should be the unanimous choice of the bishops and that although Milner's critics should be heard, in the last analysis, if Rome would not listen to the bishops then what hope would there be for the retention of law and order in the church."[14] Although six months had elapsed between Milner's recommendations and these letters indicating acceptance of his ideas, the bishops had not been idle. The English College in Rome had been seized by the French

[12]Letter, John Milner to William Gibson, 25 April 1799. Archives, Leeds.
[13]Letter, William Sharrock to John Douglass, 25 October 1799. Archives, Westminster Cathedral.
[14]Letter, William Gibson to John Douglass, 26 October 1799. Archives, Westminster Cathedral.

in the spring and the vicars had spent the summer in negotiating the return of the faculty and seminarians, and the completion of St. Edmunds, the new school to accommodate them near London. While the situation in the Midlands was grave and important, it was not, however, the only problem the vicars were faced with.

Despite the apparent desire of the vicars apostolic to have Milner succeed as the vicar of the Midlands, when the actual appointment was finally made, Gregory Stapleton received the post. This choice, approved by Pius VII on 7 November 1800, introduced a man who had not appeared on either the Midland clergy's list or on the list submitted by the vicars apostolic. The long delay in making the appointment is more than understandable, but what is not so easy to understand is why Milner did not get the post and why Stapleton did. The latter had been president of St. Omer College until the Jacobin Directory caused it to be closed in August of 1793. After a brief sojourn at Douay he accompanied the group from there back to England, where he was appointed president of St. Edmund's College, Old Hall Green, in Hertfordshire. Stapleton came to the notice of Pius VII and Propaganda as the result of a secret mission he undertook in May of 1800 relating to the validity of the marriage between the Prince of Wales and Mrs. Fitzherbert. In addition to the good impression he apparently made on the pope in the course of that assignment, he also had the merit of being somewhat remote from the arguments and partisan loyalties of the Midland District. At any rate, Pius VII appointed him in November of 1800 to be vicar apostolic of the Midland District.

Why, in the light of the vicars' evident desire, Milner was not selected is not completely clear. Ward suggests that Milner's controversy with the Anglican Chancellor of Westminster, Dr. Sturges, over the former's history of Winchester may have made him *persona non grata* with the English government which in 1800 was held in high regard by Rome. "It appears," wrote Ward in his history of the Catholic church, "that Propaganda, acting on the advice of the other vicars apostolic, had decided upon recommending Milner for the post, and according to Mr. Smelt his briefs were being actually drawn out when, by the wish of the pope, a change was made."[15] The reason given, according to Ward,

was connected with his controversy with Dr. Sturges. Representations were made to the pope that the appointment of Milner at that time would not be acceptable to the English government; and remembering all that the Papacy had owed to England during the late wars, he consented to be guided by this consideration.

"He therefore cancelled the appointment of Milner, and nominated Dr. Gregory Stapleton," explained Ward, "who during his late visit to Rome had increased the already high opinion entertained of him."

The controversy with Dr. Sturges concerned Milner's book, *The History of Winchester*, published in 1798. In it Milner had attacked the controversial Anglican, Benjamin Hoadley, bishop of Winchester from 1734 to 1761, who, according to Milner, "both living and dying undermined the Church of which he was a prelate."[16] Dr. Sturges took great offense at the criticism. A vigorous exchange of public letters ensued, and Milner claimed that as a result of this public argument and of his criticism of the established church, bills were introduced into Parliament seeking to control the growth of Catholicism and the spread of Catholic religious houses.[17] The bills proved abortive, but the painful discussion continued for some years. In a letter to Gibson, Milner indicated that he thought that his *History* was the reason he was not appointed to the Midlands. "About a fortnight ago," he wrote on 22 September 1800,

a strong report was current here and in London that both Mr. Stapleton and myself were named to the dignity in question, and I cannot help suspecting that this and similar reports heretofore have been raised by Monsignor [Erskine] himself, for the purpose of sounding the public pulse on the said matter.[18]

[15]Ward, *Dawn*, 2:228.
[16]Quoted in Ibid., 2:202.
[17]John Milner, *Supplementary Memoirs of English Catholics*, 104, quoted in Ibid., 2:202.
[18]Letter, John Milner to William Gibson, 22 September 1800. Archives, Leeds.

"But Bishop Douglass has been active in suppressing this rumour," Milner went on to explain, "and he repeats to me his opinion that I shall be left where I am in this city. I judge that he founds this opinion on hints which he has gathered from the Italian agent, and that the latter fancies I am obnoxious to government by my late publications."

In any event, Stapleton was appointed Vicar Apostolic of the Midland District. He was consecrated on 8 March 1801, by Bishops Douglass, Moylan, and Sharrock, and proceeded immediately to his new assignment. His efforts to bring peace to the troubled district unfortunately ended abruptly when he died on 23 May 1802, just a little more than a year after taking over the government of the district. Once more the Midlands was without a bishop.

Again there was a long delay in the appointment of a new bishop for the Midland District. William Poynter of the London District had been Stapleton's choice for vicar general and, accordingly, he attempted to govern the district. Bishop Gibson believed that the appointment was not valid because Poynter was not a priest from the Midland District and, under his prerogative as senior vicar, he, too, tried to govern. Poynter himself was doubtful about the wisdom of the assignment and hoped to escape from it. He sent the letter of appointment to Bishop Sharrock with the wish that the bishop try to find something irregular in it so that he would not have to serve.[19] All three bishops recommended Milner for the post, as much to settle the conflict between Poynter and Gibson as for any other reason. In the meantime, Cardinal Gerdil, prefect of Propaganda, died on 12 August 1802, and his successor, Stephen Cardinal Borgia, had strong prejudices against Milner. "Rev. Mr. Milner of Winchester was presented by Mr. Gibson and self to the Propaganda," wrote Douglass in his diary on 20 November 1802, "to fill the Vicariate of the Midland District, vacant by the decease of Bishop Stapleton."[20] "Cardinal Borgia, Prefect of the Sacred Congregation de Propaganda Fide," Douglass added,

[19]Letter, William Poynter to Gregory Sharrock, 11 June 1802. Archives, Clifton.
[20]Diary, John Douglass, 20 November 1802. Archives, Westminster Cathedral.

THE VICARS AND JOHN MILNER

having signified to us that Mr. Milner must not be chosen to the vacant Vicariate, *"quippe qui in multos isthic incidet simultates,"* Mr. Milner has drawn up a well composed memorial in explanation of his conduct and writing; asked what other kind of conduct etc. they at Rome would have wished him to have pursued when the VVAA called him to their assistance, viz., during the contest with the Committee, etc., etc.

Nearly a year elapsed before Milner was appointed to suceed Stapleton and the delay infuriated him. He repeatedly expressed his desire not to be appointed to the Midland District, although he was anxious to vindicate himself before Rome. In a letter to Gibson on 13 November 1802, he expressed hope that someone else would get the position. "With regard to myself," declared Milner,

I confine my hopes to the object I have announced, namely that, the Congregation having implicitly censured my conduct and writings to the exultation of my enemies and the confusion of my friends, should in some public manner, declare the contrary. This object I mean to pursue with unabaiting vigour.[21]

Despite his protestations about his unworthiness to have the Midland position, however, Milner expressed real anger when for the second time it seemed that the prize which was so nearly his would be snatched from his grasp. "A second time has every rule by which our little body is conducted been set aside," he wrote with evident distress to his friend Sir John Coxe Hippisley in October of 1802, "on purpose to mark me out to my fellow Catholics and fellow subjects as a man under the displeasure of the Court of Rome."[22] "In a word, Sir," he explained as though Hippisley might not understand,

The Middle District or Episcopacy, to which I had before been recommended by the three Catholic Bishops whose business it is

[21] Letter, John Milner to William Gibson, 13 November 1802. Archives, Leeds.
[22] Letter, John Milner to Sir John Coxe Hippisley, 26 October 1802, quoted in Bernard Ward, *The Eve of Catholic Emancipation 1803–1829*, 1:23.

to present, having become again vacant by the death of Dr. Stapleton (who was irregularly appointed by Rome in my place), and I having a second time been unanimously recommended by the same Prelates, I have just now received the affront of an exclusion from the President of the Propaganda.

Milner went on to say that he was thus rewarded because of his loyal defense of orthodoxy, but that nothing else could be expected from the court of Rome under its present management. He was referring here to Cardinal Borgia, at whose door he laid the blame for his failure to receive the Midland appointment. "This circumstance renders it impossible that I should stand forward again as the advocate of Rome," warned Milner in his letter to Hippisley, "and makes me wish for an entire dismissal from her Ministry, which I have an intention of applying for, after a formal justification of myself."

The appointment, when it finally did come, appeared to have resulted from the good offices of Erskine, who had been raised to the cardinalate in January of 1803. Milner and Erskine were by no means friendly or in sympathy with each other, but Erskine's recommendation no doubt resulted from the willingness, at long last, of the three vicars apostolic to make their plea through him. The proof that he did recommend Milner appeared in a letter from Douglass to Sharrock on 24 January 1803. Douglass reported to Sharrock that Rev. Mr. Smelt, the English vicars' agent in Rome, had written that "Monsignor Erskine, since his return to Rome, has recommended Mr. Milner."[23] A month later in another letter to Sharrock, Douglass announced the actual appointment of Milner. "We are peculiarly obliged to Cardinal Erskine for his nomination," he explained to Sharrock, "for though besides our recommendation from England, the Irish Bishops addressed Propaganda in his favour, but the prejudices against him were so deeply rooted, that little attention would have been paid to such solicitation, had not Cardinal Erskine exerted his influence with great activity."[24]

[23]Letter, John Douglass to Gregory Sharrock, 24 January 1803. Archives, Clifton.
[24]Letter, John Douglass to Gregory Sharrock, 26 February 1803. Archives, Clifton.

THE VICARS AND JOHN MILNER

At the same time that Milner was appointed vicar apostolic in the Midland District, William Poynter received the nomination as co-adjutor to Bishop Douglass in London. There had been some controversy over which man should get which post. Poynter had been Stapleton's choice for the Midlands for not only had he appointed him his vicar general but had suggested him as his successor. On the other hand, when Bishop Douglass had requested a co-adjutor, he had listed the names of Stapleton (now deceased), Poynter, and Thomas Smith. Since Douglass had recommended Milner for the Midlands and had wanted Poynter for his own co-adjutor, his wishes prevailed. Milner was consecrated at Winchester on 22 May 1803, with Douglass, Gibson, and Sharrock as consecrators. A week later, on 29 May, Poynter was consecrated at Old Hall Green, and Milner preached the sermon.

Almost immediately, however, Milner found himself at odds with his fellow bishops. Indeed, the sermon for Bishop-elect Poynter was, for all practical purposes, the last expression of unity heard in the English church until Milner, Poynter, Douglass, and Gibson were all dead. Milner had been the staunch friend and advocate of the bishops against outside interference. For this they recommended him for the episcopacy. Apparently it did not occur to them that he might turn against them with the same vigor, intensity, intransigence, and unscrupulousness which he had demonstrated against their common enemies.

Before touching on the story of one of the most important controversies among the vicars, it might be well to make an observation about them. As a group and to a man, the bishops throughout the entire period dealt with in this study were without any sense of humor. They seemed quite incapable of being humorous with or about one another, much less laughing at themselves. In the almost 2,000 letters researched for this essay, there is hardly a lighthearted remark, let alone a humorous one. Bishop Poynter well described the proper decorum for bishops when he was considering his new co-adjutor. "Dr. Bramston," he wrote in 1823 to Bishop Collingridge of the Western District, "is equally zealous and prudent, strictly conscientious, and a man of solid and tender piety."[25] "He is, indeed, sometimes jocular," Poynter noted,

> but he knows when to be serious. I have heard him sometimes say when he has made one with me that it would never do for the Bishop (alluding to me) to crack jokes as he did. I doubt not if he were a Bishop he would conduct himself as a Bishop should do.

There is no way of knowing, of course, how different things might have been had the bishops been able to see humor as well as solemnity and dignity in their own positions.

Milner's difficulties with the other bishops had begun before his consecration. Although Bishop Douglass joined the others in recommending him, their differences had been of long standing. They had argued as early as 1801 about the ways of handling the Staffordshire clergy. "It is certain that some degree of coolness has taken place between me and my good superior, Bishop Douglass," Milner admitted to Sharrock at that time.[26] "I am free to confess," he candidly explained,

> that the reserve in question originated with myself. I am not insensible of his great merit, and innumerable favours conferred upon me, still I cannot help feeling that the flexibility of his disposition which makes him always to be on the opinion of his last adviser, betrays me no less than himself into a constant scene of inconsistency.

"Whence I conclude," he added, "it is better not to intermeddle at all than to have my plans marred and counteracted in the very execution of them."

Later Douglass assumed the same attitude toward Milner: to avoid the issue if there could be no agreement. "It is, I am convinced," Douglass wrote to Sharrock in 1805,

> much better for Mr. Milner and myself that no letters pass between us. You would be greatly hurt by the perusal of some letters which

---

[25]Letter, William Poynter to Peter Collingridge, n.d. but bound with the 1823 letters. Archives, Clifton.
[26]Letter, John Milner to Gregory Sharrock, 18 September 1801. Archives, Clifton.

have been written by him.... The violence, bullying and insults I have seen in his letters have determined me to decline keeping the correspondence.[27]

As vicar of the Midlands, Milner found himself in a most awkward position, for he was at one and the same time a vicar apostolic of the English church and the agent for the Irish bishops in their dealings with Parliament. The chief problem of a union of English and Irish Catholics lay in their totally different positions relative to the government. In Ireland, the Catholics, by far the majority, looked upon further emancipation as a right and as the only possible way to remedy the restrictive political and economic position in which they found themselves. On the other hand, the English Catholics, few in number and without even the potential for political power which the Irish Catholics had, viewed emancipation as a privilege or a reward granted to them by a beneficent government in exchange for unending expressions of their loyalty to the Protestant establishment. Unable, even if they had been permitted in Parliament, to exert much influence, and not connecting their religious status with their economic condition to the degree to which the Irish did, they viewed emancipation with a good deal less urgency and a much greater willingness to compromise. The English Catholics, particularly the hierarchy, were always loath to upset the known status quo for some unknown and possibly less desirable situation. Under such conditions, in his dual role as English bishop and Irish agent, Milner's own penchant for argumentation and disagreement was well provided for by being called upon to support two opposing points of view. Characteristically, he failed to see the awkwardness of his position or the necessary contradictions in his obligations to both sides.

Even worse, Milner failed to comprehend the resentment of the English bishops over his position and over his severe criticisms of the English church to the Irish bishops. Milner had long represented the nearly thirty Irish bishops in their

[27]Letter, John Douglass to Gregory Sharrock, n.d. but bound with the 1805 letters. Archives, Clifton.

business with the English Parliament, both before and after the Act of Union. As their agent, he claimed a certain precedence over the four English vicars (of whom he was one), for while each of them was independent and not subject in any way to a common leader, all lacked the faculties granted to bishops in a national hierarchy such as the Irish had. Milner from time to time expressed the belief that the real salvation for the English church lay in submitting it to the care of the Irish bishops, who were, in his view, at any rate, far more orthodox, more loyal to Rome, and less influenced by the laity than were the English. This point of view could hardly have been popular among the English who certainly did not, especially in matters of religion, consider themselves in any way inferior to the Irish. "I have again and again in the report I have made to Rome," wrote Milner to Archbishop Troy of Dublin in 1807,

of the state of religion in England, represented those evils under which it groans, viz., the frequent and notorious publication of heterodox and schismatical doctrine in this city, without the slightest discouragement, the diversity of discipline and practice that prevails amongst the clergy, the opposition of Bishop Douglass to the holding of any synod or other meeting of his episcopal brethren for remedying these ... evils.[28]

"It was from this general view of the state of religion amongst us," continued Milner,

that I long ago mentioned to your Grace my earnest wish that some one or more of the enlightened and illustrious Prelates of your Island might be deputed by the Holy See to visit us Vicars Apostolic and to report to it your observations and discoveries in this essential business.

Archbishop Troy wisely declined to interfere with the internal matters of another hierarchy over which he had absolutely no jurisdiction. But the knowledge that Milner, one of

---

[28]Letter, John Milner to Archbishop Troy, 1807. Archives, Dublin, quoted in Ward, *Eve*, 1:25.

their own, was inviting what could only have been construed as interference by the Irish, hardly endeared him to Douglass, Gibson, Poynter, or Sharrock.

This connection with the Irish bishops led Milner to make another of his bold but tactless moves. Before his appointment to the Midlands, there had been some thought of making Milner co-adjutor to Douglass in London and naming Poynter to the Midlands. It was no secret, however, that Milner would have preferred London to the Midlands, which had its headquarters at Wolverhampton. London was certainly where the action was both with regard to the church and especially between church and state. Moreover, the Midlands was provincial, inconvenient, and, worse, noted for its liberal and unorthodox interpretation of Catholicism. Never a modest or prudent man, Milner had few doubts about his ability to correct the abuses that had grown up in the church or to promote the most advantageous and orthodox settlement with Parliament. To effect all this, however, he needed to be in London. According to Ward, Milner requested two of his Irish friends, Archbishop Troy of Dublin and Bishop Moylan of Cork, to petition the Holy See to permit him to be transferred to London.[29] There were two possible ways this could be accomplished. One was for Milner to live in London and govern the Midland District through a co-adjutor. The other was for him and Bishop Poynter to exchange places. The latter solution, on the face of it, appeared more gracious since it would be a promotion for Poynter, who was only co-adjutor in London. It failed, however, to take into consideration the feelings of Bishop Douglass, who had never been particularly fond of Milner and who by this time had already engaged in several acrimonious rounds of correspondence with him. In 1805 Bishop Sharrock reported of Milner to Gibson that there was need for joint action on a number of church problems but "unhappily he is again involved in some unpleasant way with Bishops Douglass and Poynter, so that the unanimity of our little Episcopal College is interrupted, which I lament as a very great misfortune."[30]

[29] Ward, *Eve*, 1:28.
[30] Letter, Gregory Sharrock to William Gibson, 11 February 1805. Archives, Leeds.

Although Douglass did not want Milner in the London District, he never questioned either his ability or zeal. When asked directly if he wanted Milner for an assistant, he answered that he did not, but his acknowledgment of Milner's talents was unequivocal. "With respect to Mr. Milner's concerns in the Agency way," Douglass replied to Sharrock on 18 February 1806, in reference to the proposal that Milner reside in London as agent of the English as well as the Irish bishops in Parliamentary matters, "I doubt much if his idea will be realized."[31] "He is very ardent on that subject himself," Douglass continued,

> and as it had been proposed by the bishops of Ireland, he imagines to himself that the business is settled. He is certainly a very active man with abilities equal to the situation, and will be perseverant. If an agent be appointed, I deem him a very proper and well qualified person for the post.

"You rejoice to hear," concluded Douglass, "that we are on the most friendly terms. I hope you never entertained an idea of any ill will being entertained by me in his regard." On the other hand, there was no doubt precisely what Douglass thought about the whole notion of Milner as his coadjutor. "At the end," Milner recorded of Douglass in his memoirs about the situation in 1806, "he put the question to me in plain terms, 'Did you think it would be more for the honour and glory of God that I should not be your Coadjutor?' I asked. He answered, 'I did think so, and I do think so.' "[32] Although such open opposition to him might have discouraged another man, it was typical of Milner that no amount of adverse action or critical comment would cause him to swerve from his own course.

Some idea of the lengths to which Milner was prepared to go to secure the London position can be learned from a letter of Robert Smelt, the agent in Rome for the English bishops,

---

[31] Letter, John Douglass to Gregory Sharrock, 18 February 1806. Archives, Clifton. This appears to contradict Douglass' letter of 1805 (page 95, above), but Douglass was extremely ambivalent about his feelings and tried, except when harassed, to hide his dispute with Milner from public notice.

[32] John Milner, *Memoirs*, 133, quoted in Ward, *Eve*, 1:33.

to Douglass. Commenting on the decree ordering Milner to stay in the Midlands, Smelt wrote in September of 1806, "I mentioned [Milner's] application to Cardinal Erskine for support and the positive refusal he received."[33] "I lately had a long conversation with the Cardinal on this business," Smelt explained, in which Erskine had raised objections to Milner's appointment to the London District, objections similar to those raised by Douglass. Milner, according to Smelt, had done all he could in Rome to persuade Erskine and others to support his plan to exchange places with Bishop Poynter. "Bishop Milner," Smelt observed, "complains much of the decree preventing his removal to London where he thinks he could do so much more good than those who at present are there."

Milner himself was well aware of the opposition of the vicars to his removal to London. Such matters as the approval of his colleagues, however, bothered him not in the least. "It is plain," he explained to Archbishop Troy on 8 November 1806, "that the Cardinal and Secretary wish me and Dr. Douglass to settle matters together, being ready to approve of any such agreement."[34] "I am of opinion, however, (if I must speak plain)," Milner confided to Troy, "that he has now and had even whilst I was his subject, a sort of jealousy of me which will always induce him to keep me as far as possible from the scene of action." "Amongst other things," Milner further confided,

> he fears that if I were in London I should be for reforming many things which he thinks it best to overlook, and I must own he is not deceived in his conjectures. For really the state of things there with respect to doctrine as well as discipline is almost like that of the Israelites when the latter were without a judge, and every one did that which seemed good in his own eyes.

"As for my worthy, but still weaker friend, Dr. Gibson," Milner went on to say, "his opposition to my agency is mere

---

[33]Letter, Robert Smelt to John Douglass, 13 September 1806. Archives, Westminster Cathedral.

[34]Letter, John Milner to Archbishop Troy, 8 November 1806. Archives, Dublin. Quoted in Ward, *Eve*, 1:34–35.

wrongheadedness, in consequence of the representations of Dr. Douglass. It would be an easy matter to conciliate him to the measure." "With respect to Bishop Sharrock, who is the most clear-headed man of us all," concluded Milner in his evaluation of all the vicars,

> he has for years lamented to me the want of a proper ecclesiastical agent in London, and has lately in a formal manner appointed me to be his representative in all public concerns of religion. At the same time he professed himself afraid of giving offence to our two colleagues by supporting this opinion in the face of Propaganda.

Milner confessed the same sentiments about Douglass and Gibson shortly afterwards. "I suspect," he summed up for Sharrock on 17 November, "they will think it better that good should remain undone than that I should be employed in doing it."[35]

Although the matter of Milner's move to London was finally negated by a decree from Propaganda in December of 1806, the issue did not die. Milner still hoped to go to London, if not as co-adjutor to Douglass, then as agent to Parliament. "Undoubtedly, it would be more for my credit and emolument to retain this district and to manage it by a resident co-adjutor, than to descend to the latter rank myself," he dutifully explained to Sharrock on 4 March 1807, "but unless my superiors recommend this measure, and in some degree impose it on me, I should have difficulties of conscience about it."[36] "On the other hand," he was quick to observe about Douglass, "I am sure from what I know of our good brother's disposition . . . that were I to reside in London in an independent situation much more violent dissensions would ensue than any we have yet withstood." In the end, Milner did spend some time in London acting as agent for the Irish bishops, although he never did receive a co-adjutor.

The ill feeling lingered on between Douglass and Milner and was eventually the basis for much future mistrust between the two men and between Milner and Poynter, who

---

[35] Letter, John Milner to Gregory Sharrock, 17 November 1806. Archives, Clifton.
[36] Letter, John Milner to Gregory Sharrock, 4 March 1807. Archives, Clifton.

took over more and more of the work of the London District as Douglass' health failed. (Douglass died in 1812 and Poynter succeeded him as vicar apostolic.) Neither Douglass nor Milner would ever admit that the problem stemmed from a mutual temperamental dislike—almost a chemical reaction. "I have spoken to Bishop Douglass," Poynter informed Gibson in September of 1807, obviously in a fit of weariness about the whole nasty business, "concerning the difference which is said to exist between his Lordship and Bishop Milner."[37] "Bishop Douglass tells me," Poynter explained, "that it is all on the side of Bishop Milner, that he knows of no other cause, than that he imagines that Bishop Milner considers him the chief person who opposed Bishop Milner's being removed from the Middle District to the co-adjutorship of the London District." "If therefore, Bishop Milner has laid aside all thoughts of renewing this subject," he added, "I conceive that all cause of difference is at an end." This was merely wishful thinking on the part of Poynter, for the battle was just beginning, especially as far as he was concerned.

The last word on the subject of Milner's being agent for the English bishops, however, came from Douglass. "You tell me," he observed to Gibson in March of 1808, "that Bishop Milner says I have consented to his being Agent for the English with Bishop Poynter. I don't comprehend what is here meant. The English don't intend to petition (that I know of), what need then of an Agent? In all cases, wherein business is to be done, Bishop Poynter will act."[38] "With Bishop Milner's being Agent for the Irish," continued Douglass,

I have nothing to do. With his coming to London or staying what time he pleases in London, I have nothing to do. He has the same right of coming up to London and remaining at pleasure in London, as all the other people have. *It was the being my co-adjutor that I opposed*. I would not yield to part with Mr. Poynter, and accept Bishop Milner in his stead. This it was that gave so much offense to Bishop Milner. This it was that *occasioned* all the evil which has followed thro' the malevolence of Satan. If Bishop Milner be dis-

---

[37]Letter, William Poynter to William Gibson, 2 September 1807. Archives, Leeds.
[38]Letter, John Douglass to William Gibson, 1 March 1808. Archives, Leeds.

posed to act with Bishop Poynter when ever any business *may come on*, I don't oppose that cooperation. There is all I say, or will say.

But Poynter and Milner agreed and cooperated no more often than Douglass and Milner had done.

The presence of the French *emigre* clergy and particularly the French emigre bishops provided Bishop Milner with an especially good excuse for disagreement with his fellow vicars. He felt, almost from the beginning, that the English vicars were lax and unorthodox in their handling of the French, most of whom were in the London District. The problem of the French did not lend itself to easy solution. The Civil Constitution of the Clergy had gone into effect in France in July of 1790 and it was condemned by Pope Pius VI in April of 1791. Under the terms of the Constitution, French priests were employees of the state and subject to national rather than papal direction. Immediately there was a great exodus of priests from France. In the years between 1791 and 1797 more than 5,000 clergymen relocated in England, most of them supported by grants from the English government. Of these men, about twenty were bishops. The English, Catholic and Protestant, lay and clerical, greeted the exiles with almost uniform kindness and generosity. Douglass issued a pastoral to the London Catholics appealing for aid. "The feelings of compassion which you have shown," wrote Douglass in commendation to his people in 1792, "and the corporal relief which you have given to the suffering clergy from France have filled your Pastor with joy."[39] "Consider the example they hold out to us," he exhorted them in conclusion, "for they have not hesitated to forego every advantage of a worldly nature to preserve their conscience unstained. . . ."

At first, the presence of the French clergy gave rise to no jurisdictional trouble. For the most part, the priests administered to their own people, and their own bishops acted as superiors. Some curtailment of their priestly functions was necessary because of the shortage of chapels, altars, sacred vessels, and so forth, for so great an influx of clergymen, but

[39] Pastoral letter of John Douglass, 8 October 1792. Archives, Westminster Cathedral.

Douglass, in particular, made every effort to accommodate all those who wished to say Mass. Many of the priests formed communal groups in various donated houses near London. Complications with the French clergy, especially the bishops, arose after the signing of the Concordat between Napoleon and Pius VII in 1801. Under the terms of the agreement, all the French bishops were to offer their resignations to the pope, who in turn would make new appointments according to the terms agreed upon in the Concordat. Of the nineteen bishops living in the London District, fourteen refused to resign, among them the bishop of St. Pol de Leon, who had become the unofficial leader of the French episcopate in exile. Bishop Douglass explained their refusal in his diary. "The French Bishops," he wrote,

> assert that the Pope is imposed on by Bonaparte, that the Cardinals of character and merit in Rome are amazed at the Pope's proceedings in the business, that they have the best intelligence from Rome that Bonaparte has gained over some of the Cardinals, and by the influence of these bad men, deceives the Pope.[40]

The pope, of course, deposed these fourteen, and when some of their countrymen returned home, they, with one exception, remained in England, for there was no hope for them in France in their present state. The majority of the deposed bishops were old men and death solved the problem of their episcopal status before too long. Naturally, there were some exceptions, and among the most vocal was a group led by the Abbé Blanchard. These dissidents, including both laymen and clergy, believed that Pope Pius VII was a schismatic by virtue of his having signed the Concordat. They expected the restoration of the royal line in France—and the accompanying restoration of the royal bishops—and kept their hopes alive while waiting by uniting against the pope. In an age when the pope was a temporal as well as a spiritual ruler, it was not hard to collect an anti-papal following, and Blanchard soon became the leader of the Blanchardists who by any orthodox standard of the times were in schism because

---

[40] Diary, John Douglass, 1802. Archives, Westminster Cathedral.

they refused to accept the orders and directives of Pius VII. In other words, they were schismatic because they considered the pope to be schismatic.

It was at this point that it became necessary for the English vicars to take some measures to prevent public scandal. So long as the disagreements had remained fairly quiet, they had tried to ignore them. Two events, however, made that impossible. The first were the deaths in rapid succession of the two exiled bishops who had been leaders of the French clergy, the bishop of St. Pol de Leon in late 1805 and the Archbishop of Narbonne in early 1806. Leadership then fell to the bishop of Uzes, a man of less prudence and one more inclined to work actively against the Concordat. The second event was the arrival of Louis XVIII in England in November of 1807. His presence lent great strength to the pro-royalist, anti-concordat groups and brought the deposed bishops who had not gone so far as Blanchard had in condemning the pope into a position of greater sympathy with the Blanchardists. The discord finally became public when these bishops, especially the bishop of Uzes, began to censor those *emigre* priests who wrote or preached in support of Pius VII and the Concordat.

Characteristically, Douglass and Milner formed opposite views about the way to handle this French problem. Douglass, only with great reluctance, took any action to condemn the French. He was hopeful that time, old age, and death, if nothing else, would settle the issue before too much damage was done. Milner, on the other hand, pushed for some positive denunciation from the English vicars. While it could be said that Douglass acted with a certain want of determination and with a phlegmatic acceptance of time as the cure for most evils, it was equally true that Milner acted with a certain naivete in thinking that a group of priests who had ignored the pope would pay heed to him. Moreover, he acted clearly outside the realm of his own jurisdiction, for the Blanchardists were active in the London Distrct, and under the prevailing mode of government in England, he had absolutely no right to make judgments about the problems of a district other than his own. Needless to say, such lack of juridical competence bothered Milner not in the least. In a pastoral published in June of 1808, he spoke to the Catholics of the Midlands concerning the dangers of the French schism. "I have long lamented that the conduct and character of our Holy Father has been grossly misrepresented in this kingdom," he wrote in reference to the accusations made by Blanchard against the pope,

> not only by persons of other communions, but also by many professing themselves to be of our own, and that the most scandalous and schismatical doctrines in this regard have been openly, repeatedly and pertinaciously proclaimed from the chairs of truth, and published from the presses of the metropolis, by preachers and theologians calling themselves Catholic. . . .[41]

As Douglass had predicted, such open condemnation increased the activity and popularity of the French, who responded to Milner's pastoral with even more outrageous criticisms of Pius VII. The new outbreak forced Douglass to issue his own pastoral against the French schism in August of 1808. Mentioning Blanchard and his writings specifically, Douglass exhorted Catholics of the London District to be loyal to the pope. "What dutiful child of the Church, what living member of the mystical body of Christ," exclaimed Douglass,

> can, without horror, hear unauthorized individuals, even Priests, who should be an *example to the Faithful in word and conversation*, libelling the character of our common Father and Head, impeaching and condemning his public and official conduct, insulting him by the most opprobrious epithets, inviting the Pastors of the Church to abandon him, and publically disclaiming his authority. . . .[42]

"It is proper to inform you, beloved Brethren and Children in Jesus Christ," Douglass explained,

> that we called upon the said two Clergymen (Pierre-Louis Blanchard and M. Gaschet) to give us satisfaction concerning their adhe-

---

[41]Pastoral letter of John Milner, 1 June 1808. Archives, Westminster Cathedral.
[42]Pastoral letter of John Douglass, 24 August 1808. Archives, Clifton.

sion to the communion of Pope Pius VII.... As neither of these two Clergymen gave us the satisfaction required, we accordingly pronounced them both suspended.

In his pastoral Douglass had made the distinction between works that were schismatical, those of Gaschet, and those which only had a tendency towards schism, those of Blanchard. Milner made no such fine distinction and was highly critical of the mildness of Douglass. Blanchard answered the condemnation of Douglass by sending him a declaration of approval of the works in question signed by seven French priests. Douglass then had no choice left but to suspend those seven also. The French clergy further objected to Douglass's action and the situation only became more public, more scandalous, and more difficult to control. Douglass recorded two attempts made by the French to have the censure lifted from the seven signers. "The Bishop of Angoulême has called upon me two different times," he noted in his diary for 24 November 1808,

and pressed me earnestly to admit Monsieur J. Trevaux (one of the seven) without any public acknowledgement of his error in signing the approbation, etc., or any notice give to the public in order to do away with the scandal. I wrote to him [the bishop], this day that I could not accede to his wishes.[43]

A few weeks later three other bishops appealed to Douglass to lift the suspension. Douglass was willing, if the priests would express sorrow for their action and allow the fact of their apology to be made public, but the priests were not agreeable. In fact, Douglass and Poynter, who was present at the interview and privy to the whole controversy, drew up a series of possible forms of retraction, all of which the group refused to sign.

In the meantime, Milner kept the storm brewing by making more and more statements about the French schism, all of which implied a certain want of vigilance and orthodoxy on the part of the London bishops for not rectifying the situa-

[43] Diary, John Douglass, 7 December 1808. Archives, Westminster Cathedral.

tion. There could be no doubt that his action constituted interference in another bishop's affairs, and in this case without the excuse that the concerned bishop was ignoring the matter, for Douglass had taken positive action to condemn and curtail the dissident priests. But this action Milner did not deem sufficient. He published a condemnation made by the Irish bishops, one which they had had no particular obligation to make either, for Blanchard worked and wrote in the London District, not in Ireland. Such interference from the Irish further estranged Milner and Douglass, for it was only too clear that the Irish had written in response to a request from Milner.

Still Milner was not satisfied. All through the winter of 1809 he agitated to persuade all the vicars to unite in a joint condemnation. First he attempted to influence bishops Sharrock and Collingridge to mention the problem in their Lenten pastoral, although it was unlikely that any Blanchardist had ventured into the remote Western District. Would it not be proper, Milner asked Sharrock, "in your ensuing instructions for Lent, to say a few words in support of our common religions, and in defense of our Holy Father?"[44] "Will you say two or three words in your answer to me which I may cite," he requested in a manner which seemed to indicate that he was doubtful of Sharrock's orthodoxy, "signifying that you hold communion with Pius VII and with those Bishops who are in communion with him." In a postscript he added, "Blanchard says again and again in his new book that he shall consider the silence of the Bishops as a proof that they support his doctrines." Nor did Milner neglect Gibson and the North in his efforts at universal agreement and condemnation. "As I am on the point of publishing a Pastoral myself on the subject," he noted in a letter to Gibson on February 23,

in which I shall assert upon due authority (except as far as your Lordship is concerned) that all the Bishops of England and Ireland condemn Blanchard's system, I wish you would inform me by re-

---

[44]Letter, John Milner to Gregory Sharrock, 1 January 1809. Archives, Clifton.

turn of Post whether I am to put in *except the Bishop of the Northern District*.[45]

What was at stake here, it is important to remember, was not the orthodoxy of Blanchard and the French. They were clearly advocating and encouraging opposition to papal authority. By everyone's standards, except their own, they were wrong. The point of concern for the English bishops was the manner in which the condemnation took place, by whom it was made, and with what degree of harshness. Blanchard and his associates were resident in the London District. Technically, the problem then belonged to the vicar apostolic of the London District, Bishop Douglass. Even if he had chosen to take no notice of the antipapal writing of Blanchard, the problem would not, in the strict sense, have passed to a neighboring bishop. In the unique English situation where each bishop was sole ruler in his own district, subject to no superior authority in England, no other English prelate had the right or the power or the obligation to interfere in the affairs of another bishop's jurisdiction. Douglass, however, was far from ignoring the problem of the Blanchardists. He had publicly condemned them. He had demanded public retraction from Blanchard and Gaschet. He had suspended the seven French clergymen who had approved the writings of the schismatics. He had demanded of them some tangible evidence that they admitted their error. On the other hand, Douglass was willing to make compromises in his demands. His object was to avoid giving so much publicity and notoriety to the Blanchardist problem that it would spread and grow. If the matter could be settled quietly, with a minimum of public display and recrimination, he felt that would be the best way to solve it. After all, for the most part, it was a difficulty which concerned only the French who were at best a passing phenomenon on the English scene. It is believable that Douglass was even moved by pity for the French priests who, wrong though they might be, had been exiled from their homeland, faced with

---

[45]Letter, John Milner to William Gibson, 23 February 1809. Archives, Westminster Cathedral.

a political decision which they found incomprehensible, and no less interested in the salvation of their souls than those who had found it politically or spiritually feasible to accept the new situation. Douglass attempted to solve the problem with the least furor possible, a program which appears now to have been eminently wise and kind.

That was not the method of Milner, however, who agitated for the most public denunciations of the Blanchardists, the most widespread possible publication of the errors under which they had labored, the most total and abject retractions of their false teachings, and, unfortunately, censure of Bishop Douglass for his supposed neglect of the faith and morals of the people. Milner enlisted the aid of the Irish bishops with whom, at this point, he was closely allied, in this vendetta against Douglass which reached all the way to Rome. "Bishop Milner informs Bishop Gibson," wrote Poynter to Collingridge in 1810, "that his Holiness has received in his solitude an account of the late transactions and that the Irish have saved our religion here. The account sent may prejudice his Holiness and the Cardinals very much against the other Vicars."[46] "I therefore think," he continued,

> that it will be very proper and even necessary to draw up a statement of what has passed for many years back and to show . . . that Bishop Douglass was employing every prudent and efficacious means to suppress Blanchard's party, when Bishop Milner, ignorant of what Bishop Douglass was doing, interfered and ignited a flame.

One of Milner's greatest complaints against the other English vicars had been their supposed unwillingness to meet as a group to discuss common problems. On the face of it, that was a justifiable complaint, but the other vicars, particularly Douglass, believed, with some reason, that meeting with Milner was pointless. They felt little could be achieved when he was so adamant in his views about the Emancipation problems, so positive about the only possible measures to take against the French, so involved with and torn by loyalty to

---

[46] Letter, John Poynter to Peter Collingridge, 24 April 1801. Archives, Clifton.

the Irish bishops, so critical of all the efforts the vicars made, and so ready to interfere in and take over other bishops' districts. They felt, understandably, that meetings under such circumstances would be worse than no meetings at all. It is always necessary to remember that such meetings were voluntary and did not bind the bishops to any course of action except by a sort of gentleman's agreement. But finally, in February of 1810, the four vicars were all present in London, brought there for the presentation of a new Catholic petition to Parliament. Bishop Douglass recorded the meeting in his diary, listing the clergy in attendance; the four vicars apostolic, their co-adjutors in the case of Douglass and Gibson, and theologians from each district, in all thirteen men.[47] For nine days the bishops met and while they spent the majority of their time discussing the ramifications of emancipation, the Blanchard schism came in for some share of their attention. Again according to Douglass's diary, the vicars accepted the proposals made by Bishop Poynter that

> any priest adhering to Blanchard or his system should be required: to acknowledge that Pope Pius VII is head of the Church . . . that Pope Pius VII is neither a heretic nor a schismatic, nor the author or abettor of heresy or schism . . . that no person has jurisdiction in the respective districts of the Vicars Apostolic in England except by delegation from them or immediately from the Holy See . . . that those who refuse to acknowledge the above articles be forbidden to exercise any ecclesiastical functions.[48]

Despite this clear warning not to interfere, Milner went back to his own district at the end of the meeting and demanded that all the French priests acknowledge the resolution. This he did, even though the resolutions which he had in person approved of clearly state "that a priest adhering to Blanchard or his system should be required . . ." and not that "all French priests should be required. . . ." Milner reasoned, apparently, that since he could not have first hand knowledge that every priest had not adhered to Blanchard, he could

[47] Diary of John Douglass, 20 February 1810. Archives, Westminster Cathedral.
[48] Ibid.

only be satisfied if every priest individually declared that he accepted the resolutions. Having overreacted in his own district, Milner voiced disapproval that Douglass, especially, did not lay down the same requirements in the London District, where, according to Milner, Blanchardism was rampant. "Religion will be the gainer," he exhorted Douglass. "The great number who were on the brink of schism will start back with horror, and the few obstinate schismatics will become known and marked as they ought to be."[49]

Trouble erupted again between Milner and Douglass over the restoration of faculties to the Abbé de Trevaux, one of the seven who had signed the approbation of Blanchard's writings. Douglass finally reinstated Trevaux without requiring him to make public his retraction of his signature on the approbation. The bishop justified this because it seemed obvious to him that Trevaux had signed without knowing that Blanchard's book had already been condemned, and his orthodoxy was personally attested to by the highly orthodox Bishop of Angoulême. In addition, Trevaux was an old man waiting to make his peace with God and die and his restoration in the light of the continued exclusion of the other six signers gave tacit acknowledgment of the fact that he had made satisfactory explanations to Douglass. In what looked like an act of charity and graciousness, Douglass lifted his suspension. Naturally, Milner objected. He wrote a scathing letter, phrased in the third person, to Douglass, accusing him of injuring the church, deserting the unanimous resolutions of the four vicars, and favoring the growth of the Blanchardist schism. He ended by threatening, if Douglass would not take action to heal this further break in church authority that, "he the undersigned . . . will consider it his duty to circulate the same among his episcopal brethren as opportunity may serve, and especially to make it known to the chief Pastor his holiness Pope Pius VII."[50] Douglass replied within the month saying, "I beg leave to observe that I did not consent

---

[49]Letter, John Milner to John Douglass, n.d. Archives, Westminster Cathedral, quoted in Ward, *Eve*, 1:159.

[50]Letter, John Milner to John Douglass, 29 June 1811. Archives, Westminster Cathedral.

to the restoration of spiritual faculties to the Abbé de Trevaux until I received such satisfaction as I deemed sufficient for what I did."[51] Anyone but Milner would have been put down by this.

Justification for Douglass's action concerning Trevaux came in a letter from Poynter to Gibson in which he explained the entire matter, apparently so that Gibson would be neither disturbed nor moved to listen to Milner's accusations. The point at issue, according to Poynter, was not Trevaux, but interference in another vicar's district. "Bishop Milner has written to me and Bishop Douglass," wrote Poynter to Gibson on 18 July 1811, "for an explanation of Bishop Douglass' conduct in this affair."[52] "What is this, My Lord," Poynter demanded, "but an act of inspecting the conduct of Bishop Douglass and of *interference in the Government of his District.*" "Bishop Milner has been acting on this system of his, for several years past," he complained,

and we have felt the disagreeable effects of it. Ignorant of the measures Bishop Douglass had adopted and was pursuing to suppress Blanchardism in its beginning, Bishop Milner interfered, disturbed Bishop Douglass in his endeavours to stifle the evil and raised a flame, which he has been fanning ever since.

"Bishop Douglass is willing," Poynter concluded,

to give an account of his conduct to proper authority, to his Holiness or to those who may have ecclesiastical jurisdiction over him; but not to Bishop Milner or to the Bishops of Ireland, until he or they prove that they are authorized to call him to an account. If Bishop Milner were Archbishop, he would not be allowed to interfere in the Diocese of one of his suffragans as he had interfered in the spiritual government of the London District.

The Irish bishops had, indeed, asked for explanations of Douglass's conduct. Archbishop Troy wrote a fairly long letter to him in which he expressed his "pain, astonishment and

---

[51]Letter, John Douglass to John Milner, 22 July 1811. Archives, Westminster Cathedral.
[52]Letter, William Poynter to William Gibson, 18 July 1811. Archives, Westminster Cathedral.

concern" over the restoration of Trevaux's faculties. We "think it necessary," he demanded in conclusion,

> to ascertain the fact by requesting your Lordship to state distinctly in a reply to this letter, with which we expect to be honoured, whether spiritual faculties have been restored to Rev. J. de Trevaux and upon what conditions? that we may determine . . . whether we continue in Catholic communion with your Lordship.[53]

Douglass could hardly have been blamed had he reacted with counter threats to such an extreme provocation, but his reply was characteristically mild. Ill at the time, he instructed Poynter to write to Troy in very much the same vein as in the 18 July letter to Gibson. Among the directives was the one to state that Douglass "was much surprised at the receipt of such a letter calling on me to say if I had required a retraction and threatening to break off communion."[54]

The vicars all expressed their concern over Milner's behavior, even though Gibson did admit that if Milner sincerely thought that the vicar of London was acting in an heretical fashion, in conscience, he would have to interfere. The point, according to Gibson, was whether Milner was making any proper effort to know the truth of the situation. He wrote in this vein to Bishop Poynter early in August of 1811, shortly before the bishops met in Durham. Poynter relayed his message to Bishop Collingridge in his request that the vicars meet. Gibson, wrote Poynter, "says he has written to Bishop Milner, and told him that his misrepresentations precluded all probability of unity, that his misrepresentations were spread wide, even to America, that even peaceful silence was become a cause of remonstrance."[55] "But, my Lord," continued Poynter in dismay,

> Bishop Milner is not inactive. When we see your Lordship, we shall, I think, convince you that he is [the creator] of a plan that will

---

[53]Letter, Archbishop Troy to John Douglass, 30 July 1811. Archives, Westminster Cathedral.
[54]Letter, John Douglass to William Poynter, 6 August 1811. Archives, Westminster Cathedral.
[55]Letter, William Poynter to Peter Collingridge, 2 August 1811. Archives, Clifton.

cause the greatest confusion in the London District and in the whole mission. Mr. Hodgson has heard, and it seems, on very good grounds, that the Irish bishops have access to the Pope, or to some person who acts with full power from the Pope, and that they are actually negotiating to have Bishop Milner transferred to the London District.... If he were here, he would, we are persuaded, be with Archepiscopal powers over the others, and then what confusion and mischief.

There had long been plans for various changes in the ecclesiastical government of England with the aim of restoring the national hierarchy. Obviously, the threat that if such a restoration were to be made, Milner might possibly gain the ascendancy, alarmed the other vicars and may well have made them slow to advocate any change.

As a result of worries of this sort, and of Milner's and Troy's threats and accusation, the vicars met in Durham in August of 1811. They were truly alarmed about the dangers to peace and good order which Milner was causing and felt that immediate steps must be taken to decide upon some method of stopping or silencing him. For this purpose they arranged the Durham meeting. A brief note to Collingridge from Poynter indicates the urgency of the situation. "Please come ... immediately," he wrote on 6 August 1811.

A letter from Troy in behalf of all the Bishops of Ireland threatens a breach of Catholic communion, unless Bishop Douglass satisfies them on their demand concerning Trevaux. Bishop Milner in London, will be here this evening, *probably to declare a breach of communion* unless we either retract faculties from Trevaux or publish his retraction.[56]

"If you *can*," pleaded Poynter, "pray do prepare to go with me to Durham. It is a general cause; the greatest the English Catholics have seen since the Reformation. All private duties must yield to this moment."

In attendance at the Durham meeting were Poynter from London (Douglass being too ill to come), Gibson and his co-

---

[56]Ibid., 6 August 1811. Archives, Clifton.

adjutor Thomas Smith from the North, and Collingridge from the Western District. Milner did not receive an invitation, which technically gave him a legitimate complaint, but the purpose of the meeting was to discuss ways and means of dealing with him and the Irish so that his presence could hardly have been possible. It is true, though, that he would probably have attended even knowing or, perhaps, particularly knowing the subject-matter, had he been invited. At this conference, the vicars drew up a series of resolutions in which they reaffirmed that they held their jurisdiction from the pope, were responsible to him for their official conduct and not to each other, and that they had an obligation to resist unwarranted interference. They resolved, moreover, that since the bishop of London had acted in a canonically regular fashion with regard to Blanchard and also with regard to Trevaux, interference from the vicar of another district was not acceptable. They stated further that "a system of interference in our Districts has been set on foot and for some years past has been persevered in by some neighbouring Bishops and their Agent, who is one of our Colleagues, who have over us no kind of jurisdiction or authority."[57] "Of this a strong instance has occurred," they explained, referring to the Irish bishops,

when a Synodical declaration censuring our public conduct was issued by them, not addressed to their own flocks, but expressly issued to be sent to their agent in England and to be here by him circulated among our people.... We are credibly informed that certain neighbouring Prelates and their above mentioned Agent have by frequent applications to the Holy See ... attempted to procure a novel establishment of jurisdiction over us.

Finally the bishops resolved

that therefore we, the undersigned Vicars Apostolic of the Northern, London and Western Districts, with the Co-adjutors of the London and Northern Districts, do feel it a conscientious obligation

---

[57]Resolutions of the Vicars Apostolic Assembled at Durham in August 1811. Archives, Westminster Cathedral.

to protest . . . against these past acts of interference of which we complain, and against any future attempts that may be made . . . to interfere in the government of any of our Districts, to exercise any control over us, or to subject us to their authority.

Clearly what bothered the vicars more than anything else was the interference of the Irish bishops who had no legal connection with the English Catholics and who, embroiled with the English as they were over the definition of Catholic emancipation, were *personae non gratae* with the English vicars. The latter might have forgiven Milner for his own interference. He was, after all, one of their own and they had been largely responsible for his rise to prominence in the church. But for his enlisting the Irish against them, they could find no excuse. Thus at the meeting Poynter also made clear why Douglass steadfastly refused to tell Milner or indeed the other vicars either of the terms of the satisfaction he had received from Trevaux. "The conditions on which they were restored have not been explained," Poynter pointed out,

partly because Dr. Douglass is not responsible for the administration of his district to Dr. Troy or Dr. Milner; and partly because as Dr. Troy communicated every letter to Dr. Milner, there was good reason to think that Dr. Milner would publish the answers, and from our past experience of the effects of his misprepresentations, we all judge it unsafe to commit ourselves to him, or to make him the interpreter of our sentiments or conduct.[58]

Unfortunately, the Durham meeting did nothing to silence either the Irish bishops or Milner, and the battle raged on throughout the fall and winter of 1811–12. Milner reacted with his customary pugnacity to his exclusion from the Durham gathering. He apparently wrote objecting to the affair to Gibson whom he considered the senior vicar, and to his co-adjutor Smith. Gibson reported Milner's comments to Bishop Poynter and Poynter in turn relayed them verbatim to Collingridge. "Bishop Smith received today a letter from Bishop Milner," Gibson wrote to Poynter in October, 1811,

[58] Ibid.

"I think more extraordinary than ever. it is principally addressed to me. He calls ours a packed meeting at Durham. It is filled with mistakes and falsehoods. He will I fear, do much mischief. . . ."[59]

In March of 1812 Milner published a "pamphlet" of 108 pages entitled "An Explanation with Dr. Poynter" which attacked the behavior of Poynter and Douglass in their handling of both the emancipation question and the Trevaux case. In the publication, Milner offered his explanation of why Douglass and Poynter had, in the first place, made so many mistakes in their handling of church problems, and second, why they refused to accept and be guided by the superior knowledge and ability of Milner. "The different wrong measures of my friend your VA and yourself," Milner accused Poynter,

which have been productive of so much dissension in the Catholic church of the United Kingdom and of such severe wounds to your character and feeling, as you pathetically lament in your different letters to Ireland, are clearly traced to that affectation of independency and superiority in consequence of the civil advantages of London, which has so long marked most of my friend's and your behaviour, an affectation which has been openly encouraged and promoted by certain intriguing laymen.[60]

Plainly Milner had never forgotten that he had been passed over for the superior London position and relegated, instead, to the backwaters of Wolverhampton.

A second meeting of the vicars apostolic held in Durham in August of 1812 attempted to heal the differences. Milner attended this meeting as did Bishops Moylan and MacCarthy from Ireland. Douglass had died the previous May and Poynter was now vicar of London. Collingridge, apparently because of illness, was absent and so there was no representative from the Western District. The bishops concerned themselves once again with the issues of emancipation and the French

[59] Letter, William Poynter to Peter Coolingridge, quoting William Gibson, 22 October 1811. Archives, Clifton.
[60] John Milner, "An Explanation with Dr. Poynter," quoted in Ward, *Eve*, 1:51.

schism. Their chief effort was not so much to solve either of the problems themselves, but to mend the unity, now so broken, of the bishops. Moylan of Cork opened the meeting, according to the notes recorded by Poynter, by pleading for harmony. "Dr. Moylan expressed his earnest desire of seeing perfect harmony established between the prelates of the United Empire," wrote Poynter, "and proposed that all that is past should be forgotten and that in future we should be united and go on hand in hand."[61]

No one could have taken exception to such kindly hopes for cooperation. Poynter wrote that he himself,

entirely and from his heart forgave all injuries that affected him *personally*, but did not think it just or reasonable that the statements of the *official* conduct of the VVAA of the Northern, Western and London Districts with the charges contained in Dr. Milner's pamphlets should pass uncontradicted or unrevoked and thus become a part of our Ecclesiastical History.[62]

Milner, recorded Poynter, "observed that this tended to renew all the disputes concerning the Fifth Resolution, Trevaux and to protract the work of pacification." An indication of the fruitlessness of the efforts at healing the disputes came from Poynter's last note on the first day of the meeting. "The first day's Conference," he commented succinctly, "broke up abruptly without coming to any conclusion."

The meeting continued for two more days and the report of Poynter indicated that it was nothing more than a continuation of the same arguments, and that it never did come to any satisfactory conclusions. Milner maintained that Douglass and Poynter had acted negligently and in opposition to their agreed upon decision of February 1810, in restoring Trevaux's faculties, and that he and the Irish bishops were well within their rights in attempting to restore orthodoxy to a district where the resident vicar was not only ineffective but in error as well. Poynter continued to argue that it was Milner, not Douglass, who had misconstrued the meaning and in-

[61]Minutes of a Conference at Durham, 21–23 August 1812. Archives, Westminster Cathedral.
[62]Ibid.

tention of the 1810 resolution, that Trevaux had given satisfactory evidence of his orthodoxy to Douglass, that only Douglass needed that evidence, and that Milner and the Irish had completely overstepped the bounds of justice and legal jurisdiction in their interference. As Milner spoke at length on the danger to the church from the enemies within and the scandal given by the restoration of Trevaux, of the wounds unity had suffered, Gibson, according to Poynter, "exclaimed with emphasis, 'what *stuff* he talks.' " The meeting ended on the third day when Milner, again in Poynter's report, "had expressed his conviction that no good would be produced by this meeting."[63] Gibson's and Milner's comments were undoubtedly the truest statements made that day.

The demands upon the vicars' time and energy made by the efforts to submit a satisfactory emancipation bill to Parliament pushed the problem of the French schism into a position of secondary importance in the next few years. A further meeting was held, again in Durham, in August 1813. The French matter received practically no mention, but the dispute with Milner continued. He was not invited to the meeting which was concerned with emancipation, another issue over which he and the other vicars were in total disagreement. The correspondence concerning his invitation to the meeting illustrates well the complete impasse into which the vicars had fallen and the absolute breakdown in effective communication among them over Milner. "I should ask," wrote Poynter to Collingridge on 3 July 1813, "whether, knowing the temper and spirit of our colleague Dr. Milner, it would be advisable to invite him to the meeting."[64] "In the regular course of things," Poynter affirmed,

> he should certainly be there. But unless he could be bound to secrecy, he would communicate everything to the Irish Bishops, and even to the public in some pamphlet or letter in a newspaper; and, moreover, as it is more than probable that he would be in opposition to us all, if we should think proper to write to Rome, he would—to judge from his past conduct—endeavour to be before

[63] Ibid.
[64] Letter, William Poynter to Peter Collingridge, 3 July 1813. Archives, Clifton.

us with a counter-statement, which from experience we may judge without rashness would be a misstatement. Hence I am at a loss to say, whether it would be advisable to invite him.

Collingridge responded, "I consider it would defeat the very purpose of the meeting, were he to come to it."[65] The vicars plainly expected that Milner would oppose them on any issue they might introduce.

As Douglass had thought all along, the French schism died a natural death as the participants in it, one by one, either returned to France as conditions changed there, or died themselves. Trevaux, fully restored to his priestly faculties, died peacefully in 1814, and interest in the whole matter diminished. The problems of Catholic emancipation were so much more central and the bitterness they created between Milner and his fellow vicars so all encompassing, that there was little energy left for the somewhat theoretical battle over the *emigre* French clergy's opinion of the papacy. Moreover, a new subject for disagreement soon appeared on the scene, for Milner and the other vicars were about to do battle over the newly restored Jesuits.

In conclusion, a statement of Dr. Poynter's explaining why Milner was not invited to the 1813 Durham meeting adequately sums up the entire situation. Milner was not invited, wrote Poynter in his memoirs,

First, because one of the Vicars Apostolic absolutely refused to meet him. Secondly, because in the former meetings he had conducted himself in a manner highly arbitrary and offensive to the other Vicars. Thirdly, because he had printed and circulated among the public mutilated and untrue accounts of what was said or done at the former meetings.[66]

In short, Milner could not be trusted, would not cooperate, and was so boorish in his manner that he could not be tolerated.

In the issue of the French schism as well as in most other

---

[65]Letter, Peter Collingridge to William Poynter, n.d., quoted in Ward, *Eve*, 2:59.
[66]William Poynter, *Apologetical Epistle*, 40, quoted in Ward, *Eve*, 2:60.

matters of Catholic concern, neither Milner nor the other vicars acted except as they thought the good of the church demanded. Both sides, without doubt, lacked charity in their dealings, but the vicars were at least willing to try. They could discuss, would compromise, did not deliberately seek to oppose Milner. They learned to their sorrow, however, that to discuss with Bishop Milner was to be misquoted, to apologize to Bishop Milner was to begin the battle again, to accept an apology from Bishop Milner was to admit their own error. They were simply not men of sufficient strength and stubbornness and cunning to break, control, or contain a man who in 1813 could write,

Thus deserted, assailed and wounded as I am in the most sensible part, by the natural friends of the Church, after having for these twenty-five years past combated her declared enemies, I nevertheless will not yield to dejection of spirits; for I am conscious of having still not only a good, but also a clearly victorious cause.[67]

Milner never suffered from doubts about the worth or the ultimate triumph of his causes. His devotion to the church could not be faulted. If only he had not considered every man who disagreed in any fashion with his own position a "declared enemy," perhaps the years of his episcopate (1803–1826) would have witnessed some greater qualitative development in English Catholicism. As it turned out, these years were among the most divided years since the Reformation.

[67]John Milner, *Supplementary Memoirs*, 334, quoted in Husenbeth, *Life of Milner*, 250.

CHAPTER V.
THE VICARS AND THE JESUITS

The strained relationship between the members of religious orders and the rest of the English clergy was not new when further difficulties erupted between them in the early part of the nineteenth century. The efforts of the Jesuits to provide leadership for the remnants of the church after the death of the last English bishop in 1585 had caused serious misunderstandings which have already been discussed. Although the antagonisms aroused at that time did eventually subside, the basic suspicion between Jesuits—and to some degree, other religious communities—and the secular clergy and vicars never entirely disappeared.

In the first half of the eighteenth century, religious orders had continually been in conflict with the vicars apostolic. The issue at stake was always the right of the vicars to exercise jurisdiction over all the priests who served as missionaries in the English church. In the peculiar situation of the Catholic church after the Reformation, clergy belonging to religious orders who normally would not have been acting as mission priests found themselves chaplains to families and pastors of local chapels. They were involved in this type of work mainly for two reasons. As members of religious communities with foundations on the continent, the Benedictines, Jesuits, Franciscans, and others were in a better position to produce trained men for an illegal and persecuted church. Second, since their ordinary manner of community life was impossible under the penal system, they had to rely on the support of the Catholic gentry whom they served as chaplains. These chaplains became in time the mission priests of England supported out of either the means of the very few wealthy Catholics or the pittances of the poor.

In reality, these regular clergy served two masters and this was at the heart of the problem. They were subject both to their religious superiors and to the vicar in whose district they served. Controversy flared in the 1740s over the necessity for the regulars to be "certified" by the presiding vicar before they could administer the sacraments. The regulars, lawfully ordained by their own superiors, resented the demand made by the vicars for further supervision. The vicars, for their part, demanded certain rights of jurisdiction and control over all priests ministering to the faithful who were, in the final analysis, the responsibility of the vicars. This argument was settled partially in 1745 when Pope Benedict XIV confirmed a series of directives for the government of regular clergy working for the vicars. When this ruling did not prove sufficient, Benedict issued in 1753, the bull *Apostolicum ministerium* which laid down the rules governing the relations between seculars and regulars and clarified the jurisdiction and authority held by the vicars. Under the terms of the bull, all regular clergymen were to be subject to the vicars in every matter relating to the missions. This settled the issue in the eighteenth century. The religious orders submitted, some with grace and some without, but the issue was not entirely resolved and the resentments were buried for a time in more pressing concerns.

When the problem surfaced again early in the nineteenth century, the main difficulty was still the same: the rights of the vicars to have jurisdiction over all those clergymen who served the faithful on the missions as against the claim of the regular clergy to be subject only to their religious superiors and independent of the vicars' control. In the expanding church of the early nineteenth century, the regulations of Benedict XIV no longer covered the new problems and the new situations. In his bull of 1753 Benedict had set down rules governing the faculties of the individual priests in administering the sacraments. The controvery which developed some fifty years later centered around the management of the local missions, the establishment of new ones, and the terms under which men received the sacrament of Holy Orders. In a poor mission, where the priest eked out an extremely meager living, new chapels could create grave financial problems. Their conservative and timid economic approach to the spread of the faith led the vicars to oppose the opening of many new churches. They felt, and there was certainly some merit to their opinion, that the English Catholics could not support many missions and that to found new ones would simply dissipate the slender resources of the faithful. They did not subscribe to the theory that easier access to the sacraments and to religious instruction would increase the numbers of Catholics or their contributions to the church. They had good reason for their caution, for the mission priests frequently sent their unpaid bills and requests for additional funds to their vicars with a childlike faith in the ability of the bishops to rescue them from financial disaster.

The crucial issue centered on the conflicting claims of the vicars and the superiors of religious orders to assign the regular clergy to the various missions, to move them from place to place, or to establish new missions. Technically, in this respect, the regular clergy differed from the secular in the terms of the "title" under which they had been ordained. Every priest received the sacrament of Holy Orders under one of two titles. If he was a secular clergyman, in the service of the bishop or vicar, he was ordained *missionis*. If he was a member of a religious community he was ordained for the service of that group subject to the superior and under the title *paupertatis*. According to the rules set forth by Benedict in 1753, the secular clergy were bound to serve the vicar from whose district they had come and for whose district they had been trained. The vicar, in most cases, had been responsible for the support of the young man during his period of training. Part of the ordination promise, the mission oath, was that the priest would serve that bishop and him alone. In return, the bishop employed him in the work of the district, provided for his support, and promised to care for him in his old age. The regular clergy, on the other hand, made no ordination promise to work in any particular district, but rather agreed to go wherever their superiors might send them. Although they had to receive periodic authorization from the vicar in whose district they resided in order to administer the sacraments, regulars were not under his jurisdiction. The vicar could not move them from mission to mission. Nor could he prevent their being moved should their superiors decide to change them about. He could not even insist that they be kept within his district. This inability to control a segment of their active clergy created a certain amount of confusion and trouble for the vicars who preferred to deal with priests totally under their jurisdiction.

Obviously, not all these possible abuses of secular-religious cooperation occurred in every case. Nevertheless, the possibility was there, and it was realized often enough to keep the issues alive as a constant irritant. The English vicars were traditionally jealous of their authority and anxious to preserve what little power and prestige they possessed. A large and united body of men not under their complete control weakened their position considerably. Possibly the problem could have been solved by efforts at compromise and cooperation between vicars and religious superiors, but however reasonable such an approach might have been, it was unlikely to occur in actual fact. The vicars, totally independent juridically of one another, and quite incapable, it has already been demonstrated, of making accommodations to the needs and desires of their brother bishops, were even less inclined to cooperate with the abbots and provincials of religious orders. It was essential, nonetheless, to bring the regular clergy who were serving as mission priests under firm control if the vicars were ever to establish orderly diocesan government. In that respect, and in the battle that raged over the Jesuits in particular, the vicars had right on their side. In the light of their own shortsightedness about corporate activity, however, it seems doubtful whether the bishops understood the conflict in such far-reaching terms. To them, the struggle with the religious orders was only one part of their effort against laity, clergy, Rome, and one another to preserve the integrity of their small spiritual empires.

A most interesting letter written in 1814 to James Bramston, then a vicar general and later vicar apostolic of the London District, highlights the typical attitude taken by the vicars toward the regular clergy. The letter was written by one William Wilds, apparently a priest and friend of Bramston. It seemed to have been sent by way of advice to Bramston as he set out with his vicar, Dr. Poynter, on a trip to Rome. The letter is long, but of such significance in its expression of the feeling against the regulars that it is worth quoting at length. "Don't," Wilds counseled Bramston, "forget the Regulars." "You must speak highly of these people at Rome—they are the Pope's men," he added shrewdly,

> but you must endeavour to convince his Holiness, that it is almost impossible for a Bishop in this country to govern his district, upon any system of regularity or comfort, while he is obliged to employ men, who are not immediately under his jurisdiction, and who, from being auxiliaries become principals.

"An Agent of the Regulars, of the Jesuits, for example," Wilds went on to explain, "comes to London, gets faculties, picks out his labour, and throws the rest to the Seculars. Is this right?" "I must observe," he complained,

> that these men have, throughout, been the sworn-friends of Bishop Milner, in opposition to all the other Vicars Apostolic, and have sided generally with the Irish Church against their own, because it is their interest to keep out of the way of Episcopal and Government influence, and to carry on business by themselves.[1]

In an effort to demonstrate further the dangers of the divided loyalties of regulars, Wilds maintained that "the Regulars, as Missionaries, have two objects, in view—the Mission and their respective corporations. While they serve the one, they are bound by system and interest to serve the other, and while they take care of the flock, they will naturally inspire them, with a predilection for men of their own body." "This is so true," Wilds declared, "that I have known several instances of a Secular and a Regular, in the same town, who were hardly upon speaking terms, and whose respective flocks formed two determined parties." "I have invariably ob-

---

[1] Letter, William Wilds to James Bramston, 25 November 1814. Archives, Westminster Cathedral.

served," he continued, "that some Catholics are for one Order, others for another, in consequence of their falling into the hands of Regulars, while the poor Secular, if he is loved at all, must be loved for his own sake."

Wilds clearly had little or nothing good to say about the regulars. While his condemnation was, without doubt, exaggerated, it demonstrated well the feeling against the religious orders. In reaction, no doubt, to their more certain and secure status, Wilds went on to say,

the Regulars have an asylum, in readiness, for poverty, age, infirmity, and above all for delinquency. This last is a great point for them. They may be comfortably withdrawn from the Censures of the Bishops, and the eye of the public and be placed in another good situation, with a fair Character, and without any imputation cast on their Order.

"O! Remember this," Wilds exclaimed, "and be convinced with me, that had several of our Seculars found the same seasonable refuge, they had never been a scandal to the public, nor a disgrace to us!"

The great complaint against the Regulars was their ability to get and keep for themselves choice missions which were financially secure. Wilds had much to say on this very aggravating topic. "The Regulars," Wilds pointed out to Bramston, who he hoped would point it out to the pope, "have the advantage of us, in another very essential point. It must be allowed, that the interest of their respective orders must have great weight with these gentlemen." "Now observe," he continued,

how much they may be helped in this, by what I call a choice of places, and not only in one district, but throughout the Mission. I say, a choice of places, for it really amounts to this. They ask the Bishop for a place,—he complies; but when they find another more suitable to their plans, away goes the incumbent, and the Bishop is left to fill up the vacancy, as he can. This happened, at our Chapel—we lost a most amiable man and were six months without a Successor. You never hear a Secular speak of *our* places. The Regulars avowedly speak of *theirs*. In a word, they have the free range of the Missions, and are disposable, in every quarter, where their interest calls them.

It would, indeed, be a simple matter to document every abuse of which Wilds wrote. It was also true, however, that the abuses were isolated and individual cases and not of an incidence that would lead to disorder. Nor was it true that the seculars were blameless, since a number of their own wilfully flitted from post to post and refused to serve where and under the conditions imposed by their vicars. Nonetheless, the abuses Wilds spoke of were real, and in addition to lowering the effectiveness of the work on the missions, they added much to the tension between secular and regular priests.

Considering the prominence of the Jesuits in England even after the Reformation, it is not surprising that the conflict between the regulars and the vicars should have been concentrated in them. When the bull ordering their world-wide suppression, *Dominus ac redemptor noster*, was promulgated on 16 August 1773, by Pope Clement XIV, there were, according to Berington, 120 Jesuits working on the mission in England, about 30 percent of the total number of clergy.[2] They were, then, the single largest group of regulars in the country. Treatment of the suppressed Jesuits, who were, it must be remembered, still priests, although no longer considered members of a religious community and now under the jurisdiction of bishops, varied from country to country. In England, where they had had no official standing with the civil government before their suppression, they perhaps fared better than in those countries where the church-state relationship figured heavily among the causes for their suppression.

At the time of the suppression, every Jesuit was required by the terms of the papal bull to make an act of submission to the local bishop, or in the case of England, the local vicar. To their credit, the English vicars acted toward the ex-Jesuits, men who had done no personal wrong and who found themselves suddenly deprived of their community status, with great

---

[2]Berington, *Behaviour of English Catholics*, 162.

charity and graciousness. Bishop Challoner, the senior vicar, along with Bishops John Hornyold, Francis Petre, and Charles Walmsley, all tried to make the transfer of obedience as easy and dignified as possible. The issue, however, was not simply one of a change of personal allegiance, for the Jesuits owned considerable property. Once the order ceased to exist, this property had to be transferred in some way to the general use of the English Catholic church without its being lost through confiscation by the civil authorities. Challoner sent for the London Jesuits to receive their submission and conferred with Father Henry More, their provincial, about the property settlement. They reached satisfactory agreement about the use of former Jesuit funds for the support of the retired or infirm members of the defunct community and arranged for the surplus to be applied to the work of the London District.[3] Bishop Hornyold exhibited the same consideration for the ex-Jesuits in the Midlands. "As to the temporalities which belonged to your late body," he noticed with great kindness in a letter of 25 October 1773 to Father John Gage, who had directed the Jesuit mission at Bury St. Edmund's, "I have nothing to say to them but am desirous that those who have care or administration of them will go on in the same manner as they were used to do."[4] In the same letter Hornyold exhorted Gage, "to take courage, and not be cast down, but let us resign ourselves to the will of Divine Providence, and go on labouring in the vineyard of our Lord with the same zeal and fervour as you have done for so many years past." "I was well assured before you signed the formula," concluded the vicar, demonstrating his own confidence in the Jesuits with whom he had worked, "of your sincere submission to the Holy See and its Vicars; and I do hereby renew and confirm the usual faculties."

Challoner set the example for his fellow bishops by appointing More to govern and supervise the ex-Jesuits in London under the ultimate supervision of the vicar. Apparently he encouraged the others to do likewise, for he explained his

[3] Burton, *Challoner*, 2:165.
[4] Letter, John Hornyold to John Gage, 25 October 1773, in Henry Foley, *Records of the English Province of the Society of Jesus* 5:540.

method of procedure in a letter to William Walton, co-adjutor of the Northern District. "I have made him [More] my vicar over his quondam brethren in my district," he wrote to Walton on 21 October 1773, "as I take him to be a very worthy man; and believe this will be the best means to cement us together."[5] In Challoner's day, the ex-Jesuits peacefully accepted the suppression and continued to service their missions under the authority of the vicars. As the former Jesuits gradually died, the missions were staffed by new priests trained in the schools once held by the Jesuits, mainly from the one at Stonyhurst in the Northern District. It was thus that the problems of the Jesuits were postponed for other vicars to arbitrate forty years later. Unfortunately, not all of them were to be blessed with Challoner's wisdom and prudence. It is important to remember here two essential changes resulting from the suppression of the Jesuits relative to later English problems with the regulars. First, the former Jesuits were now subject to the vicar of the district in which they resided, even though in most cases, that vicar delegated his authority to a superior from among the former Jesuits. Second, any men ordained from Jesuit seminaries were now required to take the mission oath—to serve the vicar of the district—and were ordained under the title *missionis*.

The existence of the school at Stonyhurst was the one trouble spot in the early years of the Jesuit suppression and came to be the focal point for the misunderstandings after their restoration in 1814. Stonyhurst had come into existence in 1794 when the seminary at Liège managed first by the Jesuits and then, after 1773, by the ex-Jesuits, was forced to close because the revolution in France had spread to Belgium. Stonyhurst, therefore, was not a new school with a new charter, but simply the old school of Liège in a new geographical location. Conflict arose immediately between the superiors of the school and Bishop Gibson in whose Northern District the college was now located. At Liège, even though the Jesuits had been suppressed, the teachers had, for all practical purposes, continued to live and act as Jesuits. They had enjoyed

---

[5]Letter, Richard Challoner to William Walton, 21 October 1773. Archives, Leeds.

a special designation there as a "pontifical" college, a term never clearly defined. Its practical effect, however, had been to remove the Liège men and their students from the authority of the local bishop. In other words, the newly ordained priests were free to contract to work anywhere. In actual practice, most of them had returned to England and had taken the mission oath to work for the vicar from whose district they had originally come. When the Liège school moved to England, confusion abounded. England lacked any clear legislation for the establishment of seminaries—even those under the jurisdiction of local bishops. The presence of a "pontifical" seminary—whatever that meant—staffed by men from an order which no longer existed, ordaining two kinds of priests—those sent to it by the local English vicars and who took the mission oath, and those who came there to be "ex-Jesuits" and who owed allegiance who knew where—was really more than poor Bishop Gibson could contend with. His very natural solution was to consider Stonyhurst a seminary for the training of secular priests and, since it was located in his district, one that would train and present to him for ordination men for his district. The Stonyhurst men, however, would have none of this and proceeded to have their former status as a "pontifical" college not subject to the local bishop reaffirmed by Rome.[6] This meant that their seminarians did not need to take the mission oath and could be sent elsewhere for ordination should Gibson refuse to cooperate. It was a most irregular and unsatisfactory situation and could not but lead to trouble.

The brief which restored the Jesuits, *Sollicitudo omnium ecclesiarum*, promulgated by Pope Pius VII on 7 August 1814, did not automatically restore the Society of Jesus everywhere, nor was it the first action taken to re-establish the order. Pius VII had legitimized the Jesuits in Russia in 1802—where the civil government had never recognized the suppression—and had granted them permission to receive candidates from outside Russian territory.[7] From this point on, hope swelled in

---

[6]Ward, *Dawn*, 2:104.
[7]Bernard Basset, *The English Jesuits from Campion to Martindale*, 365.

England about the possible restoration of the order there. The Russian general had named Father Marmaduke Stone, who had been superior at Stonyhurst, to the office of provincial of the English ex-Jesuits. At this point, there were approximately sixty-six men left of the community which had existed at the time of the suppression. Of these, about half made a private renewal of the Jesuit vows under Stone.[8] This permission to reorganize under the leadership of the Russian Jesuits was never a clearly defined transaction but existed merely as a "verbal" permission, which, therefore, the English vicars believed they could ignore. Gabriel Gruber, the Russian provincial, had merely transmitted the pope's permission to the English group, making it clear that it was only a verbal grant which, furthermore, the pope would not put into writing.

The English vicars, extremely doubtful about the wisdom of reestablishing the society under any conditions, were reluctant to accept this most informal method of reinstatement. They appealed to Rome and received a rescript from Cardinal Borgia, then head of Propaganda, prohibiting them from recognizing any Jesuit claims from the men at Stonyhurst.[9] If this appeared to indicate certain contradictions in Roman policy, that was precisely what did exist then and for some years to come. Various Roman officials, motivated by their allegiance to or distaste for the Jesuits and their respect or lack of it for the English vicars, acted independently and in frequent opposition one to another. Thus the law in a given case depended upon who the litigants thought had the most power and authority to make the law. Early in 1804, Bishop Gibson corresponded with Father Stone about the legality of the Jesuit claims of restoration. "It is my duty to acquaint you that I am officially informed by the prefect of the Propaganda," he explained to Stone, "that the superior of the Jesuits in Russia has no authority whatever out of Russia and that there is no restoration of Jesuits in England and that no regular Order can be restored without the Holy

[8]Ibid., 368.
[9]Letter, Stefano Cardinal Borgia to John Douglass, 3 December 1803. Archives, Westminster Cathedral.

THE VICARS AND THE JESUITS

See or by its authority which must be notified to us by the Sacred Congregation."[10] Gibson was referring to the letter from Cardinal Borgia prohibiting the bishops from recognizing any claims of the "Gentlemen of Stonyhurst" until the vicars should receive definite instructions from the Holy See. This order of Borgia's served as the basis for the continual refusal of the vicars, with the exception of Milner, to acknowledge the Jesuits, even after the bull of restoration had been promulgated in 1814.

Two issues must here be explained. The first is why the majority of the English vicars opposed the restoration of the Jesuits, even after the brief *Sollicitudo* had made their existence legal. The second issue to be discussed is the grounds upon which the vicars could refuse to acknowledge the restored Jesuits in the face of *Sollicitudo*. One reason for the vicars' opposition can be found in the statement made by William Wilds to Bramston in the letter already mentioned. "The hope of emancipation may never be realized," Wilds wrote in 1814, "because we must be forced to have, what is obnoxious to the state, and what is not wanted in the Country—*Jesuits*."[11] "The Church of this country," he went on to say, "should be governed solely by our Bishops; but I will venture to say, that it has been equally governed by superiors of religious orders, and till this influence is done away, no Vicar Apostolic will ever be his own Master." Poynter had also noted this issue of governmental displeasure in a letter to Father Paul Macpherson, agent in Rome for the English bishops. "The Pope's bull for the re-establishment of the Jesuits was laid before Parliament about the beginning of this month," he informed Macpherson on 31 July 1815.[12] "It will be an exceedingly delicate, not to say dangerous thing," he explained, "for me to acknowledge the re-establishment of the Jesuits in England by any official act." "It is necessary," Poyn-

---

[10] Letter, William Gibson to Marmaduke Stone, 1803, quoted in Basset, *The English Jesuits*, 365.

[11] Letter, William Wilds to James Bramston, 25 November 1814. Archives, Westminster Cathedral.

[12] Letter, William Poynter to Paul Macpherson, 31 July 1815. Archives, The Venerable English College, Rome.

ter concluded, "to be extremely cautious in this respect, not to expose the common cause of religion." Poynter, and he can be considered here to express the opinions of Bishops Gibson and Collingridge, feared the restoration of the Jesuits because he thought it was likely to be prejudicial to the cause of Catholic emancipation. Another objection stemmed from the centuries old suspicion of the Jesuits as trouble makers. "I cannot conceal what I clearly forsee will follow from the restoration of this Society in England," argued Poynter in a letter to Propaganda as late as 1826, indicating how long the issue was pending, "...namely a renewal of the old dissensions and troubles, not indeed from the constitutions and mind of this most holy Society, but from the singular spirit which the English Jesuits showed of old, and which those who now wish to become Jesuits manifest."[13]

As for the grounds upon which the vicars could refuse to acknowledge the restored Jesuits, Cardinal Litta, then prefect of Propaganda, explained the matter and gave the bishops their loop-hole in a letter to Poynter in December of 1815. According to the bull of restoration, Litta noted, the society was to be considered restored only in countries "in which the civil governments consent to receive and recall them."[14] In the same letter Litta admonished Poynter to be extremely careful and to do nothing which would antagonize the government. Obviously this was substantial vindication for the vicars' reluctance to recognize the restored society. The English government, which gave no official recognition to any Roman Catholic organization, was certainly not likely to recognize the Jesuits, much less request their recall to England.

The attitude of the priests from Stonyhurst was naturally quite opposed to that of the vicars. They interpreted the bull of restoration to be in effect in any given country unless the government specifically decreed that the society was not to exist within its boundaries. They further contended that the English government was officially indifferent to the technical

[13]Copy of letter, William Poynter to Propaganda, 18 May 1826. Archives, Westminster Cathedral.
[14]Letter, Lorenzo Cardinal Litta to William Poynter, 2 December 1815. Archives, Westminster Cathedral. My translation.

status of Roman Catholic priests, whether they were subject to their own religious superiors or whether they were subject to the vicars. "The mistake," of the vicars, it was explained in one of their memorials to Rome on the subject, "consisted in confounding the notion of a religious body recognized by law—that is, which enjoys a civil establishment—and the notion of tolerating in the state private individuals who are professed.[15] "The English government," the Memorial continued,

> having established the Protestant sect as the religion of the State, does not recognize any other religious association as established, although it does not disturb in that kingdom men of other sects and individual professed Catholics, for instance Benedictines, Dominicans, and other priests.

The Memorial went on to maintain that

> provided any Catholic whatever takes the prescribed oath, no magistrate can require more from him. If a monk or one of the Jesuits be asked, "Are you a Benedictine? Are you a Jesuit?" he may refuse to answer such a question so far as relates to his own individual affairs, or, if he chooses, he may candidly reply, "I am a Benedictine, I am a Jesuit, and have a right to be so; the law permits me to be so."

When the vicars refused to recognize the Stonyhurst men as Jesuits, even after 1814, the group began a systematic effort to persuade Rome to override the English decision. The essential point of recognition lay in the ordination oath. Since the suppression in 1773, those men ordained from former Jesuit institutions had taken the mission oath pledging their direct submission to the vicar apostolic and were ordained under the title *missionis*. Although then technically under the direct control of the vicar, it must be remembered that in practice, these men worked under the supervision of

---

[15]Copy of Memorial presented to the Holy Father, Pope Pius VII, by Father Grassi, November 1818. Archives, Westminster Cathedral.

their own superior, who acted as their agent with the vicar. Once the bull *Sollicitudo* was promulgated in 1814, however, the Stonyhurst men refused to take the mission oath, maintaining that the Society having been restored, they were entitled to be ordained under the title *paupertatis*. Their justification for insisting on a legal change that really would not alter the actual conditions was that only by insisting upon such legal forms could they ever hope to see the Society function openly in its fullest form.

Interesting as it might be to weigh the opposing claims of the Stonyhurst priests to be known and governed as Jesuits and those of the vicars to treat them in every legal respect as members of the secular clergy, the purpose here is not really to judge the validity of arguments on either side. The discussion of the Jesuit problem in this context serves to illustrate once again the central thesis of this study, the disruptive effect of the persistent conflicts among the vicars themselves over matters of policy and practice. The Jesuit problem presents a particularly good example of this lack of accord, for Bishops Poynter, Gibson, and Collingridge all attempted to prevent the restoration, while Bishop Milner was from the beginning a staunch champion of the Society's return to prominence in England. More than that, Milner, in direct repudiation of his colleagues' interests, made himself privy to secret agreements between Rome and the Jesuits, agreements which undercut the vicars' authority in their own districts, were direct blows to the orderly establishment of good local church government, and were insults to the position of the vicars.

Several explanations exist for Bishop Milner's marked preference for the Jesuit cause in 1814. One was that the Jesuits had been well received by the Irish bishops with whom Milner was so closely associated. In all matters relating to government, both civil and church, Milner sided with the Irish rather than with his fellow English bishops. Likewise, unlike the other vicars, Milner was strongly ultramontane rather than cisalpine in outlook and attitude. Very naturally then, he would lean toward the Jesuits, which like all the religious orders had strong ties with Rome.[16] Moreover, whatever Milner might have lacked in the way of prudence, tact, or judgment, he could not be faulted for lack of zeal in promoting the Catholic faith. He was always annoyed by the cautious and timid approach of the other vicars to any public declaration regarding Catholicism and to their submissive attitude toward the government. It was only natural, then, that he would be favorably inclined toward a group who, as the Jesuits did, encouraged a more open and positive exercise of religion. Finally, it is not improbable to believe that Milner, who by 1814 had systematically opposed his fellow vicars in every concern of the Catholic church in England, supported the Jesuits or at least refused to support the vicars because by that time he was psychologically incapable of cooperation with them on any issue. Some indication that these were among the reasons for Milner's favorable reaction to the Jesuits is found in a letter to him from the Catholic Arthbishop of Dublin, John Thomas Troy. "The conduct of your Vicars Apostolic," commented Troy, "is to me unaccountable. Here (in Ireland) without any publication of the bull, they [the Jesuits] are acknowledged and employed in the ministry with great benefit to religion. They have a public chapel in the city, they are ordained *titulo paupertatis*, etc."[17] "There is not a whisper of opposition against them," continued Troy, "either from the clergy or laity, from Protestants of the Government. It is impossible for Lord Castlereagh not to know this. Why then does he permit it, if he be hostile to the Jesuits?"

One of the first formal discussions of the status of the Jesuits took place at the 1813 Durham meeting of the vicars, a meeting at which Bishop Milner was conspicuous by his absence. Rumors had, of course, been widespread since 1803 that the restoration of the Jesuits was imminent, and the priests from Stonyhurst had already renewed their vows and

[16]It should not be forgotten here, however, that Milner, when he felt called upon to do so, could also be highly critical and suspicious of the "Roman" methods of church government.
[17]Letter, John Thomas Troy to John Milner, n.d., quoted in Ward, *Eve*, 3:25-26.

were more and more openly considering themselves as regulars. The vicars attempted to forestall trouble by restating their position, hoping in this way to retain the upper hand. "State of Stonyhurst College," Poynter recorded in the minutes of the meeting, "considered."[18] "Agreed," he noted,

> that there are no Jesuits in Great Britain—that none are to be acknowledged as Jesuits—that all persons educated at Stonyhurst College are still subjects of their respective Vicars Apostolic . . . that the VVAA have a right to the superintendence over the Theological Studies at Stonyhurst.[19]

A little less than a year later, at another meeting in Durham in June of 1814, just weeks before the publication of the bull *Sollicitudo* and with Milner again absent, the vicars went on record as opposing the restoration of the Jesuits. "Their restoration for Great Britain," Poynter again recorded in the minutes, "would in the opinion of Bishop Gibson be hurtful to the cause of the Catholic religion in this country for various and important considerations."[20] "Bishops Poynter and Smith," Poynter concluded, "were of the same opinion."

Between 1814 and 1820 a steady stream of correspondence went to Rome both from the clergy at Stonyhurst and their supporters and from the vicars apostolic and their friends, excepting Milner, of course, over the settlement of the Jesuit question. In March of 1815, Joseph Hodgson, another of Poynter's London vicars general, wrote to Bishop Gibson. He repeated a warning sent from Rome by Macpherson to Poynter to the effect that they should be wary of "the intrigues of the Jesuits, who are aiming at Rome by the agency of

---

[18] Minutes of a "Conference at Durham," 30 October 1813. Archives, Westminster Cathedral.

[19] Although Stonyhurst drew students from a larger area than the Northern District—representing as it did the old college at Liège which had been more than a diocesan seminary, it was under the control of and supervision of the vicar apostolic of the Northern District, at this moment Bishop Gibson. Priests ordained there, since they were not legally Jesuits, were subject to the jurisdiction of the vicar from whose district they had come. This vicar might permit the Stonyhurst priest to remain in the College, but it was the vicar's decision, not the priest's.

[20] Minutes of a "Conference at Durham," 20 June 1814. Archives, Westminster Cathedral.

Bishop Milner to obtain Powers paramount to those of the Vicars Apostolic and independent of them."[21] Hodgson went on to report that Macpherson "had seen a letter from Fr. Stone denouncing or complaining of all the bishops (except Mr. Milner on whom the highest praises are lavished) as enemies of the Society of Jesus. But Bishop Collingridge is named as particularly so."

Part of the fear inspired by the Jesuits came from their alliance with Milner and the Irish bishops. There appeared to be widespread belief among the vicars that the Jesuits, Milner, and the Irish had great influence at Propaganda— and events proved that, indeed, they did. This undue influence, it was believed, placed the English church in a position of subservience and at the mercy of the desires and ambitions of these three elements. In the struggle with Rome, the resentment over the restoration of the Jesuits formed merely one part of a much greater resentment over Rome's apparent agreement with Milner and the Irish on the question of the terms of Catholic emancipation and over the proper respect due from Rome to the vicars apostolic. "I summed up the whole to Cardinal Litta one day," Poynter both explained and complained to Gibson late in 1815,

> when I told him in plain terms, that I sought no favour, or indulgence, but only that he would attend to truth and justice; that after having suffered so much in silence from Dr. Milner, we did expect, that we should obtain justice from the Prefect of the Propaganda.[22]

Poynter then went on to report that he had accused Litta of planning "to sacrifice the English Vicars Apostolic to Dr. Milner and the Irish bishops . . . and that whilst [he] is at the head of the Propaganda the Jesuits and Dr. Milner and the Irish will do what they please against us." This same strong feeling against Milner as one who had gone over to the enemy had also appeared in William Wilds' letter to Bramston, quoted earlier. In one passage Wilds exhorted Bramston to speak

[21]Letter, Joseph Hodgson to William Gibson, 4 April 1815. Archives, Leeds.
[22]Letter, William Poynter to William Gibson, 1 December 1815. Archives, Leeds.

out clearly and forcefully to the pope. "Convince him," Wilds exclaimed, "that all had been peace and harmony amongst us, had it not been for one man, and that man a Bishop! his own representative! and that the storm will never be appeased, till he is thrown into the sea."[23]

Numerous memorials reached Rome from the Stonyhurst priests requesting that the Jesuits be fully recognized in England and that they be ordained under the title *paupertatis*. The Jesuit spokesmen apparently overplayed their very stong hand. The memorial of Father Grassi, quoted above, made, for example, a number of unfounded statements to the effect that "Stonyhurst was the only suitable place of education for the Catholic laity, or that

> in these times when a certain alienation from the Holy See is become general, and particularly in a country where so much is said about independence, about reducing the Catholic religion to the level of the national Protestantism, and of causing his Britannic Majesty to become head of the Catholic religion . . . it is of great importance that there should be religious instructors of whose sincere attachment to the Apostolic See there may be every security.[24]

In the light of the existence of seminaries for the secular priests in every district, and in the absence of any shred of evidence that the instructors in these schools were not sincerely attached to the Holy See, it is easy to see why the Jesuits' memorials may have done their cause more harm than good. At any rate, on 11 June 1817 Cardinal Litta advised Fr. Stone that it was the pope's desire that the Stonyhurst novices seek ordination under the title *missionis*.[25] His Holiness, according to Litta, had no objection to the priests pronouncing the Jesuit vows privately and living within their house as members of the Society, but in all outward signs they were to be as secular priests, subject to the local vicar. If that vicar chose

---

[23]Letter, William Wilds to James Bramston, 25 November 1814. Archives, Westminster Cathedral.

[24]Copy of Memorial presented to the Holy Father by Father Grassi, November 1818. Archives, Westminster Cathedral.

[25]Letter, Lorenzo Cardinal Litta to Marmaduke Stone, 11 June 1817. Archives, Westminster Cathedral.

THE VICARS AND THE JESUITS

to allow them to be governed as in the past, by their own superior, that was his option, but not theirs to decide.

News of the Jesuit failure to achieve their goals unofficially reached the vicars in a letter from Father John Lingard, a priest from the London District who had gone to Rome to work in the archives preparatory to writing a history of England, and who had been acting somewhat in the capacity of personal agent for Bishop Poynter. "To my astonishment," he reported to Poynter on 5 June 1817, "I found here Mr. Walsh of Durham on a special mission from the English Jesuits."[26] "His object," Lingard continued,

was to obtain a decree that their young *eleves* might be ordained *sub titulo paupertatis*. This, however, has been refused. He has now demanded that they may be ordained *titulo missionis* and this he will obtain; but in that case it will be expected that before ordination they take an oath to the bishop to serve the mission."

"I see not why," concluded Lingard, "he should apply for the last grant. Probably it is that he may not appear to have been here for nothing."

Despite Cardinal Litta's communication to Father Stone, his sympathies were definitely with the Jesuits, who along with Milner, were apparently working to discredit the other bishops in the eyes of Roman authorities. In August of 1817, Poynter consulted by letter with Bishop Gibson relative to the appointment of a president for the English College in Rome and the recognition of the Jesuits. Lingard, Poynter informed Gibson, had sent word that a president should be appointed at once, "for fear Bishop Milner or the Jesuits should have time to thwart us."[27] "Mr. Lingard says," Poynter continued, "that he had been accused to Litta by a letter or letters from England, of being a notorious Jansenist, and Litta denounced him to Consalvi as such." "I shall propose writing direct to the Pope," Poynter concluded, "and com-

[26]Letter, John Lingard to William Poynter, 5 June 1817. Archives, Westminster Cathedral. It is of interest to note that in discussing the Stonyhurst problem, all participants referred to the priests as "Jesuits."

[27]Letter, William Poynter to William Gibson, 9 August 1817. Archives, Leeds.

plaining of such treatment as we and our Agents experience from those who ought to protect us."

Evidence of Litta's preference for the Jesuits and of his real finesse in ecclesiastical politics is well demonstrated in a letter he wrote to Bishop Gibson on 14 February 1818.[28] In that letter, Litta announced the total restoration of the Society of Jesus in England, thereby canceling his order of 2 December 1815, which had declared that the Jesuits were not to be considered publicly restored and were not to be ordained *titulo paupertatis*.[29] It also rescinded his direction of 11 June 1817 to Father Stone that the Stonyhurst priests were to be subject to the vicars.[30] Gibson began to suspect that Litta's 1818 order did not carry the sanction of the pope. In April of 1818 he received a letter from Robert Gradwell, who was then rector of the English College in Rome. "We have informed by a note Cardinal Consalvi of the letter written to your Lordship by Cardinal Litta," wrote Gradwell, "and have signified to his Eminence [Consalvi] the mischievous consequences which would result from acting up to it."[31] "If your Lordship thinks an answer proper," Gradwell advised, referring to a reply to Litta,

and if I may presume to suggest an idea, the answer might state, that your Lordship will always be happy to receive His Eminence's directions in matters of faith and essential discipline, but that the directions relating to the re-establishment of the order in Great Britain are neither one nor the other; that they are contrary to your own construction of the Pope's Bull and to his Eminence's former letters; that they are an unnecessary offence to the British Government, and would prove injurious to the church and therefore you think it your duty not to injure the general body of the English Catholics to gratify a few individuals, in things which are not essential to religion.

---

[28]Letter, Lorenzo Cardinal Litta to William Gibson, 14 February 1818. Archives, Leeds.

[29]Letter, Lorenzo Cardinal Litta to William Poynter, 2 December 1815. Archives, Westminster Cathedral.

[30]Letter, Lorenzo Cardinal Litta to Marmaduke Stone, 11 June 1817. Archives, Westminster Cathedral.

[31]Letter, Robert Gradwell to William Gibson, 11 April 1818. Archives, Leeds.

THE VICARS AND THE JESUITS 143

Gradwell informed Bishop Poynter a week later of the true nature of the 14 February 1818 order from Litta. "Cardinal Consalvi addressed me as follows," reported Gradwell.

"I thank you for your note. The information it gave me is of great importance and demands our immediate attention. I have just been informing his Holiness of the business and gave him Cardinal Litta's letter to read [the February 14 letter to Gibson]. His Holiness read the letter with surprise and then said: 'I never heard of this letter before. It has been written without my knowledge and without my authority.' "[32]

The cardinal added, Gradwell explained, "The Pope is exceedingly displeased with the letter of Cardinal Litta." Gradwell then recounted the rest of his conversation with Consalvi. The letter of Litta's had been written without the knowledge of either Consalvi or Pius VII. Gradwell had been directed to write to the vicars "that in a short time something will be done to neutralize the letter and make it as if it had not been written." Apparently Consalvi and the pope acted with dispatch for on 5 May 1818, Litta wrote to Gibson and retracted his letter of 14 February 1818.[33] Litta requested that Gibson "conduct yourself in this business as if you had never received the said letter, as if indeed, this Sacred Congregation had not even written it." Moreover, within a few months, Litta was removed from his post as prefect of Propaganda. It is difficult to think that Bishop Milner was not aware of Litta's unauthorized letter to Gibson. He was a close friend of both Litta's and the Jesuit superiors at Stonyhurst. He had lent his influence to the latter's request for recognition which had resulted in Cardinal Litta's 4 February 1818 letter to Bishop Gibson.[34] While it was unfortunate, it was characteristic of Milner that he chose to cooperate in a deliberate deception which confused the ill and aging bishop of the North.

Francesco Cardinal Fontana succeeded Litta as prefect of

---

[32]Letter, Robert Gradwell to William Poynter, 18 April 1818. Archives, Westminster Cathedral.
[33]Letter, Lorenzo Cardinal Litta to William Gibson, 5 May 1818. Archives, Leeds.
[34]Husenbeth, *Milner*, 358–59.

144 THE ROMAN CATHOLIC CHURCH IN ENGLAND

Propaganda. He was not kindly disposed towards either the Jesuits or Milner and their influence in Rome declined as long as Fontana was in office. The absence of friends in high places, however, did not daunt Milner, and he continued to interfere in the affairs of the Northern District in a most blatant fashion. In the summer of 1818 he chose to enter into a dispute over a chapel in Wigan, a small but almost exclusively Catholic town in the North. The chapel there had always been under the care of Jesuits—or, after the suppression, ex-Jesuits—from Stonyhurst. In 1818 the current missionaries decided to enlarge the building since it was too small for the congregation. This required the permission of the local vicar, and Gibson refused to grant it. Instead he sent secular priests to found a new mission and to build another chapel. The Stonyhurst priests proceeded to build their new chapel anyway, and the two buildings rose side by side. The rivalry spread to the laity and the surrounding clergy, and soon accusations and counter-accusations about the Wigan chapels and the whole Jesuit question were circulated widely, even among Protestants. There was some fear that the government would become interested and that the Jesuit restoration would be a topic for official consideration. News of the scandal eventually reached Rome where partisans for each side eagerly championed their causes. Gradwell wrote to Gibson begging him to give some answer to the accusations which were being made in Rome against him. These were, he said, "that the government would have known nothing about the re-establishment of the Jesuits, but for the noise which the Bishops through jealousy made about it, that the business of the chapel at Wigan . . . was an outrage on their body, etc., etc."[35] Gibson chose to do nothing at all about the complaints in Rome, and on 21 November 1818, Cardinal Litta, who was temporarily back at Propaganda because of Fontana's illness, wrote directing Gibson not to impede the building of the Jesuit chapel since they were not to impede the building of his.[36] Gibson's advance aged—he was eighty—

[35]Letter, Robert Gradwell to William Gibson, 27 August 1818. Archives, Leeds.
[36]Letter, Lorenzo Cardinal Litta to William Gibson, 21 November 1818. Archives, Leeds.

and poor health may have accounted for his refusal to answer, but Milner's actions, nonetheless, would be hard to justify under any circumstances. In October of 1818 he wrote a very offensive letter to Gibson. "There is a most heavy complaint against your Lordship and your vicar, and the secular clergy, and the Vicars Apostolic in general," he wrote rather heavy-handedly to Gibson, "that when one-third of the congregation and the people of God are perishing for want of spiritual good, we the secular Vicars Apostolic conspire to deprive them of it by our opposition to certain colleges, and to that of Stonyhurst in particular."[37] "That when we cannot supply the county towns with priests," Milner went on, specifically referring to the Wigan situation, "we encourage opposition chapels and a redundancy of Pastors . . . from mere jealousy of a rival order. I am sure your Lordship will agree with me that this is not the spirit of the great apostle. . . ."

"Your Lordship has been instructed," Milner further reminded him, "that the last named [Jesuits] are not restored. Now I am a witness to the contrary, as were Cardinals, numberless prelates, several kings and queens and 150 Jesuits. . . ." "Since my return to England," Milner went on to say, "Cardinal Litta has written to me, 'The Jesuits are generally restored, and therefore in England, hence you may ordain them either *titulo paupertatis* or *titulo missionis*. . . .' " Milner gave himself away here, for he clearly revealed that he had known of Cardinal Litta's February letter ordering Gibson to recognize the Jesuits.

Simultaneously with the Wigan chapel dispute, Milner joined with the Jesuits in another contretemps with Bishop Gibson. The missionary of the chapel in Oxford died in the summer of 1818, and since the chapel had been traditionally served by the Jesuits, Milner applied to Stonyhurst, in Gibson's district, for a replacement. The proposed man, Robert Newsham, belonged by birth, training, and ordination to the Northern District. It was necessary, therefore, to obtain a release from Gibson in order for him to be transferred from

---

[37]Letter, John Milner to William Gibson, October 1818. Archives, Leeds.

the North to the Midlands, a matter usually a mere formality in the case of a priest from Stonyhurst. Gibson, however, did not reply to Milner. There are many possible explanations for Gibson's failure to act upon Milner's request. Gibson was very old and almost incapable of signing his name, much less writing letters. He was, moreover, on unfriendly terms at the moment with the Stonyhurst superior, Charles Plowden. It is conceivable that he was irritated with the Stonyhurst priests and with Bishop Milner over the "trick" foisted upon him the previous February. At any rate, he did not answer Milner. The latter, instead of complaining to Gibson himself that his legitimate requests were being ignored, chose to discuss the matter at Stonyhurst with Father Plowden. As a result of this visit, Milner wrote to Rome suggesting a compromise in the Jesuit problem.[38] In exchange for renouncing the title of "Jesuit," suggested Milner, the Stonyhurst rectors should be granted permission to present their students for ordination to any agreeable English or Irish bishop and then be free to send them to any former Jesuit mission without regard to the district into which they had been born or from which they entered the seminary. In the long run, it would seem that such a compromise would have left the Stonyhurst men totally dependent upon the good will of unknown future bishops and would deprive them of all status, either that of recognized regulars or of seculars. At the time, however, it seemed a possible way out of the difficulty, and Propaganda appeared to be impressed. Cardinal Somaglia, who followed Litta temporarily, was friendly to Milner and the Jesuits. He met with the Congregation and persuaded them to approve the request, and a rescript, known as the Somaglian Decree, was issued on 14 December 1818.[39] By virtue of this decree, a candidate for ordination from Stonyhurst could be sent to any English or Irish bishop for ordination under the title *paupertatis*, all the while remaining subject to the superior of Stonyhurst, who could send him to any Jesuit mission or,

[38] Letter, John Milner to Lorenzo Cardinal Litta, 5 October 1818. Archives, Westminster Cathedral.
[39] Decree from the Congregatio de Propaganda Fide, 14 December 1818. Archives, Westminster Cathedral.

THE VICARS AND THE JESUITS 147

alternatively, keep him at the college. It was a great victory for the Jesuits and Bishop Milner had won it for them.

Cardinal Somaglia notified Bishop Milner of the decision in a letter dated 23 December 1818.[40] Milner was instructed to deliver the decree to Father Plowden but to keep its contents secret from everyone else. Neither Somaglia nor Milner informed any of the other vicars apostolic of its existence, not even Bishop Gibson in whose district Stonyhurst was located and who was, therefore, most directly concerned. It was impossible, of course, that the decree could be kept secret permanently, but it was not until August 1819 that it became public knowledge. Only by accident then did Bishop Thomas Smith, Gibson's co-adjutor, learn of a Northern man whom he had not ordained being sent to a Jesuit mission. Smith went to Stonyhurst and consulted with Father Plowden, who showed him the decree. Once again, then, Rome had acted without reference to the vicars and once again, too, Rome had done this at the request of Milner.

The English vicars fully realized the need for united action both to further the cause of religion in England and to convince Rome that they were responsible and competent Pastors. They realized, also, that their difficulties with Milner were stumbling blocks to that unity. Even before they were fully aware of the magnitude of his intrigue, they knew they could not rely upon him to work with them. Thomas Smith, when he was appointed co-adjutor to Gibson in 1819, admitted the impossibility of working with Milner. "I wish most earnestly," he wrote Poynter, "that I could have a conference with your Lordship."[41] "I doubt not," he continued,

> but as soon as it is known that I am empowered to act, I shall be sounded on different matters, particularly Stonyhurst, and it is of great importance for the future peace not only of this District but of the whole English Mission, that we Bishops would perfectly understand each other, and as far at least as possible proceed on a uniform line of conduct for the good of Religion.

[40]Letter, Cardinal Somaglia to Bishop Milner, 23 December 1818. Archives, Venerable English College.
[41]Letter, Thomas Smith to William Poynter, 30 May 1819. Archives, Westminster Cathedral.

148 THE ROMAN CATHOLIC CHURCH IN ENGLAND

"It would not surprise me," he speculated, "if Dr. Milner were not to consider himself as Senior Vicar Apostolic...."

Once the Somaglian decree became known, the outcry from the vicars apostolic was loud and clear. Poynter answered a letter from Gibson on 16 September 1819, in which Gibson had reported Milner's knowledge of the decree. "This is a subject, My Lord," responded Poynter, "which demands our attention."[42] "The Superior of Stonyhurst," he predicted, "will become as an Archbishop over all England, if the intrigues of these Gentlemen and of Bishop Milner assisting are not stopped at Rome." "Until Rome will agree to this," he concluded, "and constantly act up to it, viz., not to grant any thing which affects the state of the mission in England without consulting the Vicars Apostolic, we cannot go on, but confusion will be introduced and our authority will be trampled upon."

One of the great objections to the Somaglian decree in addition to the manner in which it was obtained, was to the clause which permitted the Stonyhurst superiors to have *all* students from there ordained under the terms of the decree. This would have meant that those candidates for the secular clergy educated there would be ordained without being subject to their local vicar. Poynter compiled a series of objections to this part of the decree which he sent to the other vicars for approval and then to Father John Kirk[43] in Rome to be translated and presented to Propaganda.[44] Poynter argued in this memorial that the decree gave the Stonyhurst superiors jurisdiction far exceeding that which any other regular superior had and exceeding even that power which the vicars had over their own priests. Such far-reaching powers, according to Poynter, would eventually lead to the ultimate catastrophe for the church in England, "the appointment of

---

[42]Letter, William Poynter to William Gibson, 16 September 1819. Archives, Westminster Cathedral.

[43]John Kirk, former secretary to Bishop Charles Berington of the Midlands District, was now living and doing historical research in Rome.

[44]Letter, William Poynter to John Kirk, 27 September 1819. Archives, Westminster Cathedral.

some Gentleman Priest from Stonyhurst to be made Bishop." If such a disaster should occur, said Poynter, the blame would have to be laid at Milner's feet.

Bishop Poynter attempted to gain wider support for his stand against this threat of Jesuit domination and against Milner's part in it. He apparently canvassed the vicars of Scotland and persuaded them to write in protest against the Somaglian decree. Bishop Cameron of Edinburgh, for example, wrote to John Lingard on 15 October 1819, to add his support to the volume of protest being directed to Rome. "It appears," observed Cameron, "that good Bishop Milner's zeal cannot be kept within *any* limits . . . every resistance must be made, and I trust in Scotland at least we shall be unanimous."[45] Lingard, after apparently receiving a number of similar letters, was commissioned by Poynter to draft a compromise to be sent to Propaganda by way of Robert Gradwell, who was already in Rome. In his letter to Gradwell, Lingard proposed the following settlement: "Let the President [of Stonyhurst] send his alumni where he will to be ordained, but first let him ask the bishop of the district, and only send them to another when the bishop of the district refuses."[46] "Whenever they are ordained," Lingard suggested,

let it be *titulo missionis.* Let the President send them to those places which he has hitherto been accustomed to supply. But first let him give into the bishop a list of those places, [so] that there may be no dispute hereafter. Before the bishop grants faculties to those whom Mr. Plowden shall send, let him or his vicar examine them; when once they are placed, let them be fixed there, nor removable without the consent of the bishop.

"This I think would restore peace," Lingard noted. "It would give to Stonyhurst all it can reasonably desire, and preserve to the bishop as much authority as it would be prudent to

---

[45] Letter, Alexander Cameron to John Lingard, 15 October 1819. Archives, Westminster Cathedral.
[46] Letter, John Lingard to Robert Gradwell, 23 October 1819. Archives, Venerable English College.

claim while that house has so many friends." "I think," he wisely added in conclusion, "it would be more politic first to require the revocation of the last indult [the Somaglian decree], and at length condescend to some accommodation like that I have mentioned."

The efforts of Poynter were finally successful. On 18 April 1820 a papal brief revoked the privileges granted by the Somaglian decree which was declared "surreptitious." Notice of the revocation was sent to Plowden, Milner, Poynter, and Gibson.[47] Under its terms the Stonyhurst priests were required to accept ordination under the title *missionis* or not be ordained at all. Their only other alternative was to go as students to some Jesuit house on the continent for part of their training and their ordination. This procedure was not only expensive, but carried with it the risk that upon returning to England, the priests would not receive faculties from the bishops and would thus be unable to exercise their priestly functions.

The compromise worked out by Lingard and approved by Pope Pius VII in April of 1820 continued in force until 1829, when the Jesuits were finally completely restored in England and assumed the same status as the other religious orders. The victory finally had gone to the vicars, but they bought it at a heavy price. For almost twenty years they had been fighting over the Jesuits. Immeasurable scandal had been given to the laity and their spiritual needs neglected while bishops fought with superiors of regular orders over who should be working on the mission. Numbers of young men left Stonyhurst and were never ordained because of the uncertainty of their obligations. Rome received numerous object lessons in the vicars' lack of respect for one another and their inability to cooperate. No useful meeting, no corporate action, no joint planning for the improvement of the English Catholic church took place during all these years. Bishop Milner's support of the Jesuits against the other vicars apostolic, his interference with the problems of another bishop's

---

[47]Brief of Pope Pius VII, 18 April 1819. Archives, Westminster Cathedral.

jurisdiction, his willingness to act secretly with the Stonyhurst superiors against the vicars: all this presents yet another illustration of how the English vicars apostolic were unable to work together to promote the Catholic religion in England.

CHAPTER VI.
THE DIVISION OF THE DISTRICTS

Notwithstanding varying degrees of persecution and prejudice from without, as well as incredible mismanagement, constant bickering, contradictory efforts, and conservative policies from within, the Catholic church in England did grow. The vicars apostolic had counted 54,000 Catholics in 1780. By 1840 when all four vicars again had made reports to Rome, the Catholic population had considerably increased. From a survey of the somewhat haphazard statistical accounts, it can be estimated that in the London District there were more than 157,000 Catholics; in the Midlands (where the facts are least clear) a minimum of 90,000; in the North, where Catholics were most numerous, 180,000; and in the Western District, 25,000. The total number was in excess of 450,000, an increase of more than 800 percent over the 1780 figures.[1] This meant, then, an increase of from 0.8 percent to approximately 2.8 percent of the total population of England and Wales. A variety of reasons accounted for this growth. There had been a considerable development in the total population, from 7,500,000 in 1780 to 16,000,000 in 1840, an increase of almost 100 percent. Further, a part of this Catholic increase was caused by Irish immigration—there were 420,000 Irish born in England in 1840, most of them Roman Catholic.[2] This fact would help to explain part of the disproportionate increase in the Catholic population—800 percent as opposed to 100 percent for the general population. In addition, with the repeal of penal laws and the passage of Catholic emancipation, there must have been some return of

---

[1] Brady, *Annals*, 201, 242, 280, 316.
[2] Denis Gwynn, "The Irish Immigration," *The English Catholics, 1850–1950*, 279.

nonpracticing Catholics to their religion and a greater willingness to be counted now that reprisals were less likely to occur. Moreover, Catholicism had gained a measure of respectability and there were some conversions from other religious groups.

Of more interest here, however, than what caused the increase in the numbers of Catholics, is the way in which the vicars apostolic met the problems caused by this growth. The last change in Catholic church government in England had taken place in 1688 when the single vicariate of Bishop John Leyburne had been divided into four districts, each with its own vicar apostolic and each independent of the others. This administrative structure had continued to serve the needs of the Catholic population, augmented only by assistant or co-adjutor bishops appointed from time to time to assist the vicars. By the 1830s there was clearly a need for some change in this arrangement. The work was too heavy, the numbers too great, and the distances too far for four vicars, even if they all had assistants, to serve adequately the needs of the Catholics. In 1836 two bishops died, James Bramston of London and Thomas Penswick of the Northern District. This left for the first time in more than thirty years, only four vicars to do the work of the now greatly expanded church. Of these four, Thomas Griffiths had been appointed to the London District in 1835 to assist Bramston, Thomas Walsh had labored alone in the Midlands since 1826, John Briggs had been co-adjutor to Penswick since 1833, and Peter Baines had carried on his swashbuckling administration in the Western District since 1823.[3]

[3]The story of Bishop Baines is far too complex to be treated here, although his activities were another instance of the bishops divided among themselves. For force, spirit, vigor, and contrariness, he was exceeded—if at all—only by Bishop John Milner. But Baines, unlike Milner, carried off his exploits with a verve and dash and boldness unparalleled in the history of the vicars apostolic. In the seventeen years of his reign over the West, he purchased Prior Park in Bath as a school which he conceived of as "the English Vatican and the Catholic Oxford"; begged huge sums of money from benefactors for the school's support, but left both it and the district bankrupt; antagonized all of England's clergy by obtaining papal permission to hold a national collection for his school; persuaded the superiors of the Benedictine community at Ampleforth to leave the order and become secular priests to conduct his college—and then dismissed them because he could not get along with

The obvious answer to the problem of heavy administrative duties was to change the organization. Two basic ways suggested themselves. One was the restoration of a national hierarchy with bishops-in-ordinary ruling over geographical English sees instead of vicars apostolic. The other possible change, much more simple than a restored hierarchy, was to further divide England into additional districts so that each vicar apostolic would be responsible for a smaller area and fewer people. The restoration of the hierarchy had long been discussed as the cure for most of the internal problems of the English Catholic church. The desire for such an arrangement had been the great stumbling block in the way of reform in the seventeenth century when the Old Brotherhood had stood firmly for bishops and had refused to accept a vicar. Again in the 1780s at the time of the formation of the Catholic Committee, one of that group's proposals had been such a restoration. The Committee members had polled the vicars, but finding that the bishops had little enthusiasm for such a plan, dropped the idea. During the next forty years, the proposal was made from time to time, but it was always dismissed by the vicars as either dangerous or disadvantageous. For example, when the Catholic Commitee advocated restoration in 1780, it involved the notion of domestic and even lay election of bishops, an idea repugnant to the vicars. When restoration was suggested as part of the effort to obtain emancipation, it was then seen by the vicars as a threat to their loyalty to Rome and a possible infringement by civil authorities into the sphere of the sacred. During the era of Bishop Milner, restoration of the hierarchy had often been considered as a solution to the confusion rampant because of the lack of unity and leadership, but there was far too much

---

them; brought in the Rosminian priests from Italy for the same purpose and dismissed them for the same reason; suggested a variety of plans for redistricting Catholic England, all of which would have enhanced his position at the expense of everyone else's; tried to persuade his fellow vicars to close their seminaries and let him operate one for all England; was the defendant in an official investigation ordered by Rome over the alienation of Benedictine property; was investigated for heresy; and much more.

danger then that the most compelling personality might receive the most powerful position. No one was interested in serving under an "Archbishop" Milner. Then, too, the regular-secular problem had to be considered. In any reorganization, some division of power would have to be made. Historically, the regulars had always held a number of important English sees—at one time the Benedictines had held seven. During those years when the regulars were in the more favored position in Rome, the vicars were not likely to argue for or endorse a change that might well have gone against their own interests.

Actually, the restoration of a national hierarchy at this point would have effected little change in the powers of any individual bishop. The differences between bishop-in-ordinary and vicar apostolic, never very great, were practically unnoticeable in England by 1830. For all practical purposes, the vicars ruled as bishops, were thought of as bishops by their flocks, both lay and clerical, and were considered bishops by the civil government although the fiction of their not holding geographical sees in England was carefully maintained. There were two essential changes, however, which a restoration of a national hierarchy would have automatically brought about. The first, the one desired most by the vicars, would have established a subordination of power among the bishops and made meaningful corporate action possible. Under the vicarial system, each vicar was directly responsible to Propaganda. He could exercise no corporate authority with the other vicars, nor could the vicars, acting together, really do more than advise and counsel the English Catholic body at large. Furthermore, they did not even have the right to speak collectively at Rome. Under the episcopal system, on the other hand, there would be an archbishop who could coordinate the activities of his suffragan bishops, represent them all in Rome, and, most important, as the previous chapters have indicated, arbitrate disputes among them. Bishop Milner had noted this essential element of a national hierarchy as early as 1799. At the time he was working for his own appointment as vicar of the Midland District. In discussing the various factions at work against his appointment, Milner suggested that the delay in the settlement of his situation might possibly be partly due to the proposed "alteration in our Ecclesiastical government."[4] The chief feature of this alteration would be, thought Milner, "a subordination in our Hierarchy, I mean amongst the Vicars Apostolic."

A restored national hierarchy would also have revised the method of selecting bishops. Under the vicarial system, the pope was free to make the appointment without consultation with anyone. In practice, he customarily asked the advice of Propaganda and of the other English bishops, and considered the wishes, if they had been expressed, of the deceased vicar whose place was to be filled. The fact was, however, that the pope was in no way obliged to consult with anyone from the country or district involved, nor were the vicars obliged to accept recommendations or suggestions from their priests. Vicars usually protected themselves and their districts from surprise appointments by having co-adjutors, assistant bishops who had the right of succession, appointed. These men could be more or less hand picked by the vicar apostolic, in that the vicars could make strong representations to the pope and Propaganda about their wishes for an assistant. Under a national hierarchy some more systematic method of selection would occur, with the bishops and their clergy organized into deaneries having more control over the process. A likely method had the hierarchy been restored at this time, would have been the system newly introduced into Ireland in 1829. This system involved a meeting of the mission priests of the diocese called by the vicar general if the diocese was vacant or by the bishop if the meeting was for the purpose of selecting a co-adjutor. At the meeting each priest nominated by secret ballot one person for the office. The votes were counted and the names of the three highest candidates were sent to the bishops of the province. They, in turn, considered the names, added their own comments but no additional names, and forwarded the information to Propaganda, which

---

[4]Letter, John Milner to John Douglass, 23 January 1799. Archives, Westminster Cathedral.

then recommended to the pope.⁵ In effect, this process limited the influence of Rome upon the selection, for the officials there were obliged to make their choice from among the names, the *terna*, submitted to them.

This method or some similar one would have greatly pleased the clergy of England who were becoming more and more resentful of the arbitrary appointments of their superiors. The case of the appointment of Thomas Griffiths as co-adjutor to Bishop Bramston in 1833 aroused considerable discussion over this very point. One of Bramston's own clergymen, Father John Jones, described his feelings about Bramston's selection of Griffiths to John Lingard who was actively engaged at Rome in pressing for a restored hierarchy. "Bishop Bramston is an infirm man, whose life at best is not worth six months' purchase," Jones reported to Lingard on 29 September 1833, "and he has nominated a successor who will, we conceive, be as ready to propagate the system of private nomination of the Apostolic Vicariate as he is to take it up on that principle from Dr. Bramston."⁶ A method such as that followed in the Irish church could have prevented arbitrary appointments like this one, but without some legal machinery to regulate corporate action, the bishops could not effectively execute such a process.

Lingard agreed with Jones but realized that without some very basic change in the governing system, little could be done to remedy the abuse. "I feel with you on the subject of your letter," he replied consolingly to Jones, "and as heartily disapprove of our present ecclesiastical policy. The bishops dispose of the succession as though they held their offices in fee simple, and had a right to leave them to whom they please."⁷ "But while I admit the abuse," he continued, "I know not where to discover a remedy which may not prove a worse evil. . . . To the prevailing method of appointment in general I would object, did I know to whom to transfer it." "Would

---

⁵John H. Whyte, "The Appointment of Catholic Bishops in Nineteenth-Century Ireland," *Catholic Historical Review*, 47 (April, 1962): 17.

⁶Letter, John Jones to John Lingard, 29 September 1833, quoted in Ward, *Sequel*, 1:54.

⁷Letter, John Lingard to John Jones, quoted Ibid., 55–56, n.d.

158 THE ROMAN CATHOLIC CHURCH IN ENGLAND

you rest it in our Chapter?"[8] he asked by way of demolishing alternatives. "That could never be accomplished. We should have the court of Rome, the English bishops, and the great body of the English against us." "In the missionaries at large?" Lingard suggested, "This would lead to parties, dissensions and appeals to Rome . . . and such appeals would probably suggest the appointment of a Protector for the mission who would be Cardinal Weld under the superintendence of the Jesuits."[9] Comments like this last make it very clear the real fear the clergy, as well as the vicars, had about the dangers of power falling into the hands of the regulars.

"I have sometimes thought," Lingard proposed,

that the only possible expedient for raising the clergy from their present degraded state would be the erection of a Chapter, say of twelve members in each vicariate, which Chapter should exercise jurisdiction *vacante episcopatu*, and have the right of presenting three names to the choice of the Pope whenever a bishop or co-adjutor is to be appointed.

"This would be a first step of importance," he noted in conclusion, "as it would not only produce the benefit for which it would be ostensibly established, but also give existence to an acknowledged authority which on proper occasions might check the irresponsible and unlimited authority of the Bishop." This entire discussion of Lingard's indicated that there were

---

[8]This reference to the Chapter seems to imply that there was great resentment or ill feeling against the Chapter of the Old Brotherhood. However, although this group, never sanctioned by Rome, had continued to exist even after Leyburne became vicar and was expressly forbidden to consult with it, there is no evidence to suggest that it ever attempted to interfere. By this time it had evolved into a social club, albeit a highly selective and most exclusive one. It was not, to be sure, a representative body of all or any part of the English church. Lingard himself had been a member since 1811 so his comments cannot be interpreted as those of an envious outsider.

[9]Thomas Cardinal Weld (1773–1837) belonged to a prominent English Catholic family. After the death of his wife, he was ordained in 1821. In 1830 he was made cardinal and spent the remainder of his life in Rome. He had received his early education from Charles Plowden, who later became the superior of Stonyhurst. The college itself was presented to the Jesuits by Weld and his father. Weld's extreme fondness for the Jesuits caused him to be looked upon with some suspicion by the secular clergy of England.

serious internal problems in the relations of vicars to their clergy which went deeper than mere appointment. The vicars, although they sometimes did voluntarily, were under no obligation to share the administration of their districts with their priests. They did not even have to listen to their priests either individually or collectively. In effect, the vicar was absolute ruler in his district.

The second possibility for improving the administrative system other than the restoration of the English hierarchy was merely to divide England into additional districts so that each vicar would be responsible for fewer people and a smaller area. How this could be done was the crucial question. Such a change would necessitate a vast reorganization of existing districts, missions, and personnel, while a host of minor administrative and jurisdictional rights and privileges which had grown up over the centuries would have to be adjusted.[10] While these changes would result in better order and possibly in a greater share in the government for the clergy, they would also bring the English church more closely under the supervision of Rome, as procedures and policies became more and more regularized. Hence the ambivalence of the English vicars and their clergy to reform, and their tendency to prefer to live with the devil they know than the devil that they did not know.

The attitude towards some form of change was least uncertain among the clergy of the Northern District, which had been the stronghold of a dwindling Catholic population since the Reformation. Both in terms of absolute numbers as well as in the relative number of Catholics in relation to the total population, the Northern District had the distinction of being first. Recent immigration from Ireland and the natural increase in the population had greatly augmented the number of Catholics in the North, especially after 1830. Consequently, the clergy were hard pressed to minister to the needs of the people. Numerous appeals to the vicar of the district and to Rome that some relief be afforded appeared in the

[10]It seems necessary to make the point here that had the administrative change taken the form of a restored hierarchy at this time, these same problems would have had to be met. They were in no way unique to the division of districts.

Catholic press and in petitions sent directly to Bishop Briggs or to Pope Gregory XVI. An editorial, for example, in the *Catholic Magazine* for January 1835 noted that "unfortunately this island once lost its hierarchy, and notwithstanding the universal aspirations of the second order of the clergy, it is to be feared that measures are not yet contemplated for its restoration."[11] "It may be well indeed to intimate," the article went on to say,

> to those whom it may seem to concern more immediately that the clergy are becoming restless upon this subject; that their wishes which lately were but whispered, are now spoken; that a movement strong but orderly is daily making progress.

In November of 1836 a group of Northern clergymen forwarded to Bishop Briggs a series of resolutions. They informed him that "this meeting is of opinion that some change in our ecclesiastical administration is expedient.[12] They added in another resolution, explaining the kind of change they thought most necessary, "that it is expedient that the number of bishops in the Northern District be increased." A third resolution then emphasized what their own role in the proposed reform would entail. "It is expedient," they maintained, "that the Clergy should have a voice in the election of their bishops." This petition was only one of many which were sent to Briggs between 1833 and 1840 when the district was finally divided. A like petition "from English Catholics" was sent to Pope Gregory XVI in April of 1837 making the same request.[13]

Although most of the agitation and most of the need for division came from the North, the other vicars also understood the advantages of additional districts. "I am much inclined to apply for a division of my district into two," wrote Thomas Walsh of the Midlands to Briggs in January of 1837, "to be called the Midland and the Eastern District."[14] "I have

[11]*Catholic Magazine*, January, 1835, 3.
[12]Letter, Francis Trappes to John Briggs, 28 November 1836. Archives, Leeds.
[13]Copy of Petition to Gregory XVI from Certain English Catholics, 3 April 1837. Archives, Vatican, Rome.
[14]Letter, Thomas Walsh to John Briggs, 4 January 1837. Archives, Leeds.

had no application to this effect from any of my clergy," he explained, "but I am of the opinion that religion would be much promoted by such division." Bishop Baines of the West, who as early as 1829 had advocated a redistricting and/or the establishment of a fifth district, was still in favor of such a plan. When Bishop Griffiths of London asked him his opinion early in 1837 about a division and a change in government, he responded by presenting his earlier plan. "Your Lordship is aware, I think," he replied to Griffiths on February 9, "of my strong conviction that an additional district in England would be highly advantageous."[15] "More than one," he added, "I do not think would be advisable *at present*." Baines's opinion on the number was directly related to his 1829 plan, unanimously vetoed by the other vicars apostolic. The difficulty, as Baines had seen it in 1829, and he had not changed his mind, was not too many Catholics, but rather a poor distribution of Catholics. His remedy was to take the overpopulated Northern District and his own Western District which comprised the West of England and Wales, and divide them into three areas. In that way, his underpopulated Western District would receive additional Catholics and he would be rid of Wales. Needless to say, none of the other vicars, either in 1829 or in 1837, was interested in his proposal.

A further discussion of the needs of the North reached Rome in March of 1837, just as English influence there was changing hands. Prior to his death in April of 1837, Thomas Cardinal Weld had been the leading English prelate in Rome. A staunch supporter of the Jesuit claims, he had never lent much support to the requests or petitions of the English vicars apostolic. After Weld's death and even before, Charles Cardinal Acton, a personal friend of Gregory's, assumed more and more influence with regard to English affairs. He was held in great respect by Propaganda and the Holy Office as well as by the pope and any change in English church government would have to pass through his hands. Unfortu-

---

[15]Letter, Peter Baines to Thomas Griffiths, 9 February 1837. Archives, Westminster Cathedral.

nately, he had little respect for the capabilities of the English clergy (with whom he had never really worked) to manage their affairs. He tended to advocate, then, the least possible degree of self government for England. He had once declared that "the English throughout their history had been factious, and opposed to authority, and were not to be intrusted with more and more independent power."[16]

Francis Trappes, a priest from the Northern District who often served as spokesman for the clergy of the North, wrote to Acton in March of 1837 to report to him the dissatisfaction of the priests in the Northern District. They had many complaints: confusion in regulations, dislike of the methods used to select candidates for the episcopacy, absence of well organized district chapters, but their greatest complaint was that the size of the district made the vicar's task impossible, and their work, therefore, unnecessarily difficult and ineffective. "The enormous extent of our District and the incapacity of even two vicars apostolic to perform its duties," complained Trappes, "was the most serious hardship."[17] "In consequence," he explained to Acton,

there has not been in the memory of man such a visitation for confirmation as to put that sacrament within the convenient reach of many considerable congregations. Other ecclesiastical business is generally still more in arrears. Whence also the impossibility of a general meeting of the clergy to secure anything like union of action.

"As a remedy to the above," Trappes went on to report,

there exists a strong wish among many leading secular clergy that our district should be divided under three Vicars Apostolic; viz., one for Yorkshire, one for Lancashire, Cheswick, and Man, and one for Northumberland, Durham, Westmoreland, and Cumber-

---

[16]Notes from a letter to the 2nd Earl of Shrewsbury made by Charles Acton, 26 February 1839. Archives, Vatican.

[17]Letter, Francis Trappes to Charles Acton, 10 March 1837. Archives, Vatican. Here Trappes was apparently referring to the state of affairs prior to 1836 when Thomas Penswick was Vicar Apostolic and John Briggs was co-adjutor. If even with two vicars there was too much work, how much worse it must have been with only one.

THE DIVISION OF THE DISTRICTS 163

land. And they are persuaded that each would be fully employed and easily supported. . . .

There appeared to be no real objection in Rome to the idea of some change in the government of the English church. Griffiths reported to Bishop Briggs in June of 1837 that Pope Gregory XVI had directed him—and the other vicars—"to make a further division of Districts to meet the increasing numbers and wants of the Catholics."[18] "They are to make," Griffiths reported what seemed to be a *carte blanche*, "whatever other arrangements relative to the election of future vicars apostolic and the government of the clergy they may judge necessary." But despite the fact that Rome, English vicars and clergy all wanted some change, the affair dragged on until well into 1840. It is not difficult to understand why the hierarchy was not to be restored at this time. Weld was a friend of the Jesuits and both he and Acton were opposed to the idea of raising the vicars to bishops-in-ordinary. Moreover, there were serious problems pending in Rome over the rights of the Jesuits to establish missions, particularly in London and Liverpool, and over the claims of the Benedictines to English sees if a national hierarchy were to be reestablished. In most of the letters of the vicars, while there is definite desire expressed for improved methods of administration, there is a notable absence of enthusiasm for a national hierarchy. The hierarchy would mean an English leader and the vicars did not yet appear willing to surrender some of their individual autonomy, nor were they sure about the man they could accept as archbishop. Bishop Baines they did not trust. Griffiths was not regarded as qualified. Walsh was too much a Jesuit. Briggs was too young. Nicholas Wiseman, later to be England's first resident archbishop since the Reformation, was just beginning to make his presence felt. He was well known enough to be respected as an effective promoter of the Catholic faith with influence at Rome and among Protestants, but his Roman ways and evident ambition made him suspect among the more conservative and traditional vicars apostolic.

[18] Letter, Thomas Griffiths to John Briggs, 22 June 1837. Archives, Leeds.

Despite the reluctance to restore the national hierarchy at this time, practically no objection existed to a simple partition of the districts. Nevertheless, it was not until 1840, at least seven years after the first serious requests were made, that this relatively minor change came into effect. An analysis of the correspondence, especially between 1837 and 1840, seems to indicate that the delay could be attributed both to the vicars and to the Roman officials. The vicars failed to act decisively in this period, not so much, however, because of the usual internal disagreements, but rather because of a failure to realize the urgency of the problem and a reluctance to assume corporate responsibility. The Holy See, on the other hand, seemed unwilling to move ahead without the advice and suggestions of the English vicars, but nevertheless acted in an impatient and precipitous fashion, scarcely giving the vicars time to react before beginning to complain about vicarial neglect of correspondence. Cardinal Weld wrote to Bishop Briggs in March of 1837 about the likelihood of a division of the Northern District and pointed out to him the need for some action, not only from groups of English clergymen, but from the vicars themselves. "We have heard much here from England on the necessity of dividing some of the Districts in that country," Weld explained to Briggs, "but nothing has come officially on the subject before the Sacred Congregation de Propaganda Fide."[19] "We have been hoping to see both Dr. Walsh and Dr. Griffiths here soon," Weld continued, "but I fear there is no immediate prospect of the arrival of either. I wish your Lordship could make us a visit. It would not be right to make a division of your district till you had had an opportunity of fully expressing your sentiments upon it."

In the meantime, Griffiths had received similar information about the need for vicarial action and consulted Briggs as to what should be done. "By a letter from Dr. Wiseman dated 15th February, 1837," reported Griffiths to Briggs, 16 April, on his way to Rome, "it appears that Mgr. Mai, Cardinal Fransoni and the Pope had spoken openly on the division of England into more than four Districts, and likewise on the

---

[19]Letter, Thomas Weld to John Briggs, 26 March 1837. Archives, Leeds.

establishment of a Hierarchy if this latter measure were not disagreeable to the English government."[20] "In consequence," Griffiths continued,

Dr. Wiseman had an audience of an hour with His Holiness who spoke strongly on the propriety of the division. Since the audience, the pope had mentioned his expectation of seeing two of the English bishops soon after Easter to treat of the further division of England.

"In these circumstances," Griffiths explained to Briggs,

I have to request your Lordship to give me your free advice on the propriety of a journey to Rome. Could I inform His Holiness more effectually of our serious consideration being turned to the subject? And could I by suggesting a few of the difficulties attending a Division from the state of Catholics in different counties, from the college, the clergy, and induce His Holiness to wait patiently another year before any statement of our opinion was sent to Rome?

Despite the fact that this letter seems to indicate a great sharing of opinions and advice among the vicars, it is a bit misleading. Since the letter was dated 16 April, three days after Griffiths and Walsh had left London to begin their trip to Rome, Griffiths's request for Briggs's counsel was obviously not much more than formality.

It seems clear, also, that although the vicars did not oppose in principle the idea of division, they thought the proposal inexpedient at the moment. Griffiths's letter to Briggs also indicated certain "difficulties" he could foresee. These difficulties were never totally spelled out, but they appeared to have been those concerning the selection of qualified vicars—both the manner of selection and the discovery of good candidates, the financial support of an increased number of vicars, the distribution of property among new districts, the management of colleges and seminaries currently autonomous in each district. The bishops felt quite decidedly that they needed time to consider and plan for such changes and

[20]Letter, Thomas Griffiths to John Briggs, 16 April 1837. Archives, Leeds.

that they should not be hurried into hasty action. In January of 1837 when they had met for a general discussion of mutual problems, they had determined to prepare a plan of division to be discussed at their next meeting, scheduled for Easter week of 1838.[21] Obviously the vicars were in no great hurry.

When Bishops Griffiths and Walsh arrived in Rome in the spring of 1837, they learned that Weld had just died. They did, however, have an audience with the pope and discussed the possibility of governmental change in England. "The Holy Father," Griffiths recorded in his diary for 12 June 1837, "though not wishing to originate the further division of England into Districts, approved and sanctioned a further division, saying that as the number of Catholics increased, there was cause for an increase of bishops to govern them."[22] "His Holiness," Griffiths noted further, "wished the vicars apostolic at their meeting after Easter, 1838, to make every arrangement, except the name of bishops-in-ordinary, which they judged proper for the present state of the English Catholics." In concluding his entry, Griffiths also noted that the pope assured them "more than once that there was no obstacle with himself to the placing England in every respect, saving the name of bishops-in-ordinary, in the same situation with Catholic countries. . . ."

Clearly the pope's words were a mandate to proceed with some reorganization of the English church in a manner which the vicars thought most suited to their situation. But still they delayed. They spread—but not too efficiently—the news from Rome to their fellow vicars in England. On 22 August 1837, Thomas Walsh commented in a note to Bishop Briggs, "Doctor Griffiths, with whom your Lordship corresponds on the subject, has no doubt clearly explained to you the sentiments of his Holiness on the division of districts, election of bishops, etc."[23] But in November Briggs was still trying to acquire information about the pope's attitudes, and he indicated that

---

[21] Minutes, meeting of Vicars Apostolic in London, 24 January 1837. Archives, Westminster Cathedral.

[22] Diary, Thomas Griffiths, 12 June 1837. Archives, Westminster Cathedral.

[23] Letter, Thomas Walsh to John Briggs, 22 August 1837. Archives, Leeds.

Bishop Baines was also as yet unenlightened. Briggs, writing to Griffiths, reported that he had heard from Baines who "agrees with me on the importance of our being put in possession of what passed at Rome on the subjects of the division of districts and of the ecclesiastical government of this country. . . . He [Baines] thinks it would be best for your Lordship to give as good account as you can in writing."[24] "Under these circumstances," Briggs went on to ask of Griffiths, "I presume to request that your Lordship will be so good as to inform me on the following points, which I beg leave to submit in the way of questions:

1. Did His Holiness, Cardinal Fransoni, and Mgr. Mai express a wish that the districts of England should be divided?
2. Did they mention this wish respecting any district in particular?
3. Did they say how many districts they wished to be formed in England?
4. What is the favorable mode of effecting this division?
5. What mode of electing the future VVAA appears to be wished by His Holiness?
6. If elective by whom are they to be elected?
7. Did His Holiness seem to wish to have bishops-in-ordinary instead of Vicars Apostolic?
8. Were Chapters mentioned for the ecclesiastical government of England?
9. If so, are these Chapters to act only *sede vacante*, or are they to assist the bishop in the management of his district?
10. Was anything suggested by His Holiness as to the manner of governing the clergy in this country?"

An analysis of these questions, of Baines's lack of information, of the comments made by Griffiths in his diary all seem to suggest a certain reluctance on the part of Griffiths and Walsh to share their information. Certainly, the pope was not opposed, indeed, understood the need for some further division of districts in England, but he wished the initiative for such changes to come from the vicars—presumably

[24]Letter, John Briggs to Thomas Griffiths, 29 November 1837. Archives, Westminster Cathedral.

all the vicars. Bishops Griffiths and Walsh, however, who had received this information directly from the pope in a personal interview, had not communicated its content or tone to their fellow bishops, Briggs and Baines. Why they failed to do this is not completely clear. They did not, of course, trust Baines. He was at that time in serious trouble with Propaganda over problems in his own district, but he had powerful friends in Rome who could speak for him. Prior to this time, he had made numerous suggestions about possible changes in the English church, none of which the other vicars were enthusiastic about. He was clearly ambitious and all too willing to assume the position of leadership if it were offered to him. It may well have been that the others, at least Griffiths and Walsh, wished to have their plans well laid before allowing Bishop Baines into their confidence. In that way they could retain the upper hand.

In the case of Bishop Briggs, it was not that Griffiths or Walsh disliked or distrusted him. Nonetheless, he presented a certain real danger to them, for it was from his district that most of the agitation for reform originated. It was the second order of clergy, not the bishops, who wanted specific changes beyond the mere subdivision of the four districts. They were clamoring for a voice in the selection of vicars, a place in the government of the district, and a more regularized system for handling clerical problems. Such claims on power could be a threat to the position of the vicars. Since the loudest clamors came from the Northern District, it seems not unreasonable to think that Girffiths and Walsh would be slow to bring Briggs into their early discussions. Quite obviously he could not control the forces demanding change in his own district. It would not do to create a situation there which would allow these somewhat unruly clergymen to discover how very free the pope had left the English church to solve its problems in its own way.

All this, then, would help to explain why Griffiths and Walsh had been somewhat dilatory about informing Briggs of what had passed in Rome. For, certainly, Briggs was the one really most involved. The agitation for change not only had originated mainly in his district, but there was every likelihood that the greatest part of the division would take place in his area. In that respect, Briggs's questions to Griffiths have another interesting implication. From their tone, it would appear that Briggs was hopeful that the pope had spelled out the manner and form of the changes. It seems not unreasonable to think, then, that he was unsure of what sort of a division he should ask for, what new rights the clergy might be safely granted, and of his own ability to govern and control his priests unless the orders came from Rome.

In the meantime, the bishops proceeded unhurriedly with their plans for a future reorganization. In January of 1838, Griffiths answered Briggs's questions with brief replies.[25] The pope did, indeed, want the districts to be divided and that was why he had deferred appointing any new co-adjutors. The pope, however, had mentioned no special district nor any specific number of new districts. His Holiness, said Griffiths, left the mode of dividing up to each vicar in his own district, expecting that each would divide in such a way that the new districts would be adequate to support themselves. The vicars were to decide for themselves the method of electing new vicars; the bishops were to remain vicars and not be bishops-in-ordinary. On the subject of chapters and government, reported Griffiths, the pope had said nothing at all.

Hardly two months later, on 20 March 1838, Griffiths again wrote to Briggs explaining what his own ideas were on the proposed changes. This long and important letter is crucial to any understanding about what the Bishops were doing and thinking in this period. "I write this confidential letter with *much diffidence*," Griffiths began.[26] "I have consulted several of my clergy (under secrecy) to hear reasons and to ascertain feeling: no two have thought alike, though most agree that a change of some kind is desirable." "My own ideas are," he confided,

that even retaining our present names, the government of our country should be as much as possible assimilated to the Regular

---

[25]Letter, Thomas Griffiths to John Briggs, 29 January 1838. Archives, Leeds.
[26]Letter, Thomas Griffiths to John Briggs, 20 March 1838. Archives, Leeds.

Hierarchy. I should therefore propose:

1. To preserve union and insure uniformity, the senior Vicar Apostolic or the vicar apostolic of a determined district, should be assimilated to the archbishop of a province, and [have?] similar rights in convoking and presiding over the annual synod.
2. That besides vicars general for each district, each vicar apostolic should divide his district into eight or ten deaneries, appointing a dean to each, with vicarial powers.
3. That where more priests than one are attached to a chapel, the first should be responsible for all the duties, and charged with the inspection of his assisting priests.
4. That the faculties of the clergy, except that of administering the sacrament of penance, should be restricted to their respective chapels.
5. That the vicar apostolic with the advice of the deans . . . should nominate his vicar general, deans and the clergy to their situations.
6. That the advice of all the vicars general and of all the deans should be asked before the presentation of three names for co-adjutor.
7. That on the death of a vicar apostolic without a co-adjutor, the vicar general and deans should elect three names for presentation.
8. That the three names, whether for co-adjutor or vicar apostolic, must receive the sanction of the other vicars apostolic before they are forwarded to Rome.

"The same reasons," concluded Griffiths,

which induced the church in her wisdom to establish the different gradations of jurisdiction, viz., order, inspection, and due subordination, recommend an approach at least to the regular hierarachy. And if we cannot obtain the name, which the clergy and laity want, we shall show our desire of obtaining, what is after all principally desirable, the substance. Numbers 6-7-8 would insure the presentation of fit persons for bishops—and would avoid party feeling.

As had been planned more than a year before, the vicars met at Easter in York from 23 April to 4 May 1838. All four bishops were present: Baines, Walsh, Briggs, and Griffiths, along with their respective theologians: Fathers Thomas

Youens, Edward Cox, Francis Mostyn (later to be bishop of the Northern District), and Anthony Rey. The vicars devoted most of the meeting to a discussion of the proposed changes. The minutes, in Griffiths's handwriting, gave the following report: "Resolved: that the division of England into a greater number of districts is very desirable; but obstacles stand in the way of its immediate execution."[27] The bishops also decided "that certain new regulations should be immediately introduced in the different districts. . . ." In a series of other resolutions, the "new regulations" were enumerated. In essence they were the same as those proposals outlined in Bishop Griffiths's letter to Briggs on 20 March 1838.[28] A final resolution directed, "that a letter be written to Rome informing the Holy See of the resolutions come to by the bishops respecting the division of districts and the projected change in the ecclesiastical government." In a word, the vicars apostolic decided to concentrate in their resolutions on the internal organization of districts and the mode of electing vicars rather than on the division of districts.

From the indecisiveness of the first resolution about the proposed division—that is, there was no indication of the number of divisions, their location, or when such divisions could be effected—and from the fact that the bishops failed to notify Rome of the results of their meeting for more than a month, it would appear that they felt there was no great hurry about making the proposed change. Rome took an extremely dim view of the bishops' actions, resenting, apparently, both their leisurely approach and their failure to notify Rome before rather than after they had executed certain changes. On 19 May 1838 Cardinal Fransoni wrote to Griffiths to say that numerous petitions for division and for a change in government had reached Rome and would the vicars please send him their opinions.[29] Again on 20 June 1838, Wiseman reported to Briggs that Propaganda was dis-

---

[27]Minutes of the Bishops' meeting at York, 23 April to 4 May 1838. Copy in Thomas Griffiths' hand and dated 8 May 1838. Archives, Leeds.

[28]See p. 169, above.

[29]Letter, Giacomo Fransoni to Thomas Griffiths, 19 May 1838. Quoted in Ward, *Sequel*, 1:134.

pleased at the vicars' delay in writing Rome. Wiseman also suggested that it would be prudent to let Rome hear about changes before they took place, not afterwards.[30] A few days later Wiseman wrote to Bishop Baines "in consequence of the uneasiness expressed to me by the Secretary of Propaganda, Mgr. Cadolini, at not having heard from your Lordships since the meeting at York, upon the subjects proposed for deliberations."[31] "He gave me to understand," Wiseman recounted to Baines,

that new petitions had been received from England on the subject of increasing the number of vicariates, and that a letter was lying before the Holy Father for approbation urging in strong terms an immediate answer respecting the matter and the form of election of bishops in future.

"Further he informed me," Wiseman warned Baines, "that if no definitive result should come from the synod, Propaganda would feel itself called upon to take the matter into its own hands, and proceed to the formation of a plan to be proposed to the bishops for acceptance."

Rome, it seems probable, was hunting for excuses to take action on its own and for putting the English vicars in a defensive position. No other reason really could account for the behavior of the curial officers. The bishops ended their spring meeting on 4 May 1838 and the minutes were not ready until 8 May. On 19 May, only eleven days later, Fransoni was already displeased that he had not received a copy of the proceedings. Ten days to two weeks was the usual time for letters to reach Rome, so that he was not really justified in making the complaint. Actually, the bishops sent off their report to Rome on 11 June, certainly not with dispatch, but not with unseasonable delay either. In this report of the meeting, they included the changes in the regulations which had already been distributed to the clergy and had presumably

---

[30]Letter, Nicholas Wiseman to John Briggs, 20 June 1838. Archives, Leeds.
[31]Letter, Nicholas Wiseman to Peter Baines, 24 June 1838. Archives, Clifton.

gone into effect.³² What really was at the heart of Rome's complaint was the bishops' promulgation of administrative changes without, according to Fransoni and Wiseman, prior consultation with Rome. This complaint, however, was not altogether legitimate, for the vicars did no more in their 1838 meeting than they had been instructed to do in the spring of 1837 when Griffiths and Walsh had visited Rome. It might have been considered a breach of good manners—although a mild one—to have put the resolutions into effect without prior notification to Rome, but it was hardly a gross error in administrative procedure.

Apparently Rome did finally decide to take the initiative, for Wiseman reported to Griffiths on 14 July 1838 that a plan had been proposed which Propaganda was about to send to all the vicars for their opinions. "Mgr. Cadolini speaks of six vicariates," Wiseman explained, "but I think it probable that a plan for a division into eight will likewise be proposed."³³ "The basis on which the divisions will be regulated," he added, "seems to be number of missions and distances." "Such I have every reason to believe," Wiseman concluded, "is the outline of the measures likely to be proposed in the course I should say of a couple of months by the Sacred Congregation."

Though Rome seized the initiative, it still hesitated to act. Both Rome and the vicars wanted the division and the administrative changes, but neither one was willing to act in the face of what they considered ill feeling by the other. During 1839 another issue arose which further increased the mutual irritation. Rome had issued two special indults or decrees to the regulars in England, one to administer certain indulgences—a function formerly in the hands of the vicars; the other to establish missions on their own authority. The last, of course, had long been a sore point between the regular

---

³²Letter, Vicars Apostolic to Propaganda, 11 June 1838. Quoted in Ward, *Sequel*, 1:134. The regulations referred to are those first suggested by Griffiths. See p. 169, above.

³³Letter, Nicholas Wiseman to Thomas Griffiths, 14 July 1838. Archives, Westminster Cathedral.

clergy and the vicars apostolic, and although the pope made it clear that the regulars were expected to consult and cooperate with the vicars in the wise placement of such new chapels, there was much hard feeling and bickering.

A whole series of exchanges took place, with Propaganda and the pope expressing their displeasure at the vicars' tone and attitude, while the vicars were equally displeased that Rome was moving without consulting them. Bishop Griffiths, for example, reported to Briggs on 4 February 1839 that he had heard from Wiseman about "the strong complaint of Mgr. Cadolini at the tone and manner of the answers sent to Rome."[34] A month later Griffiths again wrote to Briggs, this time quoting a letter he had just received from Wiseman. "I had a long interview with the Pope," Wiseman had reported to Griffiths.[35] "What His Holiness spoke of with tears in his eyes were the following," Wiseman had written, "the two rescripts—the manner in which they were rejected or opposed. The tone of the letter . . . gave him great pain." A second complaint the pope had made was "the issuing of synodal decrees under the joint authority of all the vicars, without first permission of the Holy See and then submitting the decrees to it for approbation." Here the pope was referring to the resolutions passed at the 1838 meeting of the vicars after which they had promulgated their administrative changes before submitting them to Rome. Strictly speaking, the 1838 meeting was not a synod, for the vicars had no power to call such a body into existence, although it was true that the governmental changes enacted by their informal meeting were of the magnitude usually reserved for officially convoked canonical meetings. On the vicars' side of the argument were the supporting facts that the procedure was not without precedent on their part—they had been meeting on a fairly regular basis for many years, the resolutions passed in 1838 had not been totally different in kind from similar ones passed at other meetings, and their action in making

---

[34]Letter, Thomas Griffiths to John Briggs, 4 February 1839. Archives, Leeds.
[35]Letter, Thomas Griffiths to John Briggs, 1 March 1839, in which Griffiths quoted from a letter from Nicholas Wiseman received that same day. Archives, Leeds.

the changes in 1838 had been the result of Pope Gregory XVI's mandate to Griffiths and Walsh in 1837.

Gregory had still another complaint, Wiseman confided to Griffiths in his March 1st letter. It was "that he never had any communication from the Vicars that could console him, or of the progress of religion, the state of the districts, but that he had to learn what he could from newspapers while all correspondence was of a disagreeable nature and He spoke much of the tone and manner of former letters." "I cannot but think," Wiseman then advised, "that more attention ought to have been paid to forms especially such as are of usage; for, where such forms are always employed, a departure from them necessarily bears the appearance of want of respect."

Bishop Griffiths did not let Wiseman's letter go unrefuted, although he chose to make his reply to Cardinal Acton rather than to Wiseman. Acton, a far more powerful man in Rome at this time, could better defend the position of the vicars, operating as he did from a position of influence and personal friendship with the pope and many of the officials in Propaganda. "The duty of manifesting in word and action," Griffiths confided to Acton, "devoted attachment and obedience to the Holy See is one of unmixed pleasure, and I trust to the enlightened mind and impartial discernment of His Holiness, that the dutiful representation of evils resulting from any proposed measure will be regarded only as an additional proof of my devotion to him."[36] "I should ill discharge my office of vicar apostolic," continued Griffiths, "if I concealed my convictions of what was injurious to religion, from the fear of my words or motives being misconceived by the Holy See." "It is in this spirit," he concluded, referring to one of the disputed decrees which granted regulars the right to establish churches in areas where the vicars apostolic already had missions, "that I request you will, in charity to the Catholic religion in England, lay before the Holy Father the consequences of enforcing the Decree of 29 September 1838."

It was not until Acton entered the dispute that some smoothing of ruffled feelings occurred. He was instrumental

---

[36]Letter, Thomas Griffiths to Charles Acton, 14 March 1839. Archives, Vatican.

in obtaining a satisfactory explanation of the distasteful 1838 decree from Cardinal Fransoni. "With regard to the new churches of the Regulars," Fransoni had explained to Griffiths on 5 September 1839, "it is undeniable that the consent of the ordinaries is requisite; but the Sacred Congregation has thought itself bound . . . to recall to mind that such a refusal can never be made without just grounds."[37] Such an explanation offered a narrow margin of victory for both the regulars and the vicars and enabled the vicars to accept the decree without totally losing face.

After this settlement, some definite progress could be made toward a division of the districts. Cardinal Fransoni informed Bishop Griffiths on 28 September 1839 that the districts would be increased from four to eight.[38] This number was arrived at apparently through the efforts of Acton, who had been the recipient of many letters from the various vicars and from their clergy, in which they all expressed their opinions about the most advantageous division. The consensus seemed to be that the North should be divided into three districts, the Midland District and the Western District into two each, while London would remain undivided.

At this point the vicars turned their attention very naturally to a consideration of the men who might be chosen to head the new vicariates. In this they were somewhat behind the clergy themselves. As early as the summer of 1839, Acton had been in receipt of letters from priests, mostly in the Northern District, giving him their thoughts on the matter. In July, for example, four Northern clergymen had written that "the new vicars apostolic [should] *be men unquestionably attached to the Holy See*, imbued with professional knowledge, acceptable as much as may be to those whom they are to govern, and especially uncontaminated with that policy, which, to say the least, has brought our system of government into disrepute, and rendered a change imperative."[39] "It is further

---

[37]Letter, Giacomo Fransoni to Thomas Griffiths, 5 September 1839. Archives, Westminster Cathedral. My translation.

[38]Letter, Giacomo Fransoni to Thomas Griffiths, 28 September 1839. Archives, Westminster Cathedral. My translation.

[39]Letter, J. B. Marsh, Michael Singleton, M. S. Hexham, and Francis Trappes to Charles Acton, 13 July 1839. Archives, Vatican.

of the highest importance," they continued, "that they be free from all grounded accusation of partiality and factious feelings in regard to the various clerical bodies." The priests then proceeded to reject two of the names which they had heard were proposed for the new positions: Thomas Sherburne, because of "his total want of impartiality" with regard to the regulars; and Thomas Youens, because "we hold him far from being free from factious propensities, extremely inactive and dilatory in business."

Unhappily, as soon as the vicars began to attend to the specifics of the division, they began to argue among themselves over particulars. Baines offered a possible division which would have taken part of the Midlands and attached it to the West. To this, Walsh had violent objections. "Dr. Baines has proposed to me a new division of districts," Walsh complained to Briggs on 12 November 1839, "which would be the ruin of the plan I have in contemplation for the promotion of religion in Birmingham and in the neighborhood."[40] "To me," Walsh went on th explain, "part of his Lordship's plan, the separation of Staffordshire from Warwickshire I will never consent to and shall consider it my duty to oppose to the utmost of my power." "Why," Walsh asked, "is the only portion of [the Midland District] where there is a fair prospect of causing religion in some degree at least to flourish to be slashed and cut up for the purpose of assisting a barren part of the Western District?" "Why," he reiterated, "are the fairest prospects for religion in England to be destroyed to benefit Wales?" What Walsh was objecting to here was that Baines would have taken the District's college at Oscott, the vicar's home and farm from which he received his support, as well as annexing the wealthiest part of the Midland District.

Wales, part of the Western District, was apparently the Siberia of the English church. Baines, in all his attempts at division plans, always tried to separate it from the West. One of his proposals was to give Wales to the Benedictines, who would then remove themselves from the other districts—and

[40]Letter, Thomas Walsh to John Briggs, 12 November 1839. Archives, Leeds.

particularly from Baines's realm. It was true that the order did wish to be remembered when the new vicars were selected, but their plans hardly included Wales as their sole boon. "I understand," Baines informed Griffiths on 25 November 1839, "the Benedictines have been up in arms to defend themselves from the attempt of the Bishops to force them to abandon their missions and accept the District of Wales!!!"[41] He then went on to propose a division that would have partitioned Wales between two of the projected new Northern districts. "To this plan," concluded Baines, "I am not personally attached, nor indeed to any, except with a view of rescuing Wales from utter abandonment, which awaits it if handed over to a new Bishop who is not supported by all the weight of the Benedictine Body." Although this particular plan of Baines was not used, he was ultimately victorious, for Wales was set up as a single district with a Benedictine at its head.

A request to the vicars on 18 January 1840 from Fransoni for the names of men thought to be appropriate for the new districts caused a flurry in the correspondence between the vicars and from some of the clergy to them.[42] These letters indicated that there were differences of opinion among the vicars. "I beg to submit to your Lordship," suggested Briggs to Griffiths on 24 January 1840, when he received Fransoni's letter, "whether it would not be well that we should jointly but confidentially communicate the names that we each propose to send to Rome."[43] "Namely," he proposed, "to Dr. Baines and between ourselves. I omit Dr. Walsh as all the world says he is about to join the Jesuits." "The chance of our working well together," Briggs concluded, "depends very much on the choice now made and if we the vicars apostolic agree in proposing much the same, our proposing must have weight. . . . I am inclined to propose Dr. Youens and Rev. Mr. Riddell." In a letter from Griffiths to Briggs, which must

[41]Letter, Peter Baines to Thomas Griffiths, 25 November 1839. Archives, Westminster Cathedral.
[42]Letter, Giacomo Fransoni to Thomas Griffiths, 18 January 1840, quoted in Ward, *Sequel*, 7:159.
[43]Letter, John Briggs to Thomas Griffiths, 24 January 1840. Archives, Westminster Cathedral.

THE DIVISION OF THE DISTRICTS 179

have crossed the latter's to him, Griffiths underlined the importance of choosing the new vicars from the districts they were to serve and complained that Propaganda had left little time for consultation.[44] This last complaint, considering the years the topic had been under discussion, seems most unreasonable. Further, given the vicars' concern that they be heard and their opinions sought by Rome, it might have been expected that they would have long before this discussed the possible choices for the new vicars and made up their lists. But this inability either to act or think corporately was, of course, nothing new.

At the same time that Briggs and Griffiths were engaged in discussing how the vicars should present a list of names, a group of clergy from Ushaw College in the Northern District wrote to their vicar, Bishop Briggs. The college priests were insistent that all the secular—not the regular—clergy be heard on the matter and proposed two names for consideration, William Thompson and William Hogarth, "as gentlemen well adapted to fill the high station of vicar apostolic and as very likely to prove acceptable to the great body of the clergy."[45] Bishop Briggs himself contacted the same William Hogarth to ascertain his opinion about various names which had been sent by Propaganda, which had in the meantime sent out its own list for the vicars' approval. Hogarth replied to Briggs on 8 February 1840 with a series of comments on the proposed men which is not without interest. "Dr. Wiseman," Hogarth began, "no one will object to as fit though he may not be the *most* fit."[46] "Dr. Baggs," he added, referring to the rector of the English College in Rome, "is too young and totally inexperienced in missionary affairs." "Weedall, Mostyn, Wareing may, for anything I know," he continued,

do for the Middle District. They know nothing of ours. Tate will do for the North. G. Brown too old and infirm—one foot in the

---

[44]Letter, Thomas Griffiths to John Briggs, 25 January 1840. Archives, Leeds.
[45]Letter, Charles Newsham, Robert Tate, John Kirk, and Thomas (last name is illegible), all of Ushaw College, to John Briggs, 29 January 1840. Archives, Leeds.
[46]Letter, William Hogarth to John Briggs, 8 February 1840. Archives, Leeds.

grave. . . . Morris a Jesuit and far too old and infirm, Newsham, unfortunately, I fear on account of his nerves and hand will not do.

"I know nothing of the monks," Hogarth went on to say,

but am quite sure . . . that nothing but confusion will be the consequence if a regular of any description be appointed bishop in these Northern parts. I think as they have named so very few from the North, your Lordship should question the propriety of their considering that bringing a Rev. Gentleman from another district would be a great disadvantage both to him as Bishop and to the District to which he is sent.

In the same month Walsh notified Acton that he wanted Wiseman, not for one of the new districts, but for his coadjutor.[47] Wiseman, so Walsh believed, could do much to improve Oscott College and, moreover, had a good idea of how to send missionaries throughout England to stimulate religious fervor among the people. Both Briggs and Wiseman felt the central location of the Midlands would be advantageous to this plan. At this same time Griffiths indicated to Briggs that the Benedictines must take Wales whether they wanted it or not and that Thomas Brown of that order should be the vicar.[48] The intrigue increased with a series of letters from Robert Newsham, rector of Ushaw College, to Briggs. Newsham had little faith in the integrity of Roman officials and believed that anything the vicars wrote concerning new bishops would ultimately be passed on to the men concerned. "My conviction is that what you say will have little weight," wrote Newsham to Briggs, "except in the way of defending your own district from obnoxious individuals."[49] Newsham went on to say, "I agree with you in all you say about Dr. Wiseman. He is much devoted to the regulars. . . . He would refuse to be vicar apostolic in the North for I happen to know that he is quite bent on residing near London." In another letter to Briggs, Newsham's misgivings about Rome were even

[47]Letter, Thomas Walsh to Charles Acton, 20 February 1840. Archives, Vatican.
[48]Letter, Thomas Griffiths to John Briggs, 14 February 1840. Archives, Leeds.
[49]Letter, Robert Newsham to John Briggs, February, 1840. Archives, Leeds.

more in evidence. "I think very ill of the Propaganda," he wrote with some heat, "forwarding lists of either divisions of the Districts or of the persons they propose to elect for vicars apostolic to the regulars."[50] "The whole business is carried on in an underhand way," he maintained, "a way perfectly detestable to an Englishman." "But I say again," he concluded, "Fight your own battle with your clergy to back you. Exhort the other Vicars Apostolic to do the same and *you* at least will beat the Romans."

Such maneuvering continued all through the spring of 1840, especially in the North and in the West. In the latter district, Thomas Brown, abbot of the Benedictine monastery at Downside, forwarded his suggestions and comments to Rome through Cardinal Acton. He believed that conditions among the clergy in England were deplorable, largely because there had been such a poor choice of vicars apostolic in the past.[51] In this comment he was clearly referring to Bishop Baines for whom he had little if any respect. Brown went on to say that he did not wish to be appointed as vicar of the Welsh or any other district.

Finally, by a decree dated 11 May 1840, four new vicariates were created in England, bringing the total number to eight.[52] The London District remained almost the same, losing only Bedford and Bucks counties to the new Eastern District, which also contained Lincoln, Northampton, Cambridge, Norfolk, Suffolk, Rutland, and Huntingdon, formerly part of the old Midland District. The Midland District's name was dropped altogether, and its counties were divided between the Eastern and Central Districts. The old Northern District was divided into three parts, with the name of Northern retained by Northumberland, Cumberland, Westmoreland, and Durham. The county of Yorkshire comprised the entire Yorkshire District, while Chester, Lancaster, and the Isle of Man became the new Lancashire District. The Western District

---

[50]Letter, Robert Newsham to John Briggs, February, 1840. Archives, Leeds. Neither letter has a more definite date, but this one makes reference to the letter in note 49, above.
[51]Letter, Thomas Brown to Charles Acton, 2 April 1840. Archives, Vatican.
[52]Brady, *Annals*, 323, 327, 333–34, 337–38, 341–42.

was divided with the new Welsh District being formed of Herford and Monmouth as well as Wales. The decree appointing the new vicars was dated 3 July 1840.[53] By that order, Thomas Walsh of the old Midland District continued as vicar of the new Central District, while William Wareing became vicar of the Eastern District. In the West, Peter Baines held the old Western District, and Thomas Brown, O.S.B., assumed the care of the unpopular Welsh District, despite his protests. In the North, Briggs became vicar of Yorkshire, Henry Weedall, president of St. Mary's College, Oscott (in the old Midland District) was appointed vicar of the Northern District, but he declined to accept the post. In his place, Propaganda appointed Francis Mostyn, also from the Midlands. For the new district of Lancashire, Propaganda selected George Brown.

None of these appointments appeared to have been a surprise to the people or districts involved. Most of them caused little comment, except in the North, where there was strong opposition to the selection of men from outside the district. Even before the official notification arrived, the Northern clergy were busy writing letters of objection to the appointment of Weedall. William Hogarth wrote to Briggs on 3 June 1840, a month before the appointment was announced, lamenting the choice of Weedall as a stranger who could not possibly understand the problems of the area.[54] In Hogarth's opinion, the only thing worse than Weedall would have been a regular. Two days later Hogarth wrote again warning Briggs that the clergy were about to hold a general meeting to express their opposition to Weedall, and that it was very possible that should he be appointed, the clergymen of the district would withhold their obedience.[55] On 8 June 1840 he sent Briggs a statement formulated by the clergy, expressing their displeasure with Weedall. The priests demanded, wrote Hogarth, a man from their own district.[56] Some of the clergy, he warned Briggs, would ask to move out of the district if

[53] Ibid., 319–22.
[54] Letter, William Hogarth to John Briggs, 3 June 1840. Archives, Leeds.
[55] Letter, William Hogarth to John Briggs, 5 June 1840. Archives, Leeds.
[56] Letter, William Hogarth to John Briggs, 8 June 1840. Archives, Leeds.

they did not get their way. His unpopularity with the clergy of the Northern District did not go unnoticed by Weedall himself. He wrote to Acton on 6 June to ask that the appointment not be made. His reasons were that his health, both physical and mental, was not strong enough to bear the burden of any vicariate, much less one in which he was so strongly opposed.[57] The attacks upon him, largely because he was not a Northern man rather than from any objection to him personally, continued until finally, on 9 September 1840, his resignation was accepted by Gregory XVI.

Once successful in forcing Weedall to decline the appointment, the clergy of the Northern District appeared to have lost their taste for opposition. Weedall's replacement, Francis Mostyn, was also a Midland man, but aroused little disturbance when his appointment was announced. The reasons for the sudden passivity of the Northern clergy are not entirely clear, but certainly the fear on their part that if they continued with their protest, they might even be worse off, was a telling point. What would have been worse, of course, even than Weedall or another Midland man, would have been the appointment of a regular.

An obvious question, in face of the opposition of the Northern clergy to the appointment of men from another district, was why Rome persisted in appointing Midland clergy to Northern vicariates. The answer can be partially found in the need that existed to find a place for Nicholas Wiseman. Almost all the vicars recognized his importance to the progress of the church in England, but they were wary of his influence and his foreign ways. Only Thomas Walsh was anxious to have him, and the new Central District was an important post, containing as it did Oxford, where the movement of Anglicans toward the Roman church was just gaining momentum. In order, however, to appoint Wiseman to the post even of co-adjutor and to provide him with a base for his preaching and teaching, some suitable positions had to be found for the president and vice president of Oscott College, Weedall and Wareing. Hence, they were appointed to

[57]Letter, Henry Weedall to Charles Acton, 6 June 1840. Archives, Vatican.

vicariates in the Northern and Eastern Districts, so that Wiseman could be brought into the Central District as co-adjutor to Walsh and president of Oscott. In a long letter to Acton, Wiseman himself explained why it was necessary for him to be in the Central District and not take, as Baines was suggesting, Weedall's place in the North.[58] Among the reasons, explained Wiseman, was the fact that he did not want sole responsibility for setting up a new district; that, indeed, he had publishing commitments that prohibited such a total occupation with vicarial problems. Moreover, he continued, he needed a central location in order to carry out his plans for educational and missionary activities among the English clergy, and that Oscott and the church of St. Chad in Birmingham with its ample capacity had been planned by Walsh with Wiseman and his preaching in mind. Furthermore, maintained Wiseman, it was essential that he be near Oxford for he was responsible for carrying on the "controversy with the Puseyites" there. Finally, it was proper that he should remain in the Central District, Wiseman explained, because Walsh had borne the expenses of his consecration and it was only right that he should get the benefits of his services.

Another possible reason for the failure to appoint Northern men to the new districts stemmed from the agitation the clergy from the North had engaged in. They had formed clerical groups, drawn up petitions, besieged Rome with demands and resolutions for changes in their government. It seems not unreasonable to suppose that Rome, not happy with their militant attitudes and their unbecoming aggressiveness, chose to discipline them and curb their power by appointing vicars from outside their own group. This would have the double effect of depriving them of leadership and of demonstrating Rome's disapproval of the methods employed by the Northern clergy.

At any rate, after five years or more of bickering and misunderstanding, the vicars apostolic had, at last, a division

---

[58]Letter, Nicholas Wiseman to Charles Acton, 2 September 1840. Archives, Vatican.

THE DIVISION OF THE DISTRICTS 185

of their districts. Along with that division they had certain opportunities for experimentation with new methods of vicarial administration, for their proposals sent to Rome in 1838 had not been overruled. It was presumed that the eight vicariates were but a step toward the eventual restoration of a national hierarchy, an event which Propaganda hopefully planned to accomplish within a year or two. Yet it was not until 1850 that the restoration took place. Looming large among possible reasons for the unseemly delay were the further examples of vicarial disagreement. For no sooner had the new districts accepted, graciously or otherwise, their new vicars, than these men began to quarrel with one another over the problems of property settlements and the distribution of clergymen.

Until the time of the division, Ushaw College had served as the seminary for the Northern District. When that district was subdivided into three parts, one of the first issues to be settled was the manner in which the college would function for all three districts. It was, at that moment, quite impossible for the districts to open separate schools. The problems to be faced were spelled out in an interesting letter from Andrew Scott, vicar apostolic of the Western District of Scotland, who had been faced with similar problems when his vicariate had been divided. "But how are you to settle about Ushaw College?" Scott asked Briggs shortly after the division had taken place.[59] "Will the vicars of Yorkshire and Lancashire," he further inquired,

have anything to say in the management of the College? Will the whole of its funds belong to the new Northern District? As long as it continues a common college for the three new districts, by whom are the superiors and professors to be appointed? Are they to be taken proportionally from the three vicariates into which your Lordship's district had been divided? Will the vicars of Yorkshire and Lancashire have the power of recalling to the mission any of their own subjects who may happen to be professors at Ushaw, whenever they see cause? Or will the vicar of the new Northern

[59]Letter, Andrew Scott to John Briggs, 20 August 1840. Archives, Leeds.

District have the sole power of appointing, retaining, and of dismissing whatever superiors or professors he thinks proper?

"Unless the management of the college has been settled by Propaganda when they divided the vicariate into three districts," Scott warned Briggs, "the above, in my humble opinion, are grave questions, which from my little experience in the management of a joint seminary, require the grave and serious consideration of the three vicars."

Bishop Scott made a good prophet, for almost every issue he mentioned was a matter for discussion and dispute among Briggs, Brown, and Mostyn. What was essential was that the vicars come to some agreement about the handling of problems in which all three had a mutual interest. The difficulty, so well predicted by Bishop Scott, of the assignment and dismissal of professors at Ushaw, remained unsettled for some time. Of the many cases, the one of John Glover will serve to illustrate the problem. Glover, who had come to teach at Ushaw in 1840 before the division, was now, in 1841, trying to leave the college to serve at a mission in Yorkshire, which was the place of his birth. "I do not see the use of noticing means of education or fund," Glover wrote Briggs on 29 October 1841, "for then both were common to the whole northern district."[60] "I contend," he argued, "that, choosing Yorkshire, I fulfil and discharge every duty entailed upon me, both by nativity and the means of education." "I was born in the old Northern District," he continued, "I was educated and ordained on a fund supposed to belong to the old district, and I shall give my labours in the old Northern District." While it was true that Glover and many others were technically correct in their reasoning, it was manifest that every priest could not be left to select his own mission in one of the new districts.

The problem became even more complex when the vicars attempted to divide the income from funds and property held in common by the three districts. Finally in 1842, after

---

[60]Letter, John Glover to John Briggs, 29 October 1841. Archives, Leeds.

THE DIVISION OF THE DISTRICTS 187

two years of argument, Rome was forced to render a canonical decision on the distribution of the assets of the old Northern District. Thomas Grant, who was serving as Acton's secretary in Rome, and who was also a protégé of Bishop Briggs, reported the papal decision to Briggs. "Yesterday morning I received a final answer respecting the division of the funds of the District," Grant reported on 14 April 1842.[61] "I will put the question and answer," he explained to Briggs, "that your Lordship may see whether I have rightly represented the doubt." The question as Grant explained it stated that

the district of _____ is divided into three parts, during the lifetime of the bishop who had governed the whole district. As the funds are not annexed to the territory but are merely the fruits of capital invested in the public securities for the benefit of the bishop who for the time being is bishop of _____ , the bishop of the third part of the district, after its dismemberment inquires, whether he can retain the whole revenue.

The answer, according to a board of canon lawyers was that the bishop, that is, Briggs, could retain the revenues since they were not annexed to the land. This decision, as can be imagined, was most unpopular with Bishops Brown and Mostyn who as late as June 1843 were still attempting to get the decree reversed.

Three years, therefore, after the first significant reform in the administration of the English church in 150 years, the English bishops were still hamstrung because of their own inability to set their own church establishment in order. The division of the districts which was supposed to have been the first step in the return to the ancient form of government, a mere prelude to greater changes, only served for years to divide and estrange the bishops from one another. For the North was not a unique case. The two western districts fought over the apportionment of funds and personnel, the London and the Central Districts locked horns in a struggle for power

[61] Letter, Thomas Grant to John Briggs, 14 April 1842. Archives, Leeds.

in any further division of the church administration. The bishops could not unite in common cause, would not cease their crippling and divisive attacks upon one another, and any further administrative reform in the government of the English Catholic church was postponed for another decade.

CONCLUSION

The story of the actual restoration of the English hierarchy which took place on 29 September 1850 has often been told and there is no need to repeat it here. What is important in relation to the preceding years was that it marked the end to an era in the life of the English church. Beginning in 1780, there was a gradual relaxation of constant and publicly approved persecution from within. It was a time of special trial for the church in England, when its development was severely hampered because of jealousy and lack of cooperation among the vicars and serious misunderstanding between them and Rome. It is the thesis of this essay that these conditions curtailed the orderly development of the English church. It seems quite possible, furthermore, that they changed the entire direction of the church's growth, for by the time this situation was remedied by the restoration, the English church was in the midst of an Irish inundation which totally submerged most of its native tendencies and fundamentally altered its nature and tone.

The question to be answered, however, is why the English church after the Reformation and prior to the restoration was so prone to internal disagreement? What peculiar combination of factors thwarted the peaceful growth of this small religious organization? A whole series of reasons can be adduced to explain the extraordinary propensity for conflict among the English vicars. In the first place, they came into existence under the most unfavorable conditions imaginable. Vicars apostolic were created at a time when the English church was poor, oppressed, illegal, and identified with an unpopular monarch, King James II. The office was without prestige, power, or precedent, and without any clearly defined rights or responsibilities. Worse than that, it was an office resented by the English clergy, most of whom had wanted bishops-in-ordinary.

If the office of vicar apostolic was not much appreciated in England, it might be supposed that this would be compensated for by the strong support it would receive from Rome. Such was not the case, however. Between 1600 and 1800, the various departments of the Roman curia were involved in a serious struggle for power. The conflict was particularly vigorous between the Holy Office and the newly founded *Congregatio de Propaganda Fide*. One of the chief objects in this contest was control over the "mission" areas of the church. Frequently it happened that the needs of these lands were subordinate to the ambitions of the cardinal prefects who headed these departments. The sharply divided factions in England often found themselves willingly or unwillingly caught up in this kind of political maneuvering.

The problems of England and the church were, moreover, both new and unique. Rome had not yet learned how to deal with a church which had no official position relative to the civil government. None of the proven methods or established procedures were applicable to this strange new kind of church. For years Rome continued to hope that a Catholic king would ascend the throne and England would once again be a Catholic country. Hence, the appalling neglect of England between 1623 and 1685, during which time the internal difficulties crystallized—the misunderstandings between regulars and seculars, the dependence of the clergy on the charity of a few laymen, the isolation of English Catholics from the mainstream of religious life in the universal church. Even when the short-lived hope of a Catholic monarch in the person of James II persuaded Rome to appoint first one and then four vicars between 1685 and 1688, conditions did not really change. The fall of James and the establishment of a Protestant succession left the new vicars almost as powerless as they were vulnerable. The history of the eighteenth-century relations between the English church and Rome were marked with evidence of both Roman neglect and internal weaknesses. It required heroic efforts on the part of Bishop Challoner to persuade Rome even to interest herself in the

CONCLUSION 191

bitter quarrels between the vicars and the regulars which finally resulted in the decrees of 1653. These regulations, however, did little to solve the problems, for in them, Rome equivocated and avoided facing the basic issue—that vicars apostolic must have authority to govern their districts, authority which was clearly defined and not subject to being compromised by the efforts of pressure groups operating in Rome.

Two centuries of neglect and mismanagement by Rome, moreover, found the English church ill prepared to meet the challenge posed by the radically changing environment after 1780. From that point on the penal laws which frequently had not been enforced to their fullest extent were gradually removed from the statute books. Catholics were as last free to practice their religion publicly, educate their children without fear of reprisals, be married and buried with ceremony, and, in general, take their rightful place as loyal subjects of their monarch. At the same time, the Catholic church in England was changing. Both the religious difficulties connected with the revolution in France and the economic difficulties of the Irish peasants brought new Catholics to England. Demands for improved pastoral service, for more catechetical instruction, for more and larger chapels made imperative the need for better methods of district organization and improved communications with Rome.

The English vicars apostolic were unable to meet these new demands. They exemplified all the limitations of timidity and conservatism which years of penal restriction had bred. In addition, the vicars who governed between 1780 and 1850 seemed more than usually cursed with personality problems. The Talbots, James and Thomas, who governed between 1781 and 1795, though good and honest men, were weak, vacillating, and ineffectual. There was no doubt that they had been chosen more for their ability to support themselves by private means than for their skill in governing the newly emancipated church. Charles Berington, their contemporary, succeeded in making only trouble for himself, the other vicars, and the whole Catholic community as he drifted in and out of schism. His uncertain position in the Midlands, relative to the validity of his authority as vicar apostolic, kept that district in constant turmoil for a decade. William Gibson, whose reign in the North lasted from 1790 to 1831, suffered for at least half that time from severe and disabling strokes. For years he was the senior vicar in terms of age and length of service and, as such, exercised great psychological influence over the other vicars. Yet he was frequently unable to travel to vicarial meetings, to tend to the business of his own district, to communicate meaningfully with his fellow bishops. His writing, for many years, was totally illegible, yet he insisted upon taking care of his own correspondence. Even after Thomas Smith was appointed his co-adjutor in 1810, an appointment Gibson agreed to with reluctance, he refused to permit the younger man to exercise even secretarial duties. Time and time again, the other vicars complained to him and to each other and to Smith that although Gibson's opinion and advice were wanted, they found it impossible to understand what it was he was trying to tell them. His speech and handwriting became so bad during the last years of his life that it was not even possible to know if he was mentally competent.

Worse than these defects which were, after all, lack of talent, weakness of character, or physical debility, were the problems created by those vicars who were clearly psychologically disturbed. John Milner, vicar in the Midlands between 1803 and 1826, manifested obvious mental disturbance. His extreme vindictiveness, his almost paranoic attacks upon those who disagreed with him, his total inability to compromise, his propensity to intrigue, his fanatical devotion to any cause he espoused, his suspicious nature—all these were the characteristics of a sick mind. Peter Baines, vicar in the West from 1829 to 1843, while more likeable, was almost as sick as Milner. His financial irresponsibility, his inability to work with subordinates, his grandiose and impractical schemes and ambitions made any meaningful cooperation with him almost impossible.

Those other vicars upon whom fell the ordinary burden of the daily management of the church, who were obliged to deal with the splenetic outbursts of a Milner, the irrespon-

CONCLUSION 193

sibility of a Baines, the incapacities of a Gibson, the ineptness of a Berington or a Talbot, were ill suited to their role. They were characterized, almost without exception, by stubborn, conservative natures, not really capable of imagining a church which could do more than preserve the remains of English Catholicism. None of them had the skill to contain a Milner or control a Baines. All of these men, the ordinary, the ineffectual, the aberrant, might have been absorbed by the system under other circumstances. Their co-existence at a time when there was particular need for strong and creative leaders severely crippled the orderly development of the English church. Given such leadership, what but chaos could have been the result?

Both of these situations—the Roman contest for power and influence in a changing and increasingly complex Vatican bureaucracy as well as the English problem of weak, inept, or sick vicars—might have been less damaging to the English church had there not existed a third situation which was crucial to all the problems of the English Catholics. That was, of course, the absence of any central focus for leadership in the church. The problem appeared as soon as the bishops ceased to be effective rulers—almost the instant Elizabeth succeeded in 1559, continued through the period when the bishops lived but exercised no authority, that is, until 1585. Under William Allen's guidance between 1581 and 1594, England's Catholics enjoyed some semblance of responsible leadership, but the external conditions were so unfavorable that Allen could do little but lend moral support to a dying group. Although he recognized the dire need for ecclesiastical order, his appeals for the appointment of a bishop were denied. After his death, all attempts at orderly government were hampered by the increasing animosity which developed between different factions of clergy and laity. At no time between Allen's death in 1594 and 1850 was there any central leadership or government for the English church. The archpriests failed, and the long period between 1631 and 1685 when there was no leader at all, crowned their failure. The vicar in 1685 and the four vicars in 1688 never possessed more than local authority over their individual districts. There existed no method of subordination, no orderly process for taking local problems before a gradually ascending hierarchy of authority, no means of any kind for the systematic handling of issues larger than a single district or common to all districts. The entire procedure for decision-making, problem-solving, and policy-forming was a peculiar and inefficient combination of local English and top level Roman authorities. There was no middle area where less important problems could be weeded out or internal difficulties settled. It was not surprising, then, that Rome had a low opinion of the efficiency, devotedness, and skill of the English vicars. Their every local problem and disagreement was exposed to Roman eyes in such a way that they could not help but appear petty, bungling, and over-ambitious. On the other hand, the exposure of all local issues to the scrutiny of Roman officials who were not loath to use whatever means was available to further their own interests made for great difficulty in solving English problems with the good of the English church as the paramount consideration.

The question remains, of course, why England was left without this necessary leadership in the person of an archbishop. The English themselves certainly understood the problem and recognized its solution. The great cry in the late sixteenth and early seventeenth centuries was for a bishop—one who could legislate for all England. As late as 1696 the Old Brotherhood understood the need for bishops-in-ordinary which implied an archbishop rather than for vicars apostolic. Although expressed demand for a hierarchy and an archbishop lessened in the eighteenth century, Challoner's requests for settlement of the secular-regular issue and for the establishment of orderly procedures implied that he wanted some method of subordination. The mood shifted somewhat, however, in the late years of the century. When the Catholic Committee questioned the vicars in 1783 about the feasibility of a national hierarchy, most replied no. Even the Bishops Talbot, who agreed to it, did so with evident lack of conviction concerning any possible advantages. All through the early years of the nineteenth century until the negotiations for the 1840 division of districts began, the subject of

CONCLUSION

a national hierarchy was skirted. The vicars appeared to recognize its advantages. Milner and Baines, for example, both understood the need and the possibility for such a reorganization. No one, though, worked actively to accomplish the change.

Several reasons can be offered, first for the early enthusiasm, then for the later indifference. In the sixteenth and seventeenth centuries the memory of another era was still fresh. The Catholics' position as an illegal and persecuted minority group made them nostalgic about better days in times past with the natural yearning to return to that happy state. Gradually, though, this memory dimmed and the clergy as well as the laity became accustomed to their condition. When it began to improve—the repeal of penal restriction, the increased toleration on the part of the general public, the granting of emancipation—there was an understandable tendency to refrain from changing a *modus vivendi* which allowed them to survive. All these improvements had been gained under a system of vicars apostolic without benefit of a hierarchical organization. Two things, then, were apparent to Catholics. First, advances could be made under the existing system. Second, a more structured system and one which tied England more closely to Rome just might cause a reversal in the trend toward equality.

As the degree of toleration increased and as the church grew in numbers and needs, it might have been thought that this persecution mentality would cease and the vicars would actively seek to regularize their position. It was at this point, however, that the vicars themselves divided and became virtual enemies. Charles Berington, censured by the Vatican; Milner, a constant thorn; Gibson, infirm but immovable—which one of these men could be expected to suggest a hierarchy in which he would take a subordinate position, or to which one of them would the others submit as a bishop to his archbishop? Together with this was the great fear—it matters not how groundless—that a change in the status of English vicars would result in the regulars' assuming a larger share of the power, perhaps even that of archbishop. Given conditions like these, it was understandable that the vicars and even the clergy kept their discussion of the advantages of a national hierarchy on the theoretical level and avoided any real efforts at implementation. It was a fine topic for episcopal meetings, a good scapegoat for clerical complaints, but it was not to be sought with genuine enthusiasm. The evils which might accompany it were too great, and the good too doubtful, to be risked.

Although England was content without a more formal and more structured system, why was it that Rome did not make greater attempts to bring the English church more fully into the pattern established for other countries? Certainly in the early years after the Reformation, Rome's ignorance about the best ways of dealing with a new kind of church prevented her from acting. Moreover, until the middle of the eighteenth century, at least, the hope—however futile it might really have been—that England's monarch would once again be the defender of the Roman faith, kept alive in Rome hope that all could be as it once had been. This dream, in itself, would have persuaded Rome to make no permanent adjustment to the new conditions.

The reason for the failure to establish England as more than a mission land, once the dream of Catholic restoration had died and once the threat of persecution had disappeared, seems to lie in the politics of Rome, both within the church and with her relationship to the civil government. Without belaboring the issue, the opportunity, particularly during the years of Napoleonic domination, of England and Rome being mutually helpful was greater if questions of religion were ignored or at least subordinated to questions of a military, economic, and political nature. Internally, the issue was more complex. In the period prior to the reigns of Gregory XVI (1830) and his successor, Pius IX (1846), there was less centralized power in Rome and more competition and rivalry among the various branches of the Roman curia. Especially was this true between the Holy Office and Propaganda. In their efforts to gain and maintain power and authority, these offices found it advantageous to keep control of certain mission lands. England was a prime example. The ability to make decisions about the church there, the power over appointments, the influence which either office could bring to bear upon the pope, the regulars, or other curial departments, was a valuable sort of patronage which both found it useful to perpetuate. The same kind of political power was found useful by the cardinals as they competed for positions of prestige. A kind word in the right place from a Jesuit provincial whom one had befriended with a favorable decree, or a judicious decision rendered on an English vicarial dispute could bring one into high favor in places where it really counted. An attentive ear to an English vicar such as Douglass or Poynter who lacked the sophistication to make his way through the maze of Roman protocol; a promise to carry an English grievance such as one either from Milner or about him to the pope guaranteed, or at least so the Roman bureaucrats believed, commendations from the vicars to authorities who held power over the Roman curia. On the other hand, a miscalculation, such as the one Somaglia had made with regard to the Jesuits, could help to banish one from the scene of the action and the position of importance in the Vatican system. Roman officials, therefore, had little to gain, much to lose, in encouraging the establishment of a more systematized hierarchy for England. The English church's anomalous position quite clearly had many advantages for the ambitious both in Rome and England.

From about 1835 on, however, the attitude toward a restored hierarchy changed. More and more, vicars and the second order of clergy alike were beginning to see the need for better organizational techniques for dealing with church problems. The cumulative experience of trying to cope with a Milner and a Baines, with the Jesuits, with schism and heresy, all helped to make the vicars realize that alone and separately they could not competently handle the issues which arose. Before and after the 1840 subdivision of districts, the clergy became increasingly insistent in their demands for control over their own lives and for more planning and order in the management of the mission work of the church. The involved negotiations required to settle the property disputes in the North after 1840 made it only too evident that some better method was essential if the work of the English church was not to bog down in internal confusion. Compounding this series of difficulties was the growing pressure on the vicars and the clergy to meet the demands of a church swelling rapidly with the hordes of Irish immigrants fleeing to England as the famine swept more often over more and more of Ireland.

All this, however, would not have been sufficient to bring the vicars to an acceptance of a restored hierarchy had there not been other factors lending strong impetus to the restoration. One was the trend in Rome, under Pius IX, toward a more centralized church. A paramount demand in such a system was uniformity of administration. The mission status of the English church was clearly an obstacle to any true reorganization along such lines. Rome needed a single person responsible for the English church, one who could cope with local problems at the local level, synthesize English opinion before it reached Rome, protect Rome from the ever-increasing barrage of memorials, appeals, delegations, and complaints reaching the Holy City from the English church, and—most important of all—promulgate and implement Roman decisions and Roman attitudes to English Catholics. Rome recognized, in other words, the advantage of having an English archbishop, primate of all England, to act as her agent.

In addition, Rome was changing her mind about the English church. The growing importance of the Oxford Movement and of men like John Henry Newman placed the whole question of England's mission status in a new light. If it were true, and Pius IX believed it was, that great numbers of Anglicans, men of superior intelligence, with sound education and great devotion to religion, were about to cross from Canterbury to Rome, then it was imperative that the English Catholic church be prepared for their arrival. A first essential and obvious move was to restore Catholic England to its position of importance in the eyes of the world.

Coupled with these new Roman attitudes about the English church was the emergence in England of men who had the experience and the drive to achieve the necessary changes. None of the bishops who governed between 1840 and 1850 possessed the intransigence of character or the timidity of approach that distinguished so many of the earlier men. Two of them, at least, William Ullathorne and Nicholas Wiseman, possessed genuine ability and experience in the delicate sphere of Roman politics. They both had, moreover, knowledge of the way things were done in other countries, first-hand training in administration, and the skill—one so rarely found in former English vicars apostolic—to win the cooperation and consent of their fellow vicars. Ullathorne, who had for many years served as vicar apostolic to Australia, had been responsible for much of the work which resulted in the establishment of a national hierarchy in that country in 1840. Declining to accept a bishopric in the newly formed administration, he returned to his native England where he became vicar apostolic of the infamous Western District in 1845. There he labored with fair success at untangling the confusion left by Bishop Baines. In 1847 Ullathorne replaced Thomas Walsh in the more prestigious and populous Central District when Walsh was translated to London. Brought then into close contact with Wiseman, who briefly served as his co-adjutor before being moved to London upon the death, in 1849, of Walsh, Ullathorne was able to give Wiseman the benefit of his own experience in negotiating the establishment of a national hierarchy.

Wiseman had long worked with the power structure in Rome. In addition, he was the one man the English clergy and vicars seemed willing to accept as their superior, more, however, because they recognized his greater knowledge and skill in dealing with Rome than from any personal affection they had for him. Indeed, there is much evidence to suggest that Wiseman was feared and mistrusted as an ambitious man who was too eager to achieve a high place in church politics. The English vicars finally realized, however, that their best interest lay in supporting a man like Wiseman. In promoting his own cause in Rome, he could best serve their needs. Wiseman envisioned the task of leading an orderly, fervent, and growing English church as the one position for which he had unique talent and in which he could find fulfillment of his own ambitions. The vicars, on the other hand, envisioned him as the one man who could restore English Catholicism to its rightful place in the universal church. Rome, England, and Nicholas Wiseman were all ready for the restoration of the national hierarchy.

APPENDIX A.
THE VICARS-APOSTOLIC OF ENGLAND AND WALES[1]
(1623–1850)

On the death of the last of the Marian Bishops, in the reign of Elizabeth I, the Catholic hierarchy in England became extinct. The country was ruled for a time by an Archpriest; afterwards by Vicars-Apostolic in Episcopal orders, first one for all England, then two, then four, and finally eight.

The ancient hierarchy ended with THOMAS GOLDWELL, Bishop of St. Asaph, who died in Rome, 3 April 1585, about six months after the death in prison of THOMAS WATSON, Bishop of Lincoln.

WILLIAM ALLEN, afterwards Cardinal and Archbishop-elect of Mechlin, was actually designated (as he had been in fact from 1568) "Prefect of the English Mission" by brief of Pope Gregory XIII (18 September 1581); died 1594.

In 1598 the Catholics were placed under Archpriests: 1. Rev. George Blackwell, from 6 April 1599, till his removal, 1 February 1608 (he died in prison 12 January 1613, age 68); 2. Rev. George Birkhead, 1 February 1608, died 6 April 1614, age 66; 3. Rev. William Harrison, February, 1615, died 11 May 1621, age 69. In 1623, 23 March, Pope Gregory XV appointed a Vicar-Apostolic.

202 THE ROMAN CATHOLIC CHURCH IN ENGLAND

Vicars-Apostolic of England

WILLIAM BISHOP, consecrated 4 June 1623; died 13 April 1624, age 71.
BRADY, *ANNALS*.
RICHARD SMITH, consecrated 12 January 1625; died 18 March 1655, age 88.
JOHN LEYBURNE, consecrated 9 September 1685. In 1687 the jurisdiction was divided between him and Bishop Giffard, afterwards Vicar-Apostolic of the Midland District.

Pope Innocent XI, 30 January 1688, created four districts or vicariates: the London, Midland, Northern, and Western.

London District

JOHN LEYBURNE, previously Vicar-Apostolic of England; died 20 June 1702, age 83.
BONAVENTURE GIFFARD, translated from the Midland District, 14 March 1703; died 12 March 1734, age 92.
BENJAMIN PETRE, consecrated 11 November 1721, as second co-adjutor to Bishop Giffard, on whose death he succeeded; died 22 December 1758, age 81.
RICHARD CHALLONER, consecrated 29 Janaury 1741, as co-adjutor to Bishop Petre, on whose death he succeeded; died 12 January 1781, age 90.
JAMES TALBOT, consecrated 24 August 1759; died 26 January 1790, age 65.
JOHN DOUGLASS, consecrated 19 December 1790; died 8 May 1812, age 69.
WILLIAM POYNTER, consecrated 29 May 1803; died 26 November 1827, age 66.
JAMES YORKE BRAMSTON, consecrated 29 June 1823; died 11 July 1836, age 74. Co-adjutor: ROBERT GRADWELL, consecrated 24 June 1828; died 15 March 1833, age 57.
THOMAS GRIFFITHS, consecrated 28 October 1833, as second co-adjutor to Bishop Bramston; afterwards Vicar-Apostolic of the new London District.

Midland District

BONAVENTURE GIFFARD, consecrated 22 April 1687; translated to the London District, 14 March 1703.

APPENDIX A. 203

GEORGE WITHAM, consecrated 15 April 1703; translated to the Northern District, in September 1715.

JOHN TALBOT STONOR, consecrated August 1716; died 29 March 1756, age 79. Succeeded by co-adjutor—

JOHN HORNYOLD, consecrated 10 February 1752; died 26 December 1778. Succeeded by co-adjutor—

THOMAS TALBOT, consecrated 1766; died 24 February 1795, age 69. Succeeded by co-adjutor—

CHARLES BERINGTON, consecrated 1 August 1786; died 8 June 1798, age 51.

GREGORY STAPLETON, consecrated 8 March 1801; died 23 May 1802, age 54.

JOHN MILNER, consecrated 22 May 1803; died 19 April 1826, age 74. Succeeded by co-adjutor—

THOMAS WALSH, consecrated 1 May 1825; afterwards Vicar-Apostolic of the Central District. Co-adjutor: NICHOLAS WISEMAN, consecrated 8 June 1840; afterwards co-adjutor for the Central District.

Northern District

JAMES SMITH, consecrated 13 May 1688; died 13 May 1711, age 66.

GEORGE WITHAM, translated from the Midland District, in September, 1715; died 16 April 1725, age 70.

THOMAS DOMINIC WILLIAMS, O.P., consecrated 30 December 1725; died 3 April 1740, age 80.

EDWARD DICCONSON, consecrated 19 March 1741; died 24 April 1752, age 82.

FRANCIS PETRE, consecrated 27 July 1751, as co-adjutor to Bishop Dicconson, on whose death he succeeded; died 24 December 1775, age 85.

WILLIAM WALTON, consecrated 1770, as second co-adjutor to Bishop Petre, on whose death he succeeded; died 26 February 1780, age 74.

MATTHEW GIBSON, consecrated September 3, 1780; died 19 May 1790, age 57.

WILLIAM GIBSON, consecrated 5 December 1790; died 2 June 1821, age 84. Succeeded by co-adjutor—

THOMAS SMITH, consecrated 11 March 1810; died 30 July 1831, age 69. Succeeded by co-adjutor—

THOMAS PENSWICK, consecrated 29 June 1824; died 28 January 1836, age 64. Succeeded by co-adjutor—

JOHN BRIGGS, consecrated 29 June 1833, as co-adjutor to Bishop Penswick, on whose death he succeeded; afterwards Vicara-Apostolic of the Yorkshire District.

Western District

PHILIP MICHAEL ELLIS, O.S.B., consecrated 6 May 1688; resigned in February 1705; translated to Segni, in Italy, 3 October 1708; died 16 November 1726, age 75.
MATTHEW PRICHARD, O.F.M., consecrated 9 June 1715; died 22 May 1750, age 81. Succeeded by co-adjutor—
LAWRENCE WILLIAM YORK, O.S.B., consecrated 10 August 1741; resigned 11 July 1763; died 14 April 1770, age 85. Succeeded by co-adjutor—
CHARLES WALMSLEY, O.S.B., consecrated 21 December 1756; died 25 November 1797, age 76. Succeeded by co-adjutor—
WILLIAM GREGORY SHARROCK, O.S.B., consecrated 12 August 1780; died 7 October 1809, age 68. Succeeded by co-adjutor—
PETER BERNARDINE COLLINGRIDGE, O.F.M., consecrated 11 October 1807; died 3 March 1829, age 72. Succeeded by co-adjutor—
PETER AUGUSTINE BAINES, O.S.B., consecrated 1 May 1823; afterwards Vicar-Apostolic of the new Western District.

Pope Gregory XVI, 3 July 1840, created eight districts or vicariates: the London, Western, Eastern, Central, Welsh, Lancashire, Yorkshire, and Northern.

London District

THOMAS GRIFFITHS, previously Vicar-Apostolic of the former London District; died 12 August 1847, age 57.
NICHOLAS WISEMAN, Pro-Vicar-Apostolic; translated from the Central District, 29 August 1847.
THOMAS WALSH, translated from the Central District, 28 July 1848, when Bishop Wiseman became his co-adjutor; died 18 February 1849, age 73.
NICHOLAS WISEMAN, succeeded as Vicar-Apostolic on the death of Bishop Walsh; translated to Westminster, 29 September 1850.

APPENDIX A.

Western District

PETER AUGUSTINE BAINES, O.S.B., previously Vicar-Apostolic of the former Western District; died 6 July 1843, age 57.

CHARLES MICHAEL BAGGS, consecrated 28 January 1844; died 16 October 1845, age 40.

WILLIAM BERNARD ULLATHORNE, O.S.B., consecrated 21 June 1846; translated to the Central District, 28 July 1848.

JOSEPH WILLIAM HENDREN, O.F.M., consecrated 10 September 1848; translated to Clifton, 29 September 1850; to Nottingham, 22 June 1851; to Martyropolis, 23 February 1853; died 14 November 1866, age 76.

Eastern District

WILLIAM WAREING, consecrated 12 September 1840; translated to Northampton, 29 September 1850; resigned 11 February 1858; translated to Retimo, 23 December 1858; died 26 December 1865, age 75.

Central District

THOMAS WALSH, previously Vicar-Apostolic of the former Midland District; translated to the London District, 28 July 1848. Coadjutor: NICHOLAS WISEMAN, previously co-adjutor in the Midland District; translated to the London District as Pro-Vicar-Apostolic, 29 August 1847.

WILLIAM BERNARD ULLATHORNE, O.S.B., translated from the Western District, 28 July 1848; translated to Birmingham, 29 September 1850; and as Archbishop to Cabassa, 27 April 1888; died 21 March 1889.

Welsh District

THOMAS JOSEPH BROWN, O.S.B., consecrated 28 October 1840, translated to Newport and Menevia, 29 September 1850; died 12 April 1880, age 82.

THE ROMAN CATHOLIC CHURCH IN ENGLAND

Lancashire District

GEORGE HILARY BROWN, consecrated 24 August 1840; translated to Liverpool, 29 September 1850; died 25 January 1856, age 70. Co-adjutor: JAMES SHARPLES, consecrated 15 August 1843; died 11 August 1850, age 53.

Yorkshire District

JOHN BRIGGS, previously Vicar-Apostolic of the former Northern District; translated to Beverley, 29 September 1850; resigned, 7 November 1860; died 4 January 1861, age 72.

Northern District

FRANCIS GEORGE MOSTYN, consecrated 21 December 1840; died 11 August 1847; age 47. Succeeded by co-adjutor—
WILLIAM RIDDELL, consecrated 17 March 1844; died 2 November 1847, age 41.
WILLIAM HOGARTH, consecrated 24 August 1848; translated to Hexham, 29 September 1850; died 29 January 1866, age 80.

By Letters Apostolic (*Universalis Ecclesiae*) of Pius IX, dated 29 September 1850, the English hierarchy was restored and the Metropolitan See fixed at Westminster. There were at first twelve Suffragan Sees: Beverley, Birmingham, Clifton, Hexham, Liverpool, Newport and Menevia, Northampton, Nottingham, Plymouth, Salford, Shrewsbury, and Southwark.

APPENDIX B.
DESCRIPTION OF ENGLISH SOURCES

The English sources from which this essay was written merit some brief discussion. They are all rich for this period and some of them are practically untouched. The archives at Westminster Cathedral are the most completely arranged. They are fairly well indexed and boxed or bound in chronological order. In addition, the archivist, Elizabeth Poyser, has a remarkable working knowledge of what is there. Of particular value are the diaries of Bishop Douglass and the carbon copies of Bishop Griffiths's letters.

In Birmingham, the archives have all been arranged chronologically, placed in envelopes, and boxed. This makes them somewhat difficult to scan but, no doubt, helps preserve them. They have been briefly indexed and a copy of the index placed in the British Museum. The writings of Milner are at Birmingham, although there is less material on the Midland controversy than the importance and extent of the problem would lead one to expect.

The Clifton archives form a large and very complete chronological survey. The letters which begin abruptly with 1780—everything prior to that date having been burned during the Gordon riots—are all bound. There is a volume for each year until 1829. The period of Bishop Baines's incumbency, 1829–1843, is represented by only one small collection, a perfectly predictable situation when one considers the personality of Baines. There are several very interesting topics discussed in the Clifton records and nowhere else. There is, for example, an extensive correspondence from women's religious communities which had settled in the West after the French Revolution. These letters give interesting commentary on convent life, devotional practices, and the position of women in late eighteenth and early nineteenth-century England. Here, too, are almost the only pastoral letters of a spiritual tone to appear in the English archives. Furthermore, for the Bishop Walmsley period, the archives are especially helpful because Walmsley made a brief notation on every letter of the answer he was sending.

It is in Leeds, however, that the real discoveries can be made. Unlike the other three deposits, the archives here have hardly been touched. It is only recently that an archivist has been appointed and the first attempts at sorting and indexing been made. For some reason, however, no one has used the material. When Bernard Ward wrote his seven volumes which comprise the only complete work on the period, he used Westminster, Birmingham, and Bristol, but he made no mention of Leeds. As far as I have been able to ascertain, none of the others who have worked in this area has consulted the Leeds collection. The material there, however, is of great interest and importance. It is the one place where much information can be found about parish life, local government, priests' associations, retreat movements, seminary politics, and other similar topics. Again, it is the place where evidence does exist for English efforts in the 1830s and 1840s to persuade Rome to regularize English church government. In the Leeds documents, too, is the story of the complex political maneuvering which took place at the time of the 1840 division and which resulted eventually in Nicholas Wiseman's going to London. The Leeds collection also contains an extensive correspondence from the late seventeenth century in amazingly good condition. All in all, Leeds was a great discovery, one of those marvelous pieces of luck a student longs for but rarely finds.

The records of the Old Brotherhood proved less valuable than expected, largely because of the war damage which made so much of them illegible. But they do provide valuable links in the chronology and are the only source for information about efforts to obtain a bishop for England prior to 1750.

These sources in England are unbelievably rich in historical materials. Political, theological, social, economic history

APPENDIX B.

of the English Roman Catholic church can be written from there. They are accessible, readable, complete, and interesting. They can lead the researcher to other deposits both in England and Rome, where additional information exists. I would not hesitate to say they are among the most valuable untapped collections of church documents available today to the student of English history.

BIBLIOGRAPHY

Manuscript Sources

Birmingham, England. St. Chad Cathedral. Archives, Midland District.
Clifton, England. Pro-Cathedral Church of the Apostles. Archives, Western District.
Leeds, England. St. Anne Cathedral. Archives, Northern District.
London. Westminster Cathedral. Archives, London District.
Sutton Coldfield, Warwickshire, England. Oscott College. Archives, The Old Brotherhood of the English Secular Clergy.
Rome. Archives, Congregatio de Propaganda Fide.
Rome. Archives, The Venerable English College.
Rome. Vatican Archives. The Acton Papers.

Printed Sources

ALBION, GORDON. "The Restoration of the Hierarchy," *The English Catholics: 1850–1950*. Edited by George Andrew Beck. London: Burns, Oates, 1950.
AMHERST, WILLIAM JOSEPH. *The History of Catholic Emancipation.* 2 vols. London: Kegan Paul, Trench & Co., 1886.
BASSET, BERNARD. *The English Jesuits from Campion to Martindale.* London: Burns, Oates, 1967.
BERINGTON, JOSEPH. "An Introduction and a Supplement Exhibiting the State of the English Catholic Church," in *Memoirs*, by Gregorio Panzani. Birmingham, England: Swinney and Walker, 1793.
———.*The State and Behaviour of English Catholics from the Reformation to the Year 1780*. London: 1780.
BRADY, W. MAZIERE. *Annals of the Catholic Hierarchy in England and Scotland, A.D. 1585–1876*. London: Thomas Baker, 1877.
BRIDGETT, T. E., and KNOX, T. F. *The True Story of the Catholic Hierarchy Deposed by Queen Elizabeth.* London: Burns, Oates, 1899.

BURTON, EDWIN H. *The Life and Times of Bishop Challoner.* 2 vols. London: Longmans, Green, 1909.
BUTLER, CHARLES. *Historical Memoirs of the English, Irish, and Scottish Catholics since the Reformation.* 4 vols. London: John Murray, 1822.
Catholic Magazine. January, 1835.
DE CASTRO, J. PAUL. *The Gordon Riots.* London: Oxford University Press, 1926.
DICKENS, A. G. *The English Reformation.* New York: Schocken Books, 1964.
DIETZ, FREDERICK C. *An Economic History of England.* New York: Henry Holt, 1942.
DODD, RICHARD [Hugh Tootell]. *Church History of England.* Edited by M. A. Tierney. 5 vols. London: Charles Dolman, 1840.
FOLEY, HENRY. *Records of the English Province of the Society of Jesus.* 5 vols. London: Burns, Oates, 1879.
GWYNN, DENIS. "The Irish Immigration," *The English Catholics: 1850–1950.* Edited by George Andrew Beck. London: Burns, Oates, 1950.
HUGHES, PHILIP. *The Catholic Question, 1688–1829.* New York: Benziger Brothers, 1929.
———. "English Catholics in 1850," *The English Catholics: 1850–1950.* Edited by George Andrew Beck. London: Burns, Oates, 1950.
———. *Rome and the Counter-Reformation in England.* London: Burns, Oates, 1942.
HUSENBETH, F. C. *The Life of the Right Rev. John Milner.* Dublin: James Duffy, Wellington-Quay, 1862.
MILNER, JOHN. *Orthodox Journal.* October, 1819.
Old Brotherhood of the English Secular Clergy. *A List of Members.* Privately published pamphlet, 1954. In archives, Oscott College, Sutton Coldfield, Warwickshire, England.
PHILLIPS, G. E. *The Extinction of the Ancient Hierarchy.* London and Edinburgh: Sands, 1905.
POLLEN, JOHN HUNGERFORD. *The Institution of the Archpriest Blackwell.* London: Longmans, Green & Co., 1916.
RENÖLD, P. (ed.). *The Wisbech Stirs, 1595–1598.* Vol. LI, *The Catholic Record Society.* London: The Catholic Record Society, 1958.
WARD, BERNARD. *The Dawn of the Catholic Revival in England, 1781–1803.* 2 vols. London: Longmans, Green & Co., 1909.
———. *The Eve of Catholic Emancipation, 1803–1829.* 3 vols. London: Longmans, Green, 1911.

———. *Sequel to Catholic Emancipation, 1830–1850.* 2 vols. London: Longmans, Green, 1915.

WHYTE, JOHN H. "The Appointment of Catholic Bishops in Nineteenth-Century Ireland," *The Catholic Historical Review*, 48 (April, 1962): 12–32.

INDEX

Act of Union: 75, 96.
Acton, Charles Cardinal: 161–2, 175–6, 180–1, 183–4, 187.
Alcala, University: 60.
Alexander VII, Pope: 25.
Allen, William: 11, 13, 193.
America: 113.
Amherst, William: 49.
Ampleforth: 153.
Angouléme, Bishop of: 106, 111.
Anticlericalism: 50.
Antiquaries, Society of: 76.
Apostolicum ministerium: 34, 123.
Appellants: 15–6.
Appleton, John: 81–2.
Archpriest: 14–6, 20, 23, 28.
Australia: 199.
Ayroldi, Signor: 27.

Baggs, Doctor: 179.
Baines, Peter: 153, 161, 163, 166–8, 170, 172, 177–8, 181–2, 184, 192–3, 195, 197, 199.
Bath: 32.
Bedford County: 181.
Benedict XIV, Pope: 33–4, 123–4.
Benedictines: 19, 23–4, 30, 32, 58, 122, 135, 155, 163, 177–8, 180–1.
Bennett, Edward: 18.
Bennett, John: 17–8.
Berington, Charles: 41, 58–9, 64–6, 69–73, 76, 79–83, 85, 128, 191, 193, 195.
Berington, Joseph: 24–5, 27–8, 31, 36–9, 62, 82–3.
Bew, John: 81–2.
Birkhead, George: 15–6.
Birmingham: 177, 184.
Bishop, William: 16, 18–9, 32–4.
Bishops-in-ordinary: 27, 29, 56.
Blackwell, George: 14–5.
Blanchard, Abbé Pierre-Louis: 103–12, 115.

Blanchardism: 111, 12.
Borghese, Cardinal: 15.
Borgia, Cardinal: 86, 90, 92, 132–3.
Bramston, James: 93, 125–7, 133, 139, 153, 157.
Briggs, John: 153, 160, 162–71, 174, 177–9, 180–2, 185–7.
Britannia: 20, 22.
Brown, George: 179, 182, 186–7.
Brown, Thomas: 180–2.
Bucks County: 181.
Burke, Edmund: 36.
Bury St. Edmund: 129.
Butler, Charles: 52, 56, 58, 60–1, 64–7, 77–9.
Butler, William: 52

Cadolini, Monsignor: 172–4.
Cambridge: 181.
Cameron, Alexander: 149.
Castabala, Mesopotamia: 76.
Castlereagh, Lord: 137.
Catholic Committee: 41–4, 54–61, 63–5, 67–9, 71–3, 76–7, 79, 91, 154, 194.
Catholic Dissenters of England: 63.
Catholic Emancipation: 50, 95, 109, 116–7, 119–20, 133–4, 139, 152.
Catholic Magazine: 160.
The Catholic Question: 50.
Catholic Relief Act: 35.
Central District: 2, 181–4, 187, 199.
Challoner, Richard: 31–2, 34, 40, 129–30, 190, 194.
Champney, Antony: 16–7.
Chapter of the English Church: 18–9, 24–7, 29.
Charles I, King: 24.
Chester: 181.
Cheswick: 162.
Clement VIII, Pope: 14–5.
Clement IX, Pope: 27.

214

Clement XIII, Pope: 40.
Clement XIV, Pope: 128.
Clergy, regular: 16, 19–23, 25–27, 33–35, 75, 122–8, 173, 176–7, 179–83, 190.
Clergy, secular: 12, 15–6, 19, 23–4, 34, 38, 75, 122–4, 126–7, 179.
Clifford, Lord: 58, 62–3.
Codner, David: 23.
Colleton, John: 19.
Collingridge, Peter: 93, 107, 109, 113–7, 119–20, 134, 136, 139.
Concordat: 103–4.
Consalvi, Cardinal: 141–3.
Constitution of the Clergy: 102.
Cox, Edward: 171.
Crook Hall College: 83.
Cumberland, 162, 181.

d'Adda, Ferdinand: 29.
d'Arras College: 19.
Dicconson, Edward, 32.
Dominicans: 32, 135.
Dominus ac redemptor noster: 128.
Douay College: 11, 17, 29, 60, 76, 78, 88.
Douglass, John: 41, 72, 76, 78, 80–3, 85–7, 90, 92–4, 96–114, 116–20, 197.
Downside: 181.
Dutham: 83, 113–4, 116–7, 119, 137–8, 162, 181.

Eastern District: 160, 181–2, 184.
Edinburgh: 149.
Edward VI, King: 9.
Elizabeth I, Queen: 10, 193.
Ellis, Philip: 30, 32.
Emanicipation Act: 2.
Englefield, Sir Henry: 58, 68.
English College, Rome: 87, 141–2, 179.
Erskine, Charles: 84–5, 87, 89, 92, 99.
Eyre, Thomas: 83.

Fermor, William: 58.
Fifth Resolution: 118.
Fitton, Peter: 22–3.
Fitzherbert, Mrs.: 88.
Fontana, Cardinal Francesco; 143–4.
Forrester, Charles: 42–3, 57.
Franciscans: 32, 122.
Fransoni, Cardinal: 164, 167, 171–3, 176, 178.

Gage, Francis: 25–7.
Gage, George: 26.
Gage, John: 129.
Gaschet, M.: 105–6, 108.
George I, King: 31.
George III, King: 61.
Gerdil, Cardinal Giacinto: 79–81, 85, 87, 90.
Gibson, Matthew: 43, 57, 61–3, 67, 69, 71–2, 76.
Gibson, William: 72, 76, 80–3, 86–7, 89–91, 93, 97, 99–101, 107, 109–10, 112–4, 116, 119, 130–4, 136, 138–9, 141–8, 150, 192–3, 195.
Giffard, Bonaventure: 30–2.
Glover, John: 186.
Goldwell, Thomas: 10–11, 13.
Gordon, Lord George: 52–3.
Gordon Riots: 32, 35, 52–4.
Gradwell, Robert: 142–4, 149.
Grant, Thomas: 187.
Grassi, Father: 140.
Gregory XIII, Pope: 11, 13.
Gregory XV, Pope: 17–8, 21.
Gregory XVI, Pope: 2, 160–1, 163–4, 167, 169, 174–5, 183, 196.
Grenville, Thomas: 50.
Griffiths, Thomas: 153, 157, 161, 163–71, 173–6, 178–80.
Gruber, Gabriel: 132.

Harding, Thomas: 11.
Harrison, William: 16–8.
Hayes, Bishop: 53.
Henry VIII, King: 9.
Herford: 182.
Hippisley, Sir John Coxe: 91–2.
Historical Memoirs: 77.
History of Catholic Emancipation, The: 49.
History of Winchester: 89.
Hoadley, Benjamin: 89.
Hodgson, Joseph: 114, 138–9.
Hogarth, William: 179–80, 182.
Holt, Alexander: 27.
Holy Office: 2, 19, 24, 84, 161, 190, 196.
Holy See: 24, 29, 34, 44, 56, 97, 129, 132–3, 140, 164, 171, 174–6.
Hornyold, John: 32, 41, 129.
Hornyold, Thomas: 56, 58.
Horsley, Samuel: 73.
Howard, Philip: 27.

216 INDEX

Hughes, Philip: 50–1.
Huntingdon: 181.

Ingoli, Francesco: 23–4.
Innocent XI, Pope: 21, 29.
Innocent XII, Pope: 33.
Ireland: 51, 156, 159, 198.
Irish: 51, 152, 189, 191.
Isle of Man: 162, 181.

Jacobin Directory: 88.
James I, King: 15, 54–5.
James II, King: 29–30, 32, 189–90.
James III, Pretender: 40.
Jerningham, Sir William: 58.
Jesuits: 4, 12–13, 15–17, 19, 23–4, 75, 120, 122, 125–6, 128–47, 149–50, 158, 161, 163, 180, 197.
Jones, John: 157.
Julius III, Pope: 9.

Kellison, Matthew: 17.
Kirk, John: 81–2, 148.

Lambruschini, Cardinal Antonio: 1.
Lancashire: 162, 182, 185.
Lancaster: 181.
Lawson, Sir John: 58.
Leyburne, John: 29–32, 153.
Liage: 130–1.
Lincoln: 10, 181.
Lingard, John: 141, 149–50, 157–8.
Litta, Cardinal: 134, 139–46.
Liverpool: 163.
Llandoff: 10.
London District: 30–1, 37–8, 40, 57, 69, 76, 90, 98–9, 101–5, 107–8, 111–12, 114–15, 118, 125, 129, 141, 152–3, 161, 163, 180–1, 187, 199.
Louis XVIII, King: 104.
Louvaine: 60.

McCarthy, Bishop: 117.
Macpherson, Paul: 133, 138–9.
Magdalen College: 10.
Mai, Monsignor: 164, 167.
Manning, Henry Cardinal: 1.
Marian bishops: 12.
Mary, Queen: 9, 11.
Memoirs: 52, 77.
Midland District: 30–2, 38, 41, 57–8, 69, 76, 79–88, 90–1, 93, 95, 97, 99, 101, 105, 129, 146, 152–3, 155, 160, 176–7, 179–83, 191–2.
Milner, John: 41, 76–83, 85–102, 104–7, 109–21, 126, 133, 136–9, 141, 143–50, 153–6, 192–3, 195, 197.
missionis: 124, 130, 135, 140–1, 145, 149–50.
Monmouth; 182.
More, Henry: 129.
More, Thomas: 16–17.
Morris, Father: 180.
Mostyn, Francis: 171, 179, 182–3, 186–7.
Moylan, Bishop: 90, 97, 117–8.

Napoleon: 103.
Napoleonic settlement: 75.
Napoleonic wars: 26.
Narbonne, Archbishop: 104.
Newman, John Henry Cardinal: 3, 198.
Newsham, Robert: 145, 180–1.
Non confirmatur capitulum Anglicanum: 27.
Norfolk, Duke of: 37.
Northampton: 181.
Northern District: 30–2, 38, 43, 57, 66, 69, 107–8, 115, 118, 130, 144–6, 152–3, 159–62, 164, 168, 171, 176, 178–81, 183–7, 192, 197.
Northumberland: 162, 181.

Oath of allegiance: 15, 60.
Oath of 1606: 54.
Oath of 1774: 49, 54–5, 73.
Oath of 1778: 54, 59, 70–1.
Oath of 1789: 64–9, 72–3, 76, 79–80.
Oglethorpe, Owen: 10.
Old Brotherhood: 18, 29, 32, 154, 158, 194.
Orthodox Journal: 77.
Oscott College: 177, 180, 182–4.
Oxford: 145, 183–4.
Oxford movement: 3, 198.

Parliament: 9, 36, 42, 52, 54, 59–60, 73, 76, 89, 95–6, 100, 110, 119, 133.
Paul V, Pope: 15–6.
paupertatis: 124, 136–7, 140–2, 145–6.
penal law: 36, 42, 50–2, 73, 152, 191, 195.
Penswick, Thomas: 153, 162.

INDEX 217

Persons, Robert: 12, 14.
Petre, Benjamin: 31.
Petre, Francis: 32, 129.
Petre, Lord: 56, 58, 68–9.
Pilling, Father: 66.
Pitt, William: 50, 59–60, 63.
Pius V, Pope: 11.
Pius VI, Pope: 84, 102.
Pius VII, Pope: 88, 103–7, 110–11, 131, 143, 150.
Pius IX, Pope: 1, 196, 198.
Plantin, Laurence: 25.
Plowden, Charles: 146–7, 149, 158.
Pole, Reginald Cardinal: 9, 11.
Poynter, William: 90, 93–4, 97, 99–102, 109–10, 112, 114, 116–20, 126, 133–4, 136, 138–9, 141, 143, 147–50, 197.
Prichard, Matthew: 32.
Prior Parke: 153.
promoter fidei: 84.
Propaganda Fide, Congregatio de: 2, 21–4, 37, 79, 84, 88, 90, 92, 100, 132, 134, 139, 143–4, 146, 148–9, 155–6, 161, 164, 168, 171–6, 179, 182, 185–6, 190, 196.
Protestant Association: 53.
Protestation of 1778: 61, 63–7, 69–73, 79–80.
Puseyites: 184.

Rant, Thomas: 18–19.
recusants: 15, 31.
Reformation: 44, 76, 114, 121–2, 128, 159, 163, 189, 196.
Reform Bill of 1791: 54.
Relief Act of 1778: 52–3.
Relief Act of 1791: 55, 73, 76.
Rey, Anthony: 171.
Riddell, Father: 178.
Rosminian priests: 154.
Rutland: 181.

St. Asaph, Bishop of: 10.
St. Chad, Birmingham: 184.
St. Edmunds: 88.
St. Mary's College, Oscott: 182.
St. Omer College: 88.
St. Pol deLeon, Bishop of: 103–4.
Salamanca University: 60.
Sander, Nicholas: 11.
Scotland: 149, 185.

Scott, Andrew: 185–6.
Sharples, James: 3.
Sharrock, William: 57, 62, 66, 71, 76, 82, 86–7, 90, 92–4, 97–8, 100, 107.
Sherburne, Thomas: 177.
Shrewsbury, 14th Earl of: 40.
Smelt, Robert: 89, 92, 98–9.
Smith, James: 30, 32.
Smith, Richard: 15, 19–25.
Smith, Thomas: 83, 93, 115–16, 138, 147, 192.
Sollicitudo omnium ecclesiarum: 131, 133, 136, 138.
Somaglia, Cardinal: 146–7, 197.
Somaglian decree: 146–50.
Sorbonne: 60.
Southworth, Richard: 81.
Spain: 12.
Staffordshire: 177.
Staffordshire clergy: 70, 80–1, 94.
Stanhope, Lord: 61.
Stapleton, George: 83, 85.
Stapleton, Gregory: 88–93.
Stapleton, Thomas: 56.
Stirs of Wisbech: 13.
Stone, Marmaduke: 132, 139, 140–2.
Stoner, John: 32.
Stonor, Christopher: 34, 40.
Stoneyhurst College: 130–8, 140, 142–50.
Stourton, Lord: 56, 58.
Stuarts: 35, 40.
Sturges, Doctor; 88–9.
Suffolk: 181.
Surrey, Earl of: 37.

Talbot, James: 40–1, 57–9, 61–4, 67–71, 76, 191, 193, 194.
Talbot, Thomas: 41, 43, 57–8, 61–2, 67, 69–72, 76, 79, 191, 193–4.
Tate, Robert: 179.
Teynham, Lord: 37.
Thompson, William: 179.
Throckmorton, John: 56, 58.
Townley, John: 58.
Trappes, Francis: 162.
Trevaux, Abbé de: 106, 111–20.
Troy, John Thomas: 96–7, 99, 112–4, 116, 137.

Ullathorne, William: 3, 199.
Urban VIII, Pope: 20, 22.

218 INDEX

Ushaw College: 179–80, 185–6.
Uzes, Bishop of: 104.

Vatican: 32, 193, 195, 197.
Venerable English College: 12.
Vicariate of England and Scotland: 18.

Wales: 152, 161, 177–8, 180, 182.
Wales, Prince of: 88.
Walmsley, Charles: 32, 41–3, 53, 57–8, 61–2, 65–72, 76, 129.
Walsh, Thomas: 2, 141, 153, 160, 163–8, 170, 173, 175, 177–8, 180, 182–4, 199.
Walton, William: 32, 130.
Ward, Bernard: 49–50, 59, 69, 88–9, 97.
Wareing, William: 179, 182–3.
Warwickshire: 177.
Watson, Thomas: 10.
Weedall, Henry: 179, 182–4.
Weld, Cardinal: 158, 161, 163–4, 166.
Western District: 30–2, 38, 41, 53, 57, 69, 93, 107, 115, 117–8, 152–3, 161, 176–7, 181–2, 187, 192, 199.
Westminster: 3.
Westmoreland: 162, 181.
Wigan: 144–5.
Wilds, William: 126–8, 133, 139–40.
Wilkes, Joseph: 58–9, 64, 71.
William III, King: 52.
Williams, Thomas: 32.
Winchester: 76.
Wisbech Castle: 12.
Wiseman, Nicholas Cardinal: 2–3, 163–5, 171–5, 179–80, 183–4, 199–200.
Witham, George: 32.
Wolverhampton: 36, 117.
Woodfall's *Register*: 64.

York: 172.
York, Laurence: 32.
Yorkshire: 10, 162, 181–2, 185–6.
Youens, Thomas: 171, 177–8.